- What is the cutting-edge? How can I find this
- Who are using this?
- What have people done and how this might be turned into a teachable process — can it be learnt
- Developing the tools to acquire information

IDENTIFYING HIDDEN NEEDS

- Do you have the drive and stamina for this
- There are a few things here that you have figured out yourself naïvely — maybe you can just apply them
- People before have done great work with researching and analysing to make good decisions — why can't you?
- You probably have been too lazy with not enough follow through
- How do you gain access to people
- Zaltman Metaphor Elicitation Technique (ZMET)
- Knowing what is needed but not how to do it
- You have likely been looking in the wrong place and not hard enough
- It's your mindset, effort and how you approach things that will need to improve
- Believe in yourself, trust your judgement and decision-making but back it up with work and rational analysis
- What are the cutting-edge market research techniques
- You have regularly been caught c

GW00402192

- Where can I find good business case studies
- Developing and enhancing your critical thinking is very worthwhile
- Quest for deep insights?   • You can turn situations around
- Projective techniques
- Something about projective techniques and metaphors

IDENTIFYING HIDDEN NEEDS
Creating Breakthrough Products

- Overcoming Institutionalisation   • I'm not sure how much I

KEITH GOFFIN   agree with the repetory
FRED LEMKE   grid & whether it can be
URSULA KONERS   improved / evolved

- What is a JD and what is the UK equivalent
- Chicago School of Sociology - early anthropology
- Not taking things at face-value - you got conned many times over the years by not being skeptical & critical with people
- The need to choose and the need to stick with a decision
- Finding experts and finding sources of where they are and where customers are - likely a trawl.
- Learning from mistakes and feedback
- Doing high-end positioning and analysis

palgrave
macmillan

© Keith Goffin, Fred Lemke & Ursula Koners 2010
Softcover reprint of the hardcover 1st edition 2010 978-0-230-21976-2

All rights reserved. No reproduction, copy or transmission of this
publication may be made without written permission.

No portion of this publication may be reproduced, copied or transmitted
save with written permission or in accordance with the provisions of the
Copyright, Designs and Patents Act 1988, or under the terms of any licence
permitting limited copying issued by the Copyright Licensing Agency,
Saffron House, 6-10 Kirby Street, London EC1N 8TS.

Any person who does any unauthorized act in relation to this publication
may be liable to criminal prosecution and civil claims for damages.

The authors have asserted their rights to be identified as the authors of this
work in accordance with the Copyright, Designs and Patents Act 1988.

This edition published 2010 by
PALGRAVE MACMILLAN

Palgrave Macmillan in the UK is an imprint of Macmillan Publishers Limited,
registered in England, company number 785998, of Houndmills, Basingstoke,
Hampshire RG21 6XS.

Palgrave Macmillan in the US is a division of St Martin's Press LLC,
175 Fifth Avenue, New York, NY 10010.

Palgrave Macmillan is the global academic imprint of the above companies
and has companies and representatives throughout the world.

Palgrave® and Macmillan® are registered trademarks in the United States,
the United Kingdom, Europe and other countries.

ISBN 978-1-349-30531-5   ISBN 978-0-230-29448-6 (eBook)
DOI 10.1057/9780230294486

A catalogue record for this book is available from the British Library.

A catalog record for this book is available from the Library of Congress.

10 9 8 7 6 5 4 3 2 1
19 18 17 16 15 14 13 12 11 10

Transferred to Digital Printing in 2014

Contents

List of Case Studies

Each chapter includes several short case studies to illustrate how techniques are being used by companies and the value of theories and concepts. The book contains a total of 50 case studies and many of these are based on projects in which we were directly involved, or on interviews that we have conducted with managers who have conducted leading-edge work.

From the table below, readers will see that hidden needs approaches are still mainly used in the manufacturing sector (often for B2C products) but this is changing rapidly as companies in the service sector realize the importance of deep customer understanding.

Chapter	Case No.	Sector	Main Country or Region	Organization	Type of Product or Service	B2B/ B2C	Page
1	Introduction to Customers' Hidden Needs						
	1.1	Manufacturing	UK/Europe	Clarks	Walking boots	B2C	12
	1.2	Manufacturing	USA	Skyline Products Inc.	Children's toys	B2C	13
	1.3	Service	UK/Europe	Equant	IT services	B2B	14
	1.4	Manufacturing	Thailand	Cobra	Windsurf boards	B2C	15
	1.5	Manufacturing	USA	University-led research	IT in the home	B2C	21
2	Surveys and Interviews						
	2.1	Service	Mexico	Mexican pharmacies	Pharmaceuticals	B2C	33
	2.2	Manufacturing	UK	Bentley Motors Ltd.	Automotive	B2C	36
	2.3	Service	Czech Republic	Telefónica O2	Telecommunication	B2B/ B2C	40
	2.4	Service	Germany	Deutsche Telekom AG	Telecommunication	B2B/ B2C	41
	2.5	Service	Scotland	University-led research	Internet usage	B2C	46
	2.6	Service	UK	University-led research	3G mobile banking	B2C	49
3	Focus Groups and Variations						
	3.1	Service	USA	Weatherchem	Market Research	B2C	55
	3.2	Manufacturing	Germany	Ravensburger Spieleverlag GmbH	Games and Puzzles	B2C	56
	3.3	Manufacturing	USA/ worldwide	Maxwell House	Instant coffee	B2C	64

Continued

Chapter	Case No.	Sector	Main Country or Region	Organization	Type of Product or Service	B2B/ B2C	page
	3.4	Manufacturing	Germany	Dr. Oetker	Food	B2C	67
	3.5	Manufacturing	USA	Coca-Cola	Beverages	B2C	69
	3.6	Retail	USA	Target	Products for students	B2C	71
4	**Ethnographic Market Research**						
	4.1	Manufacturing	Japan	Nokia	Mobile phones	B2C	80
	4.2	Manufacturing	USA	Astra Zeneca	Pharmaceuticals	B2C	82
	4.3	Manufacturing	USA	Panasonic	The Lady Shaver	B2C	89
	4.4	Service	Italy	Lucci Orlandini Design	Product design	B2B/ B2C	93
	4.5	Retail	Egypt	Sainsbury's	Supermarkets	B2C	103
5	**Example: Warehouse Equipment Research**						
	5.1	Manufacturing	UK/USA	Smith & Nephew	Medical devices	B2B	112
	5.2	Manufacturing	Europe	"WarehouseEquipCo."	Warehouse equipment	B2B	116
6	**Repertory Grid Analysis**						
	6.1	Service	Austria/ Switzerland/ New Zealand	National tourist boards	Tourism	B2C	127
	6.2	Service	Malaysia	Malaysia Airlines	Air freight	B2B	135
	6.3	Service	UK	Fascia Mania	Home improvements	B2C	137
	6.4	Manufacturing	Germany/UK	Beiersdorf	Skin care products	B2C	139
	6.5	Manufacturing	Italy	University-led	Wine packaging	B2C	145
7	**Involving the User**						
	7.1	Manufacturing	USA	Procter & Gamble	Consumer goods	B2C	155
	7.2	Service	USA/ worldwide	United Airlines	Cabin crew uniforms	B2B	157
	7.3	Service	USA	Sample U	Market research	B2B	158
	7.4	Manufacturing	Europe	Lego	Hi-tech toys	B2C	160
	7.5	Manufacturing	Germany	Nubert Electronic GmbH	Loudspeakers	B2C	163
	7.6	Manufacturing	Sweden/USA	Volvo Cars	SUVs	B2C	170
	7.7	Service	USA	Unconventional Films	Film production	B2B	172
8	**Conjoint Analysis**						
	8.1	Manufacturing	UK	Bentley Motors Ltd.	Automotive	B2C	179
	8.2	Manufacturing	UK/Norway	IKEA	Furniture	B2C	184
	8.3	Service	Germany	Bayernwerk AG	Electricity	B2C	189

Continued

Acknowledgements

In our teaching and research we are fortunate to come into constant contact with excellent students, companies, and managers. We benefit enormously from this interaction and from the ideas that this generates. This book is based partly on a new course on market research given to MBA students in Stuttgart in 2003 and the many ideas arising from our consultancy and project work with our students. A number of our MBA students have worked directly with us on hidden needs projects that have provided material for this book: many thanks to Ricardo Gandolfo, Jim Gould, Thomas Klatte, Hector Martinez, Anoop Nair, Amol Pargaonkar, Alejo Ribalta, and Gary Smith.

Thanks to the Palgrave designers for coming up with the cover. The sliced loaf of bread can be interpreted in various ways. Cockney market researchers will know that they have to use their *loaf*, others will know that market research is not as simple as sliced bread, and German readers will know that products based on professional market research and customers' hidden needs will be as easy to sell as sliced bread (*verkaufen sich wie geschnitten Brot*).

A significant number of managers have enthusiastically supported us with the case studies. Thanks to: Craig Bongart (Sample U), Kate Blandford (Kate Blandford Consulting Ltd.), Louise Burns (Bentley Motors Limited), Vorapant Chotikapanich (Cobra International), David Deal (Sample U), Massimo Fumarola (Fiat-Iveco), Johann Gessler (Audi), Julian Glyn-Owen (Boxer), Angelique Green (Boxer), Tomáš Hejkal (Telefónica O2 Czech Republic, a.s.), David Humphries (PDD), Ryan Jones (P&G, Geneva), Markus Kurz (Bosch Packaging), Martina Lovčíková (Telefónica O2 Czech Republic, a.s.), Roberto Lucci (Lucci Orlandini Design), Werner Mayer (Bosch Packaging), Liam Mifsud (Equant), Vernon Mortensen (Unconventional Films), Thomas Müller (Deutsche Telekom AG), Günther Nubert (Nubert electronic GmbH), Paolo Orlandini (Lucci Orlandini Design), Kiran Parmar (Bentley Motors Limited), Michael Senger (Sample U), Klaus Schreiber (Bosch Packaging), Roland Spiegler (Nubert electronic GmbH), Chris Towns (Clarks), and Klaus Ullherr (Bosch Packaging).

To help keep a practical focus to our work, two managers Dr. Ceri Batchelder (BITECIC Ltd.) and Dr. Neil Stainton (Reckitt Benckiser) reviewed drafts of the chapters and the case study material. Their help was invaluable.

We are fortunate to have very supportive colleagues in Cranfield who have helped in preparing or commenting on teaching material on hidden needs, conducted research with us, and helped in the preparation of this book. Thanks to

Dr. Alan Cousens, Professor Rick Mitchell, Dr. Marek Szwejczewski, Chris van der Hoven, and PhD candidate Helen Bruce. The management of the many improvements to early drafts was a challenging task and we are very thankful to have had Maggie Neale (Cranfield) diligently taking the lead on this.

KEITH GOFFIN; FRED LEMKE; AND URSULA KONERS
CRANFIELD, UK; SAN DIEGO, USA; AND FURTWANGEN, GERMANY.
JULY, 2010

Soun

Preface—Hidden Needs

Marketing is what you do when your product is no good.
Edwin Land Inventor of the Polaroid camera

Sounds like a heavy sales pitch

This is not a book to share with your competitors. It was written for professionals who work on new product development but, more specifically, those professionals who are frustrated with incremental improvements and want to develop breakthrough products and services.

During our careers, all three of us have been extensively involved in market research and new product development: Keith with Hewlett-Packard medical products; Fred in financial services; and Ursula with Daimler-Chrysler, Ravensburger, and now Siedle. The wide variety of projects on which we have worked, in companies and in our regular consultancy work, means that we have extensive and ongoing experience of using the techniques which we describe in this book. Many of the examples that we give are based on our own research. Every technique that we cover is described with one aim—to help companies identify their customers' hidden needs. Once these have been identified, companies will need to harness all of their creativity in generating innovative solutions. In contrast to the quote from Edwin Land above, we truly believe that marketing (or to be specific, market research) is what you *must do well* to ensure that your product or service *is good*. So good luck with the challenge of uncovering hidden needs and creating breakthrough products and services!

KEITH GOFFIN; FRED LEMKE; AND URSULA KONERS
CRANFIELD, UK; SAN DIEGO, USA; AND FURTWANGEN, GERMANY.
JULY, 2010

About the Authors

KEITH GOFFIN BSc (DUNELM), MSc, PhD

Professor of Innovation and New Product Development, Cranfield School of Management, UK (http://www.som.cranfield.ac.uk/som/).

Keith studied physics and anthropology at Durham University, graduating in 1977 with a first class honours degree in physics. Subsequently, he obtained an MSc in Medical Physics from Aberdeen University. For 14 years he worked for the Medical Products Group of Hewlett-Packard (HP), starting as a support engineer working on new product development. In subsequent management roles he gained extensive experience in market research, international marketing and, for example, took HP's defibrillator products from a 5 percent market share to market leadership position within a year. Parallel to his management responsibilities, Keith studied part-time for a PhD at Cranfield. The results of his doctoral research on customer support have been applied at Ford, NCR, and HP. In 1991 he became Product Marketing Manager at HP and focused on developing the intensive care market in Asia/Pacific, before joining Cranfield in 1994.

At Cranfield, Keith lectures on both the MBA and Executive Programmes and has developed several new courses on innovation management. He regularly lectures at other schools, including Bocconi University, EM-Lyon, Mannheim Business School, the University of Hamburg-Harburg, and Stockholm School of Economics. From 2002–2004 he worked as Academic Dean at Stuttgart Institute of Management and Technology.

His current research interests are innovation leadership, project-to-project learning, and hidden needs analysis. He has published two books, eleven reports, and over eighty articles in a number of journals and magazines, including the *Journal of Product Innovation Management* and *International Journal of Operations and Production Management*. In addition to his work at universities, he regularly acts as an innovation management consultant to companies including Agilent Technologies, Bosch, Kellogg's, HSBC Bank, BOC Gases, Rank-Xerox, Sony, and Heidelberger Druckmaschinen. Currently, he is conducting three in-depth, confidential hidden needs projects with major companies.

FRED LEMKE BCom (HONS), MBA, PhD

Assistant Professor of Marketing, Marshall Goldsmith School of Management (MGSM), Alliant International University, USA; and founder of Hidden Needs Business Consulting (http://www.hiddenneeds.com).

Fred is the founder of *Hidden Needs Business Consulting* and acts as a management consultant for international companies such as Sony, BASF, and Bosch. His business experience was in the financial services sector, in marketing and business analysis. Fred received an MBA from Oxford Brookes University, UK and later, conducted doctoral research at Cranfield School of Management, UK in marketing on a part-time basis. He has conducted research projects on the automotive industry in Germany, the pharmaceutical sector in the UK, design in Italy, and projects for the European Commission (Brussels). The results of his research have been applied at a number of leading companies.

From 2003–2004, he was Assistant Professor of Marketing and Innovation at the Stuttgart Institute of Management and Technology (SIMT, Stuttgart). From 2005–July 2009, he was faculty member at the Cranfield School of Management and Henley Business School, UK on a part-time basis and taught MBA classes in various countries, including Norway, Denmark, Sweden, Switzerland, UK, and Greenland. Fred joined MGSM as a faculty member in Marketing in 2009 and leads workshops for managers in Marketing and Innovation. Fred has published in practitioner magazines as well as in high impact academic journals (including *Journal of Operations Management*) and has won the *IJPDLM Emerald Literati Award for Excellence* Price for one of his papers. As an expert in marketing and innovation, Fred speaks frequently on international conferences on topics such as discovering hidden needs, customer experience, customer insight, market research, design, and innovation management.

URSULA KONERS, BA (HONS), DIPLOM-BETRIEBSWIRT (FH), PhD

Visiting Research Fellow at the Cranfield School of Management, Bedford, UK, and Senior Manager at S. Siedle & Söhne OHG in Furtwangen, Germany.

Ursula Koners first studied for a joint degree in European Business Administration in Reutlingen and London, graduating in 1996. She began her professional career in the project management department at the central Research & Technology Unit of Daimler-Chrysler, where she coordinated major EU funded R&D projects in the field of telematics. At the time, she also managed several projects with the Institute for Technology Management (ITEM) at the University of St. Gallen, Switzerland. From 1999 to 2006, she gained extensive international experience at Ravensburger Spieleverlag GmbH, including assignments as Financial Controller in England, special projects manager in France, and establishing the Spanish subsidiary.

Parallel to her work in industry, Ursula studied part-time for a PhD at Cranfield School of Management, focusing on knowledge and learning in new product development, with a particular emphasis on the role of tacit knowledge in R&D teams. She graduated with a PhD in management in 2006 and the results of her research have won prizes and been widely published in top journals such as the *Journal of Product Innovation Management* and the *International Journal of Operations & Production Management.*

Ursula is continuing her career in both business and academia. She is a Visiting Research Fellow at the Cranfield School of Management. Together with Keith Goffin she regularly teaches Innovation Management on MBA courses in Germany and Italy. She is also a member of the advisory board for the Executive MBA at the Hochschule Furtwangen, Germany, and regularly supervises theses of BA and Executive MBA students. In 2007 she moved to S. Siedle & Söhne OHG in Furtwangen, Germany, a manufacturer of building communication systems, where she is a member of the senior management team.

Copyright Material

The authors and publishers are grateful to the following organizations for permission to reproduce copyright material:

Figure 1.3 "Usage of Techniques by Leading UK Companies" reproduced from Goffin, K. and Szwejczewski, M., "Keep a Close Eye on the Market," *Management Focus* (Cranfield School of Management), Autumn 2009, pp. 17–19.

Figure 1.4 "Usage and Perceived Effectiveness of Methods" is used with permission from: Cooper, R. G. and Edgett, S. J., "Ideation for Product Innovation: What Are the Best Methods?" *PDMA Visions Magazine*, Vol. XXXII, No. 1, March 2008, pp. 12–17 (Exhibit 2, page 15).

Figure 2.8 "Example of an Introduction Letter for ZMET Participants" reprinted with permission from: Tung, W., Lin, C. and Wen, Y., "Applying ZMET to Explore Consumer Experience: A Case Study of a Theme Park" Conference Proceedings, International Conference on Business Information. July 11–13, 2007, Tokyo, Japan.

Figure 3.4 "Form for Capturing Observers' Analysis and Reflections" was developed by Doctoral Researcher Helen Bruce of Cranfield School of Management in 2010. Used with permission.

Figure 3.6 "Checklist for Analyzing Focus Groups" is a new diagram based on the recommendations in: Eriksson, P. and Kovalainen, A., *Qualitative Methods in Business Research*. London: Sage, 2008; and Marshall, C. and Rossman, G., *Designing Qualitative Research*, 4th Edition, London: Sage, 2006, 115.

Figure 4.2 "Field Notes for Market Research" is based on the format given by: Rust, L. "Observations: Parents and Children Shopping Together: A New Approach to the Qualitative Analysis of Observational Data," *Journal of Advertising Research*, Vol. 33, No. 4, July/August 1993, pp. 65–70. Used with permission from Dr Lang Rust.

Figure 6.1 "Example of a Repertory Grid Interview" is reprinted (with enhancements) by permission of Sage Publications Ltd. from Goffin, K., "Repertory Grid Technique" in Partington, D. (ed.) *Essential Skills for Management Research*, London: Sage, 2002. Copyright © (Keith Goffin 2002).

Table 7.1: This table was published in: Sawhney, M., Verona, G. and Prandelli, E. (2005) Collaborating to Create: The Internet as a Platform for Customer Engagement in Product Innovation. *Journal of Interactive Marketing*, Vol. 19, No 4, pp. 1–15. Reproduced with permission of Elsevier.

Figure 7.2 "The Crowdsourcing Flowchart" used with permission from: Brabham, D. http://darenbrabham.com, crowdsourcing researcher

Figure 9.2 "Comparison of Interviews and Focus Groups" reprinted by permission from: Griffin, A. and Hauser, J. R. "The Voice of the Customer," *Marketing Science*, Vol. 12, No. 1, Winter 1993, pp. 1–27. Copyright (1993), the Institute for Operations Research and the Management Sciences (INFORMS), 7240 Parkway Drive, Suite 300, Hanover, MD 21076 USA.

Figure 9.3 "Number of Analysts Required" reprinted (with enhancements) by permission from: Griffin, A. and Hauser, J. R. "The Voice of the Customer," *Marketing Science*, Vol. 12, No. 1, Winter 1993, pp. 1–27. Copyright (1993), the Institute for Operations Research and the Management Sciences (INFORMS), 7240 Parkway Drive, Suite 300, Hanover, MD 21076 USA.

Figure 10.1 "Organizational Barriers to the Adoption of Hidden Needs Techniques" enhanced and used with permission from: Batchelder, C., Pinto, C., Bogg, D., Sharples, C. and Hill, A. "Capturing Best Practice in Establishing Customers' Hidden Needs for Smith and Nephew," Manchester Business School, International Business Project 2006, December 2006.

Box Cases 1.1 (Clark's shoes); 1.3 (Equant); 1.4 (Cobra); 4.1 (Nokia), 7.3 (Lego), 9.1 (Miele), 9.3 (Boxer Creative), 9.5 (Black & Decker) were all modified from Goffin, K. and Mitchell, R., *Innovation Management: Strategy and Implementation Using the Pentathlon Framework*, Basingstoke: Palgrave, 2nd Edition, 2010, © K. Goffin and R. Mitchell.

Every effort has been made to trace all the copyright-holders, but if any have been inadvertently overlooked the publishers will be pleased to make the necessary arrangements at the first opportunity.

All of the figures and tables not mentioned above are original and have been drawn or devised by the authors.

Part 1
Introduction and Traditional Methods of Market Research

∘ There is something here about ranges of Qualitative Analysis
∘ There is something about TA
∘ There is something about triangulating /integrating different techniques

1 INTRODUCTION TO CUSTOMERS' HIDDEN NEEDS

> *We don't believe in doing market research for a new product unknown to the public.*
> Akio Morita, Sony[1]

INTRODUCTION

Many new products fail. Far too many! Products fail regularly in both the manufacturing and service sectors. By *failure* we mean that these new products *fail* to excite customers and *fail* to reach the sales and market share goals set by the companies that develop them. Research shows that the major reason that new products and services fail is that they are too similar to existing market offerings. New products which are hard to differentiate simply do not capture the customer's imagination. However, the lack of differentiable features is a symptom. The cause of the problem is a poor understanding of customers' needs. Companies need to take a radically different approach if they are to be successful at identifying customers' real needs and this book is about innovative ways to conduct market research. Specifically, it addresses how to unveil what we will term customers' *hidden needs*.

The way top companies "listen" to their customers is changing as managers realize that end-users are often unable to articulate their needs, and that customer surveys and focus groups seldom lead to breakthrough product ideas. The Sony Walkman is a clear example of a new product that resulted from insights into customers' hidden needs rather than from traditional market research. It is not that market research is bad *per se*, it is rather that the way it is conducted is in need of a complete overhaul in many organizations.

We have assembled a number of market research techniques that probe far deeper than traditional market research, which is largely based on two methods—surveys and focus groups. We call this approach *hidden needs analysis* (HNA) and its techniques include *repertory grid analysis, ethnographic market research* (including *systematic observation* and *contextual interviews*) and *involving the user,* such as *lead user* groups. Such techniques allow us to understand hidden needs—the deeper needs that customers cannot articulate and probably have not even recognized themselves. If products and services include features that address such needs, then customers will be both surprised and delighted. Each of the new market research

3

Who are the experts

Too much fluff

techniques described in this book has specific advantages, but it is in combination that they really come into their own. It is not widely known but the driving force behind some breakthrough products from companies such as Bosch, Clarks Shoes, and Whirlpool was a new approach to understanding the customer.

This book is written for professionals working in the area of new product development (NPD), and MBA and other business students studying innovation. Our message is important for departments such as marketing, design, and research and development (R&D), in companies in both the manufacturing and service sectors. It explains the need for new approaches to market research, and ways to select and apply the appropriate techniques. It also discusses why organizations should develop a deep understanding of their customers and why this is not a task that should be passed to a market research agency. Although some consultancies offer innovative ways to understand customers' needs, the process of understanding the customer should be recognized as a core competency. There are functions that you may choose to outsource but *understanding customer needs* should not be one of them.

In this chapter we will:

- Discuss why poor market research leads to product failure.
- Explain the terminology of hidden needs.
- Introduce the philosophy behind and the techniques used to identify hidden needs.
- Stress the importance of considering the ethical issues in market research.
- Discuss how different techniques can be used in combination.
- Describe the style, aim, and structure of this book.

PRODUCT FAILURE AND MARKET RESEARCH

Research shows that product failure is a major issue. One study found that 34 percent of new product developments do not fully reach their business objectives[2] whilst another study found the figure to be 90 percent.[3] As we have said, the major cause of failure for new products and services is that they cannot be differentiated. In order to appreciate root causes, Japanese quality philosophy tells us to ask "why?" multiple times.[4] Figure 1.1 shows how such an analysis can identify the problems underlying product failures. The work of Professor Bob Cooper of McMaster University in Canada has shown that 98 percent of products that managers perceived to be "superior and differentiated" succeeded, whereas only 18 percent of "me-too" products survived.[5] So differentiation is key but we need to look deeper.

If products are hard to differentiate, then this is due to a poor understanding of customers' needs. Unfortunately, this is a common problem. Many organizations do not have an adequate understanding of their customers and users and few have the deeper understanding that is necessary to develop breakthrough products. Why? The main reasons are that customers' requirements are changing fast and inadequate methods (that is, *traditional* methods) of market research

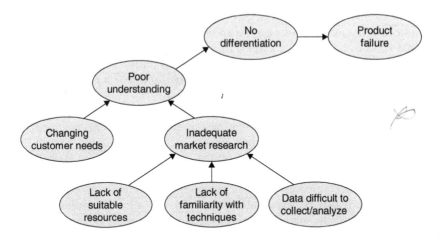

Figure 1.1   Root Cause Analysis of Product Failure

are used. A survey of 70 Finnish companies producing business-to-business products showed that the enhanced methods of market research are not widely used: 58 percent of respondents did not use any technique and 27 percent used only one technique.[6] Companies do not use innovative approaches to market research because they do not have the resources, their organizations are unfamiliar with the new techniques, or they perceive data to be difficult to collect and analyze. Such perceptions act as a strong barrier to the adoption of new approaches and we will describe solutions to these issues later (Chapter 10). Next, however, we will look in detail at the changing needs of customers and the drawbacks of traditional methods of market research.

Changing Customers and Customer Needs

The challenge of trying to understand the customer's needs is exacerbated by the fact that expectations are changing quickly in many markets and, in response, business models may need to change significantly.

The demographics for the next 50 years show that many markets will evolve. For instance the aging population in the West will have different needs. The size and nature of many markets will change: the demand for healthcare will rocket but, as the working population as a percentage decreases in many countries, healthcare funding will come under extreme pressure. This will necessitate a whole range of low-cost products and services. Other markets like Southeast Asia are now largely made up of young consumers with particular aspirations and, therefore, different product needs. As the earnings in newly industrialized countries increases, the demand for particular products and services is developing. For example, the Whirlpool Corporation recently launched the "Ideale," the world's cheapest automatic washing machine, which retails at around $150 in Brazil and China.[7] Companies that can accurately identify the needs of customers in developing markets will be at an advantage. Appropriate products and services may be low-tech and have fewer features than their Western equivalents. In many markets, understanding the customer's needs means knowing which features of a product or service are absolutely essential, and which features add cost and complexity but little perceived value.[8]

A deeper understanding of customers' needs can lead companies to adopt radically different business models. The business model for airlines has changed significantly over the last decade. Budget airlines such as Ryanair and Easyjet have rewritten the rules of the air travel business and prices have been slashed through a focus on "no frills" service, flying to airports with lower or subsidized handling fees, and also improved business processes (for example, maximizing aircraft utilization). It may be less comfortable to fly with a budget airline but the low pricing opened the market to more travelers. If the price is right, customers can be very willing to accept compromises. Conjoint analysis is a method to understand the trade-offs that customers are willing to make between, for example, service and price (by having them consider different combinations). However, the way conjoint analysis is often applied is fundamentally flawed, in that the factors used have not been appropriately elicited from customers (in later chapters we will discuss how the factors should be elicited).

Changing customers also means that traditional market segments are fragmenting and companies will need to adjust their product ranges accordingly—for example, car manufacturers now target over fifteen key segments in the U.S., as opposed to only five in the late 1960s. Contrast this to the market addressed by Henry Ford's products! At the same time, there are additional pressures such as consumer demand for more environmentally acceptable products and services. As customers' needs change, so should the approach we take to understanding them. However, most organizations continue to just use surveys and focus groups.

Traditional Market Research

Traditional market research mainly uses *surveys* and *focus groups*. Typically the questions to be asked are based on the knowledge of existing products, markets, and customers. In selecting a survey sample, companies strive to identify a representative group of customers or users, whose answers will be indicative of the whole market, or at least a segment. It should be noted that in some markets the customers and users may be different persons and, in addition, the purchase decision may not be made by a single person but rather by what is called the *decision-making unit* (DMU)—this can consist of several people. Particularly in business-to-business markets, the DMU can be complex as the decision-makers involved can have different expectations and requirements.

The main tool in the traditional market researcher's armory—the survey—has several drawbacks. Customers and users often find it difficult to articulate their needs. Asking direct questions does not help with this problem. We regularly come across questionnaires that are so poorly designed that they will not generate reliable responses. The level of skill required to design an effective questionnaire is often underestimated. In addition, a major issue with questionnaires is the low response rate. How many questionnaires do *you* fill in and return? Not that many, probably. Companies are realizing that surveys are increasingly becoming very difficult to administer effectively and Internet-based approaches do not necessarily improve the quality of responses.

The second traditional method for market research is the focus group. Focus groups are small groups of customers or users who have sufficient knowledge to discuss a specific topic, related to a product or service.[9] Normally, they are invited to meet at a neutral location, the discussion topic is introduced, and visual examples of the subject matter are often displayed. The discussion is stimulated with a broad question posed by the moderator, who also ensures that all participants contribute equally and also that the appropriate topics are discussed. Focus groups mix interview techniques with observation (with market researchers often being hidden behind a two-way mirror). Video recordings may also be used. Once the data have been collected, careful analysis leads to a list of product attributes required by customers. The majority of marketing managers say that ideas generated by focus groups are unexciting and new products based on these ideas are purely incremental innovations (which cannot be differentiated from the competition). "Customers often describe the solutions they want in endless focus groups and surveys... How sad it is, then, when the product or service is finally introduced—and the only reaction in the marketplace is a resounding ker-flop."[10] This is because there are several limitations to focus groups. The first is that discussions take place outside the customer's environment; this means that a host of clues that product designers can learn from are missing. Similarly, as focus group discussions are not aligned directly with a purchasing decision their validity is limited ("when a consumer reaches for a product... this is the only time and place that consumers' *purchase interest* and motivations are well defined and readily expressed").[11] Second, focus groups are by their nature not representative. Third, the scope of discussions is limited by participants' limited knowledge of the possibilities for new product and service designs. Consequently, the results of focus groups lead to incremental improvements rather than the breakthroughs that management hopes for.[12] Harvard Business School summarized the situation as "Focus groups have potentially enormous value, but not the way most companies use them."[13]

Although both methods have their limitations, surveys and focus groups are still valid market research techniques, provided that they are combined with a wider set of techniques that both allow deeper insights and cross-validation of results. This is the philosophy behind hidden needs analysis, which always uses a combination of techniques. The importance of new approaches to understanding customers is equally important in the service sector.[14] It should be noted that "traditional market research and development approaches [have] proved to be particularly ill-suited to breakthrough products."[15]

HIDDEN NEEDS DEFINED

Definition

Hidden needs—*issues and problems that customers face but have not yet realized.* When hidden needs are addressed by product design, customers are both surprised and delighted. It has been pointed out that hidden needs are those which "many customers recognize as important in the final product but do not or are not able to articulate in advance."[16]

Types of Customer Need

Table 1.1 shows that the customer needs that are identified in market research will range from *known needs* (which are common knowledge and addressed by the features of existing products and services), to *unmet needs* and *hidden needs* (which are not serviced by today's products and services). The needs and issues identified in market research should be viewed as problems that need suitable solutions. Procter & Gamble view market insights as "science problems to be solved."[17] We would agree except that the solutions should not only be scientific in nature, as innovation can and should come from a range of sources. So hidden needs analysis takes the problems identified (or an understanding of the tasks the customer has to complete) as the starting point and presents these in a challenging way to new product development teams, who must then create solutions,

Table 1.1 Types of Customer Needs

	Category	Explanation	Comments/Kano Terminology
1)	Known needs	• Customer needs that have been recognized for some time and are common knowledge within an industry. • Needs that are already addressed by existing products and services.	• Can be basic or performance features. • Easily identified by analyzing competitors' products and services. • Known needs are often used as the basis for customer satisfaction surveys, where companies ask their customers how satisfied they are with existing products and service features.
2)	Unmet needs	• Needs that are known and articulated by customers. • Not currently addressed by today's products and services.	• Performance features always have an unmet component.
3)	Hidden needs (also called *latent needs*)	• Needs that have not been previously identified, either by market researchers or customers themselves.	• Excitement needs, which are seldom expressed directly by customers. • Such needs provide opportunities for companies to develop products and services with features that are highly differentiated.

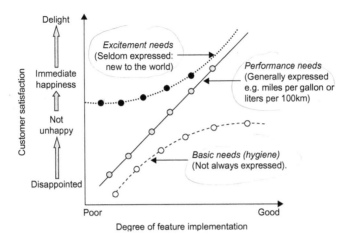

Figure 1.2   Kano Model of Product (or Service) Features

based on science, technology, marketing, service operations, or any other way that the team can create. This is very different to the brainstorming approach taken at many organizations, where personnel create ideas for product concepts without starting from a deep market understanding. Internal teams which create product concepts without true market inputs are ineffective; as such groups base their ideas on current thinking. Basing product concepts on hidden needs breaks with conventional thinking.

Insights from the Kano Model

A useful model for understanding customer needs is that from Professor Noriaki Kano. His original paper was published in Japanese in 1984 but later became available in English.[18] Figure 1.2 illustrates Kano's classification in schematic form. The horizontal axis is the degree of implementation of a feature and the vertical axis is the customer satisfaction conveyed by it: Kano identified three categories of product (or service) features and the influence they have on customer satisfaction:[19]

1. *Basic features.* These are attributes, without which a product or service would simply be unacceptable to customers. The customer perceives them as prerequisites and may not even mention them in response to direct questions about their needs. For example, cars must start readily and window-glass must not distort the view. Such product features are taken for granted nowadays (though it was not always so) and failure to provide them causes dissatisfaction. However, providing extra performance beyond the basic requirement generates no extra customer satisfaction.
2. *Performance features.* These are features that provide real benefit to the customer, and the more performance offered the better. Typical examples would

be fuel economy in a car, battery life in a mobile phone, reliable and increasing dividends for shareholders. For many products reliability or ease of use will also be performance features.

3. *Excitement features.* These features are new to the market and immediately bring high customer satisfaction. They give extra, unexpected value and may be attractive out of all proportion to the objective benefits they give. Customers are unlikely to ask specifically for such features because they are not aware of part of the way the product is normally viewed, but when offered them he may be surprised and pleased. (A recent example of an excitement feature is the *iPhone* feature that the display automatically switches from "portrait" to "landscape" format as the device is turned.)

The three categories of feature follow different curves reflecting their different effects on customer perception. A successful product needs to have an appropriate combination of basic, performance, and excitement features. Thus a sufficient level of basic features is essential but must be accompanied by an attractive level of performance and, if possible, excitement. Excitement features are often needed to capture market share.

The way in which the features of a product fit into the three Kano categories can be determined by using a questionnaire in which customers are asked how they would feel about a significant increase or decrease in its level of implementation (or possibly its presence or absence (see Chapter 2 pages 33–34)). The Kano Model is useful because it forces new product development teams to take the customer's perspective on which features are exciting, and it also reminds us that increasing the performance of basic features is a waste of effort.

THE PHILOPSOPHY OF HIDDEN NEEDS

The philosophy of hidden needs analysis is based on four main tenets:

1. Traditional market research using only surveys and focus groups is ineffective and seldom leads to exciting new products and services.
2. Newer market research techniques need to be used in combination with traditional ones, to gain deeper and more reliable insights.
3. Market insights are formulated as customer problems, issues, and cultural factors for which solutions—breakthrough products and services—can be designed.
4. To develop breakthrough products and services, the right organizational culture is required.

Behavioral sciences such as psychology and anthropology allow us to understand how individuals think, how they interact, and the functioning of social systems. And so it is techniques from the social sciences that are making inroads into market research and enabling us to understand how customers think and act. However, such approaches are not well understood by the majority of marketing and product development professionals, partly as they are seldom covered by university courses on marketing.[20]

"New" Techniques

As it is an evolving area, there is no generally acknowledged list of the "new" techniques for market research and there is some confusion in the terminology. The main techniques that are being used in leading-edge market research are:

- Ethnographic market research (including systematic observation and contextual interviewing).
- Repertory grid interviewing.
- Involving the user (including projection, user communities, and lead user technique).

In fact, some of these techniques are not "new"—for example, observation has a long tradition in ethnography and repertory grids were developed in the 1960s. However, it is the application of the techniques to market research that is still relatively new and consequently they are not widely known by marketing professionals. Each of the techniques has advantages and limitations but ideally this is taken account of by using them in combination. This allows a higher degree of confidence in the findings to be achieved through cross-checking (known as *triangulation*). Here, we will give a brief introduction to each technique and later we will explain how they can be blended together.

Ethnographic Market Research—Systematic Observation

Systematic observation is not simply watching customers and it requires a clear *coding scheme*. This is a list of the different aspects that the observer is looking out for, including, for example, the stages in which a person conducts a task, the surroundings in which they conduct it, and their reaction (as indicated by their body language). Systematic observation is a very effective technique if conducted professionally. In recent years several of the leading market research companies have hired anthropologists (ethnographers) as observers. There is more to professional observation than the "fly on the wall" approach of reality television. Ethnographers observe at many levels simultaneously, for example, they are able to pick up clues on customers' hidden needs through observing body language, spatial signals, and other subtle gestures, all of which are easily missed by amateurs. The use of video cameras is making observation easier as the analysis can be made *off-line* (after the events observed are completed and when the researcher has enough time to conduct a detailed analysis). We have worked in Germany with one of Robert Bosch's business units which designs and manufactures production line equipment. Through close observation of operators working in their customers' factories, Bosch gained much deeper insights into product requirements than it would have from interviews with production managers. Similarly useful insights were obtained by ethnographers working for Clark's shoes. They observed purchasers in sports shops and were able to identify the characteristics of walking boots that strongly influence purchasing behavior (see Box Case 1.1).

Box Case 1.1

Clarks—These Boots are (Really) Made for Walking[21]

Clarks Shoes has been renowned for the quality and comfort of its products for over 175 years. Several years ago the company was aware that the market for leisure footwear was significant and growing fast, and decided to enter what was for them a new market—walking boots. As this was a market about which they had no detailed knowledge of customer needs, they worked closely with PDD, a London-based market research consultancy. Product Manager Chris Towns said, "I needed to understand the buying habits, end use and expectations of our new consumer. Understanding the motivations of walkers can only be guessed at from within the confines of your own office."

PDD specialize in ethnographic studies and they conducted contextual interviews with walkers in UK national parks, home interviews with people who were members of walking and rambling clubs, and observed customers buying walking boots. The insights obtained from this market research allowed Clarks to clearly identify their target segments and, for each of these, to understand customer priorities. For example, "comfort," "fit," and "safety" were quickly identified from interviews as important product attributes. However, the contextual interviews in the national parks allowed the design team to understand the real meaning of each of these terms and develop product characteristics to meet them. Much of the development involved experimentation with prototypes and this was conducted directly with walkers. Similarly, customers in shops were observed to always feel the tongue of walking boots before they tried them on. Therefore, it appeared that the tongue was a feature of a boot that customers closely associated with comfort. This insight led the Clarks team to produce a particularly well-padded tongue in their final product. The Clarks range of "Active" walking boots has been well received by both hobby and professional walkers and ramblers and is selling well.

Ethnographic Market Research—Contextual Interviewing

Contextual interviews are conducted in the user's environment and semistructured questions are used in addition to observation, in order to understand the situation in which products are used. Questions are used to collect background information on the user, and then to stimulate them to describe their actions. Typical questions are: "Can you please describe what you are doing?" and "When is that necessary?" These questions produce qualitative data on product usage that might not be generated in pure observation of a single user working alone. Once again, video recording is commonly used. Contextual interviews are particularly useful for gaining insights into how the customer feels during delivery process of a service and for gaining ideas for improvement.

The London consultancy WhatIf! has made contextual interviewing easy for the manufacturers of consumer products, by negotiating access to all of the residents in one (long) street in Birmingham. All of the houses in "The Street" can be visited with minimal notice and product managers have been able to both observe their products in use and ask questions. Intel, the microchip giant has a number of projects which make use of contextual interviewing and employ a team of ethnographers, sociologists, and behavioral scientists based in Oregon.[22] This team was involved at looking at the need for a device for helping parents keep track of their children's extracurricular activities. Although such a product was known to be applicable in many Western countries, social research showed that in China, where families are restricted to one child, there was not a need. Intel now regularly uses such insights on the social background to product usage.

Box Case 1.2

Skyline Products Inc.—Making Child's Play of Market Research[23]

Skyline Products is a U.S. company that invents and designs children's toys. It organizes six-week play-group sessions, where children and parents get the opportunity to play with the latest toys for a couple of hours each week. Interestingly, participation has become so popular that parents pay for their children to take part!

Market researchers from Skyline apply a number of principles from ethnographic market research. First, they like to (literally) sit-in with the sessions and just observe, immersing themselves in what is going on. They ask a number of simple open-ended questions in their contextual interviews. Sometimes they get very direct responses from children, whereas others are shyer and might not comment until their journey home. In recording the responses to contextual questioning, the researchers not only listen to what is said but also watch for clues, such as children's and adult's expressions, the proximity children adopt to toys, the size of toys compared to children's hands, and so on. Data from the play sessions are deliberately checked for disjunctures; for example, children claim that color is unimportant but, in picking toys to play with, color is often observed to be important. Data from the play sessions are also contrasted with data collected on the homeward journey, as the researchers often ask if they can join the family.

There are several points to note from the Skyline case. Obviously, ethical issues are paramount when conducting research with children and such work needs to be carefully designed. Skyline researchers immerse themselves in the topic, use different data sources, and look for discontinuities in the data. Superficially, the research might sound like child's play but professionally conducted ethnographic market research often looks deceptively easy.

Repertory Grid Analysis

Repertory grid analysis was initially developed by psychologists to uncover individuals' *cognitive maps*—a two-dimensional representation of how an individual thinks. Repertory grid uses indirect questions to help users compare their experiences of existing products and services. The technique is ideal for developing new product ideas and revealing customers' hidden needs. Companies that have used repertory grid in their market research include Beiersdorf (the Hamburg-based manufacturer of global brands such as *Nivea*), Hewlett-Packard, and Equant (see Box Case 1.3). All were successful at uncovering hidden needs.

Box Case 1.3

Equant—Repertory Grids in Practice

One company that has used repertory grid to its advantage is Equant, the world's largest data network provider—offering network design, integration, maintenance and support services in over 180 countries. The company always placed a high emphasis on being "customer-focused" and regularly reviewed the results of customer satisfaction surveys, comparing their performance with competitors'. Although such surveys provided useful "benchmarks," Equant recognized that they did not measure performance against the criteria which were most important to customers.

In 1996, the company offered excellent network performance and global service availability. Consequently, it received better ratings than its competitors in surveys and this could have led to complacency. However, a project was launched to investigate whether there were aspects of service quality that were important to customers but were not covered by the surveys. Liam Mifsud, Business Support Manager at Equant, designed and conducted repertory grid interviews. Using the technique enabled interviewees (IT Directors and Managers) to identify a wide range of service quality criteria (far wider than those covered by the customer satisfaction surveys).

The results showed that customers' perceptions of service quality were not solely based on technical measures (such as coverage or network performance). Equant were able to identify ten new criteria on which their performance was being judged. For example, customers emphasized intangible elements of service quality, such as the responsiveness and flexibility of account management teams, and the quality and competence of the support staff they came into contact with. "This provided us with a valuable means of understanding the changing needs of customers," says Mifsud.

Involving the User—Lead User Technique

There are a number of innovative ways in which to involve the customer in product development and the most important technique is lead users. Customers who face more extreme conditions are observed or interviewed, to determine how they use products. The classic example is how many of the innovations developed for the challenges of Formula 1 racing can then be modified for general usage. In some technical situations, users may modify standard products to address their specific needs. It is particularly important to identify how the lessons learnt from lead users can be applied to the broader market: workshops and prototyping are often used in this respect. Both 3M and Texas Instruments regularly employ the lead user approach (see also Box Case 1.4).

Box Case 1.4

Cobra, Thailand—Leadership and Windsurf Boards[24]

Based in Chonburi in Thailand, Cobra International was founded in 1985 and is a manufacturer of windsurf and surfboards and a range of other items for recreational sports. Cobra's strategy has always focused on quality, technology, and a strong customer orientation.

Cobra uses professional quality management techniques, focuses on quality consistency, and is the only manufacturer in the industry with ISO 9001:2000 certification. This is one of the reasons that it has become a world leader, with over 50 percent market share today as an original equipment manufacturer (OEM) supplying the top brands. Windsurf boards must withstand tremendous loads, as top windsurfers can launch their boards up to seven meters off rolling surf. Making boards that can withstand such a buffeting requires not only good manufacturing but also an intimate knowledge of the leading technologies—such as fiber-reinforced composites. Cobra is constantly developing the "combination of methodologies and materials" says Pierre Olivier Schnerb, Vice President of Technology. "For example, Cobra Tuflite® technology applies techniques learnt from windsurfing to surfing."

The third element of strategy has come from the employees' intimate knowledge of the sports for which they manufacture equipment. Kym Thompson, an Australian, has been a champion surfer for over 30 years. In addition, for 30 years he has been professionally pushing forward the quality standards of surfboard manufacturing as Cobra's manager of surfboard production. Many other employees are active sportspeople and bring product and design ideas into the company. Being users themselves has helped Cobra develop top designs and enabled them to build very close relationships with nearly all of the top sports brands.

Vorapant Chotikapanich the founder and current president thinks innovation is absolutely essential for the company's competitiveness and takes every opportunity to stress it. In order to stay innovative, he gives employees the power to create, experiment, and decide. "I ensure that they get adequate top management support but I also drive for hot ideas to be implemented quickly," says Chotikapanich. In addition, he perceives organizational innovation as key, "we are currently organized according to technology rather than industry. So, for example, the Thermo Compression Molding Division manufactures everything from windsurf boards, surfboards, wakeboards to kiteboards. It is important to apply our technical expertise across all of our products. We also supplement our own competencies with those from a network of customers, suppliers, and designers." Encouraged by Chotikapanich, Cobra has recently used its expertise in materials and manufacturing to enter new markets. These include not only related sports equipment markets, such as kayaks and canoes, but also completely new markets such as automotive parts (using Cobra's material and process expertise).

ETHICAL ISSUES

In applying both traditional and newer techniques for market research we need to give a word of caution. Market research should always be carried out in an ethical way and researchers need to show the right respect for their respondents. Extreme care is required when children or minority groups are being investigated, or when potentially intrusive or revealing methods (for example, visits to consumers' homes using ethnographic approaches) are used. Pretending to be a normal citizen and conducting covert market research is both unethical and very likely to be uncovered (people have an uncanny ability to realize they are being watched).

Ethical issues need to be carefully considered BEFORE research starts and the appropriate permissions obtained. We recommend that researchers consult the guidelines provided by the various professional associations.[25]

USING AND COMBINING THE TECHNIQUES

Examples of Successful Usage

Over the last 15 years there have been a number of reported cases of companies successfully using new approaches to market research. Table 1.2 summarizes the main reported cases from the literature and notable successes include the development of new food products (to meet the needs of Asian workers or "on the go" families) and a new way to market zip drivers for Iomega. The techniques are not only useful for consumer products—new surgical drapes and production line equipment has also benefited.

The history of behavioral science being applied to industrial problems has been described in detail in an interesting book by Susan Squires and Bryan Byrne.[26] It goes back to the 1920s when psychologists first tried to understand the perceptual abilities of car drivers and the first anthropologists worked in industrial settings. Other industrial psychologists studied motivation at work including the famous Hawthorne studies of the factors that influence production line productivity. In the Second World War social scientists first entered the realm of product design, working on *human factors*, such as improving the design of aircraft cockpit controls. Behavioral approaches continue to play an important role in product design; largely focused on ergonomics and usability. For example, Rank-Xerox hired a PhD anthropologist in 1979 to help the company design machines that could be more rapidly understood by office users. The focus on the user-product interface has continued but, over the last 20 years, methods from social science have been increasingly applied to not only understand how products are operated but also to identify users' real needs. Now social science methods are equally valid in market research and as part of the design of the human-interface of products. However, it is perhaps in the identification of hidden needs that the techniques will bring the biggest returns. As an article in Harvard Business Review stated, "the scouting out of new opportunities and

Table 1.2   Usage of New Techniques to Identify Hidden Needs

	Technique	Companies known to be using this technique	Specific application (if known)
1)	Systematic observation (including video ethnography)	• Arm and Hammer, USA, 1960s	• Observed typical uses of baking powder
		• Sony, 1970s	• Regularly "watching" people, as opposed to formal market research
		• Rank-Xerox, USA, 1980s	• Observing the problems users encountered with photocopiers, in order to develop easier to use machines
		• NCR, USA, 1990s	• Observed people using ATMs, to improve the design
		• Unilever, 1990s	• Observed Asian workers' purchasing of afternoon snacks and developed a new soup
		• Iomega, USA, circa 2000	• Photographed and analyzed the home and office environment, to better understand data storage needs
		• Clark's shoes, UK, 2001	• Understanding the purchasing process for walking boots (see Box Case 1.1)
		• Intel, USA, 2001	• Anthropological expeditions to understand different sets of customers
		• Vodafone, Europe, 2004	• Photographed and analyzed the contents of 5000 women's handbags, as part of their design of a mobile telephone
2)	Contextual interviewing	• General Mills, USA, circa 1995	• Study of how consumers and their children eat breakfast. Led to "Go-Gurt"; a yoghurt in a tube that can be eaten without a spoon
		• Microsoft, USA, circa 2000	• Experiencing the use of technology in the users' own environment, in order to understand the user's perspective on software design
		• Whirlpool, USA, circa 2000	• Validation of the proposed name for a luxury bath—checked by gathering users' feelings whilst taking a long relaxing bath
		• Clark's shoes, UK, 2001	• Users' requirements, as observed in locations such as the Lake District, UK
3)	Repertory grid	• Hewlett-Packard, early 1990s	• Identifying key design features for medical equipment
		• Bosch, Germany, 2002	• Understanding operators' views on production line equipment

Continued

Table 1.2   Continued

	Technique	Companies known to be using this technique	Specific application (if known)
4)	Lead users	• 3M, USA, 1990s	• Design of surgical drapes—by focusing on the hygiene problems faced by hospitals in developing countries
		• Hilti, Switzerland, 1990s	• Design of industrial fixings
		• Contacta, UK, 2005	• Establishing an on-going dialog with customers—in this case hearing aid users
5)	Empathy building	• Ford, UK, 1990s	• Product designers on the Focus project wore thick "Michelin Man" suits to simulate the problems elderly drivers have in climbing into their cars.

Notes: Although not an exhaustive list, this table gives includes examples drawn from:—Christensen, C. M., Cook, S. and Hall, T., "Marketing Malpractice: The Cause and the Cure," *Harvard Business Review*, Vol. 83, No. 12, December 2005, pp. 74–83.—Fellman, M. W., "Breaking Tradition," *Marketing Research*, Vol. 11, No. 3, Fall 1999—Goffin, K., "Understanding Customers' Views: A Practical Example of the Use of Repertory Grid Technique," *Management Research News*, Vol. 17, No. 7/8, 1994, pp. 17–28.—Leonard-Barton, D. and Rayport, J. F., "Spark Innovation through Empathic Design," *Harvard Business Review*, Vol. 75, No. 6, November–December, 1997.—McFarland, J., "Margaret Mead Meets Consumer Fieldwork," *Harvard Management Update*, Vol. 6, No. 8, August 2001, pp. 5–6.—Squires, S. and Byrne, B. (eds.) (2002) *Creating Breakthrough Ideas: The Collaboration of Anthropologists and Designers in the Product Development Industry.* Westport, CT: Bergin and Garvey.

technological possibilities, arguably creates the most value. Unfortunately, it is the least understood by managers."[27]

Survey Evidence of Usage

The limitation of looking just at the reported usage of the new techniques is that only success stories are reported and also the general level of usage cannot be gauged. Reliable surveys are needed to generate this information. One author has suggested that there is an "explosion" in the use of ethnographic techniques for market research[28] but in our experience the reality is that the level of usage remains very low and there can be significant organizational barriers to the adoption of new techniques. In a survey of 36 leading companies in the UK[29] we showed that most market research is still strongly focused on customer visits (86 percent), surveys (64 percent), and focus groups (50 percent). Although nearly 60 percent reported using "systematic observation," visits to some of these companies showed observation to be informal and not to use a full ethnographic approach (only used by 8 percent of companies—see Figure 1.3).

Figure 1.4 shows the results of useful research by Professor Robert Cooper (of Stage-Gate fame). In a survey of 160 U.S. companies he looked at the usage of various ideation methods and their perceived effectiveness (on a

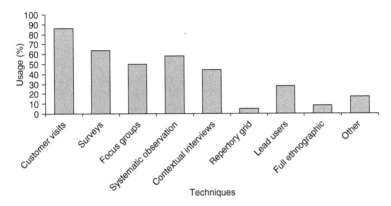

Figure 1.3   Usage of Techniques by Leading UK Companies
Source: Cranfield School of Management Innovation and Design Excellence Awards (IDEA) 2006-7

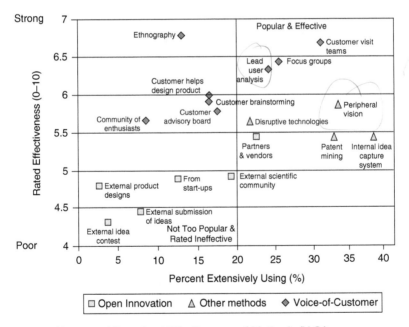

Figure 1.4   Usage and Perceived Effectiveness of Methods (U.S.)
Source: Based on Exhibit 2 (page 15) from: Cooper, R. G. and Edgett, S. J., "Ideation for Product Innovation: What Are the Best Methods?" PDMA Visions Magazine, Vol. XXXII, No. 1, March 2008, pp. 12–17. Used with permission.

scale from 1 poor to 10 excellent). Interestingly, open innovation methods (indicated by squares and including, for example, *external ideas contests* and *external submission of ideas*) are all in the bottom-left corner of the diagram— they are neither widely used nor perceived as particularly effective. The results show that ethnography is perceived as the most useful method but it is only used by about 15 percent of organizations. Lead user technique and focus groups are both highly used and regarded, whereas other methods (indicated by triangles) such as *disruptive technologies* and *peripheral vision* are relatively often used but their effectiveness is not judged as high.[30] The two limitations of the diagram are that the utility of the methods is only measured by managers' perceptions, rather than the methods having been systematically compared, and the research did not check whether different methods were used in combination.

Combining the Techniques

Figure 1.5 indicates how the techniques should be used in combination. It shows that effective market research combines traditional survey and focus group research, with techniques such as observation, repertory grid analysis, and lead users. The choice of techniques to be used depends on the aims of the research. Using different techniques allows the limitations of single techniques to be mitigated.

Once the appropriate combination of market research techniques has been selected, data collection and analysis can begin. Triangulation of the results from different techniques enables higher levels of validity to be achieved. The output of the data analysis is normally a deep understanding of customers' (or users') problems, issues, and needs (particularly hidden needs).

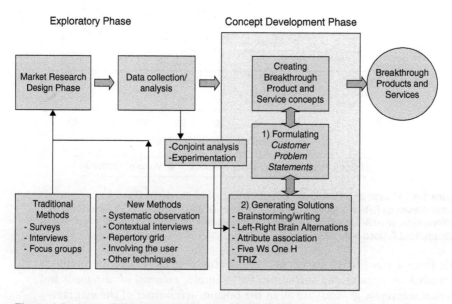

Figure 1.5 Using Different Techniques in Combination

The needs identified in the market research should be seen as problems and issues that require suitable solutions (see Box Case 1.5). This is a fundamental difference to the traditional approach to market research where the aim is nearly always to directly collect customers' views on suitable product attributes. Hidden needs analysis takes the problems identified (or an understanding of the job the customer has to get done) as the starting point and presents these in a challenging way to new product development teams, who then brainstorm solutions. Typically, brainstorming is used by companies to generate ideas for new products. In contrast, HNA focuses on solving customers' problems that have been identified in probing market research. To support this process, techniques such as *attribute association* (where each attribute of an existing product or service is considered and ideas for modifications generated focused on solving the customer's problems) may be used. The resulting attributes of the new product or service can be tested with potential customers through *experimentation* (for example, *rapid prototyping*). Similarly, customers' preferences and the trade-offs they are willing to make (for example, between features and price) can be better understood by *conjoint analysis*. The process of developing features to solve customers' problems is a complex one that can be accelerated by using what is known as *TRIZ*. This acronym is derived from the Russian for *Theory of Creative Problem Solving* and it is a technique for solving problems through looking at similar problems that have been solved in the past and documented in patents. As indicated by Figure 1.5, hidden needs analysis provides the inspiration from which breakthrough products can be developed.

Box Case 1.5

The Home of the Future[31]

Everyone knows that information technology has had a major impact on our lives but few of us are aware of the steady impact it is having on the home. Ethnographic market research, with its focus on cultural aspects is admirably suited for drawing out such changes.

In a project to understand the use of information technology in the home, researchers visited 50 families in the U.S. and used systematic observation, contextual interviews, and photography. These data were supplemented by the results of focus groups, consumer diaries, and a survey to gain a comprehensive picture. The research showed that the technical advances in personal computers were not matched by good solutions for housing the devices and printers in the home. This clearly led to some ideas for new furniture products, including a "tandem" chair so that parents could easily work with their child on one computer. However, the deeper cultural findings of the research were also interesting. The way the home is perceived is changing. It is no longer "just" a "physical space" and family "social space" but it must double-up as a "technical space." These changes have implications for architects, interior designers, and computer designers and will bring a host of product opportunities but only for the organizations that are capable of understanding the subtle needs that these changes are bringing.

Using the Techniques in New Product Development

Any innovation must progress through a number of *phases* before it is commercially viable. This is true, irrespective of the type of innovation—whether it is a new product or a new service. All innovations begin with the generation of ideas and the road to implementation and commercial success can be a long one. In addition, many ideas fall by the wayside.

Figure 1.6 shows the typical phases of innovation, with a funnel of ideas being generated and collected by an organization. Innovative approaches to market research are needed to generate ideas that help the customer "to do the job" quickly and effectively.[32] Some ideas are filtered out swiftly whereas others progress further and are developed into what are normally called concepts. An initial idea might be developed into a concept by a small team of people from different functional areas of the business working together part-time over a few weeks or, for more complex ideas, the process of developing the concept may take longer. At the concept stage, an idea for a new product or new service will have been formalized to the extent that some questions such as the size of the potential market and the best way the product or service can be designed will have been considered (although these questions will not have been answered to a high level of detail). Similarly, at the concept stage, ideas for new processes will have been analyzed as to the investments required and the returns these can bring. Normally, management takes the decision on which concepts will be chosen to become *projects* (the implementation phase), although the way in which an organization chooses the particular concepts for development may not be transparent to many of the employees.

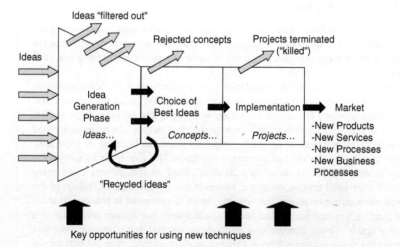

Figure 1.6   The Typical Phases of an Innovation ("The Development Funnel")
Note: The idea to compare the phases of an innovation to a funnel goes back at least to: Majaro, S., *The Creative Gap*. London: Longman, 1988.

As indicated by the diagram, there are three points where behavioral science-based techniques can add particular value to product development (see arrows indicating "Key opportunities for using the new techniques"). These are in identifying customers' hidden needs, for which suitable solutions (that is, product concepts) can be brainstormed by considering, for example, available technologies. The next area where social science methods are very useful is in the human factors of product service design (in new service design, the consumer's view is very often not adequately considered). Finally, a deeper understanding of purchasing behavior is extremely valuable in planning the way a new product or service will be marketed.

The new techniques should be seen as enhancing the possibilities available to market researchers and they will normally be used in combination, often with the traditional focus group and survey.

THE STRUCTURE OF THIS BOOK

This book is structured in three parts. Part 1 consists of three chapters covering the need for identifying hidden needs and important (but often overlooked) characteristics of the two main traditional market research methods—surveys and focus groups. Part 2 covers new methods of market research, with chapters on each of the main techniques. Part 3 then discusses how the results of using the different techniques can be used in combination to generate concepts for breakthrough products and services. Figure 1.7 shows the relationship

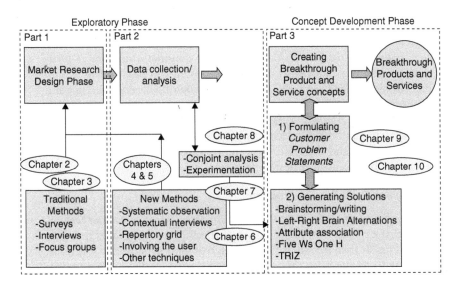

Figure 1.7 Developing Product Breakthrough and the Chapters of this Book

between the process of developing breakthrough products and the chapters in this book.

PART 1: Introduction and Traditional Methods of Market Research

Chapter 1: Introduction to Customers' Hidden Needs. This chapter explains the need to use new methods for market research and the risks of relying solely on surveys and focus groups.

Chapter 2: Surveys and Interviews. Here we explain the use of surveys and interviews in market research, including how questions should be formulated. We cover both *direct* and *indirect* questions (including *projection* and using metaphors).

Chapter 3: Focus Groups (and Variations). Focus groups are very widely used but they need to be used in the right way. We explain when and how they can be used effectively and the variations of the technique.

PART 2: New Methods of Market Research

Chapter 4: Ethnographic Market Research. Observing end-customers using products or consuming services can give excellent insights into their behavior and needs. Although the idea of observing customers is not new, systematic approaches based on ethnography are needed to maximize the effectiveness of this approach. In this chapter we discuss the history of ethnography, how it is applied in market research, and how the results can be analyzed.

Chapter 5: Example: Warehouse Equipment Research. In this chapter, we explain how the concepts introduced in Chapter 4 were applied in an actual market research project, investigating opportunities for new equipment in warehouses.

Chapter 6: Repertory Grid Technique. This technique comes from psychology—a science that investigates how humans think. We explain how it can be applied to understand how customers think. Repertory grid is particularly effective at helping customers to articulate their hidden needs.

Chapter 7: Involving the User. In this chapter, we consider a number of techniques that can uncover hidden needs through close involvement of users and customers. We discuss *lead user technique, virtual communities, crowdsourcing,* and *rapid prototyping.*

Chapter 8: Conjoint Analysis. This technique enables us to understand how customers make their purchasing decisions. The "trade-offs" they make between, for example, the price and the features of the range of products on the market helps us to make better product design decisions.

PART 3: Designing Breakthrough Products

Chapter 9: Combining the Techniques: Designing Breakthrough Products and Services. This chapter first explains how hidden needs analysis provides insights into customers' problems. It then describes the challenge of identifying viable solutions. A powerful way to do this is for the cross-functional product development teams to brainstorm the way in which the new product or new service can provide the necessary benefits.

Chapter 10: Creating a Culture Focused on Hidden Needs. There can be significant organizational barriers to the adoption of new approaches to market research and product development. This chapter first presents a detailed case study on Bosch Packaging Technology's identification of their customers' hidden needs. It then discusses what can be learnt from this case and shows that organizational barriers can be overcome in order to develop breakthrough products.

Format of the Chapters

Each chapter follows an essentially similar style:

- A particular market research technique is discussed. This includes a historical perspective, advantages and limitations and key points to consider in using the technique.
- The explanations of the techniques are backed by examples, including four or five short "box cases" (mini case studies) per chapter, selected to illustrate key aspects of how companies have utilized new methods for market research.
- Important terms related to hidden needs analysis are first shown in italics and then their meaning is explained.
- A summary recaps the main points and gives practical recommendations for managers.
- Two or three annotated recommendations for readings—either books or papers—are given, for readers who want to go deeper into the topics covered in this book.
- The references are listed at the end of the book in the order in which they were cited in each chapter.
- In some of the chapters the reader is referred to key data collection or analysis instruments (for example, forms for interview data collection) and these are in the relevant appendices.

SUMMARY

The drawback with traditional market research is that it merely reflects common knowledge. In discussions with companies we use the analogy of an iceberg: make sure your market research is taking you below the waterline as a mass of ideas for product designs is typically hidden. This chapter has shown:

- Many new products and services fail because they do not have any differentiating features.
- The root cause of product failure is a poor understanding of customers due to an overreliance on surveys and focus groups.
- Emerging techniques for market research are largely based on the behavioral sciences and these allow customers' hidden needs to be identified.

- The main techniques are ethnographic market research (including systematic observation and contextual interviewing), repertory grid analysis, and involving the user (such as lead user technique). Each has advantages and limitations and so their use in combination is most effective.

In Chapter 2 we will look at survey technique and how it can still be useful in combination with the newer approaches.

MANAGEMENT RECOMMENDATIONS

- Determine how ideas for new products and services are typically generated in your organization and identify opportunities to improve this process.
- Check which market research techniques are familiar to your marketing department and how hidden needs analysis could be applied to your next new product development.
- Ensure that the expertise to understand the customer is a core competence in your organization.

RECOMMENDED READING

1. Squires, S. and Byrne, B. (eds.) (2002) *Creating Breakthrough Ideas: The Collaboration of Anthropologists and Designers in the Product Development Industry*. Westport, CT: Bergin and Garvey. [Excellent book on how insights from the social sciences have influenced product development. Less on the techniques themselves.]
2. Leonard-Barton, D. and Rayport, J. F., "Spark Innovation through Empathic Design," *Harvard Business Review*, Vol. 75, No. 6, November–December, 1997, pp. 102–113. [Good paper on how observing customers can identify needs for which product solutions can be brainstormed but gives little detail though on how to analyze the results.]
3. Goffin, K. and Mitchell, R. *Innovation Management: Strategy and Implementation Using the Pentathlon Framework*. Basingstoke, UK: Palgrave Macmillan Academic Publishers, 2nd Edition 2010. [In this book we concentrate on the broader aspects of innovation management.]

2 SURVEYS AND INTERVIEWS

A survey researcher asks people questions in a written questionnaire...or during an interview, then records answers. The researcher manipulates no situation or condition; people simply answer questions.[1]

o Not sure this is correct

INTRODUCTION

Surveys are the classic tool for market research and because they are ubiquitous, every one of us has at some time been asked to answer survey questions. Writing survey questions is deceptively difficult and, consequently, many questionnaires are so badly phrased or designed that the results are of little value. Therefore, it is absolutely essential for marketers to become good at survey technique. Although customers may have difficulties in answering direct questions about their future product requirements, surveys and interviews remain at the heart of market research and they are essential complement to newer methods for identifying hidden needs.

Different types of surveys exist: interviews (face-to-face, telephone, or by video) and questionnaires (for example, on paper via post, or via the Internet). This chapter explains the key aspects to designing and conducting surveys and interviews covering:

- The history of surveying and interviewing.
- Applying the technique.
- Analyzing the results of surveys.
- Limitations to consider.
- Variations on surveys and interviews.

HISTORY OF SURVEYING AND INTERVIEWING

Surveys have been used for centuries and probably the first major survey—a *census* (a survey of the whole *population*)—was conducted by the Romans. At the time of Christ's birth, Saint Luke reports "it came to pass in those days, that there went out a decree from Caesar Augustus, that all the world should be taxed...And Joseph also went up from Galilee...with Mary his espoused wife, being great with child ..."[2]

Throughout history, there are several references to census data being collected. For instance, a large-scale survey was commissioned by William the Conqueror in England in 1086. The results of this survey were used to clarify land owner-ship, calculate taxes, and determine the number of inhabitants able to defend the country. The results were recorded in the *Domesday Book*, which is kept in The National Archives in London. In addition to surveys for administrative purposes, the emergence of social science led to an interest in collecting data on people's way of life. Charles Booth is regarded as one of the originators of the social sur-vey and for his monumental 17-volume study the *Labour and Life of the People of London*[3] he attempted to collect data from the whole population of London! National governments still occasionally collect data from all of their citizens but social scientists normally base their conclusions on data obtained from smaller samples and use these to infer the characteristics of the population.[4]

Surveys have been used in the U.S. to conduct opinion polls since the early nineteenth century. Newspapers often sponsored polls during presidential elec-tions and were keen on printing exclusive stories. But the theoretical foundations of survey technique were not well developed and how to analyze the data and interpret the results was not well understood. For example, in the 1936 presiden-tial election, two large-scale competing surveys were conducted, one of which was sponsored by *The Literary Digest*, a weekly magazine that shaped public opin-ion at the time.[5] Readers of the magazine, automobile owners, and households owning a telephone were selected for the survey. About two million responses were collected, and based on these it appeared that Alf Landon would win by a large margin. The *American Institute of Public Opinion*, founded by the political scientist George Horace Gallup, ran the alternative survey in which Franklin D. Roosevelt was correctly predicted to be the winner. Gallup's survey, later called the *Gallup Poll*, was based on a relatively small sample that was carefully selected to be representative of the voting population. The *Literary Digest*'s approach was flawed because magazine readers, automobile owners, and households owning a telephone were not representative of the general population of the time.

In 1948 history repeated itself in another U.S. presidential election, when the candidates were Thomas Dewey and Harry Truman. Based on a large-scale survey, the headline of the first edition of the Chicago Daily Tribune declared "Dewey Defeats Truman."[6] Truman—the actual winner—was photographed that morning after he was declared winner triumphantly holding a copy of the newspaper with the erroneous headline. Yet again a sampling error had led to the wrong conclusion—the newspaper based its headline on a telephone sur-vey and, at that time, only families with higher incomes owned a telephone.

Market researchers had started to adopt more scientific techniques in the 1930s[7] and good questionnaire design and *sampling* (selection of the people to be questioned from the wider population) were recognized to be essential. Survey techniques have greatly improved over the past 50 years but good design and appropriate sampling remain fundamental.

Our history has, up until now, only considered direct questions. In the 1880s and 1890s psychologists recognized that patients might deny their own emotions and so responses to direct questions can be unreliable. It was largely the work of Sigmund Freud (1856–1939) that created the field of psychoanalysis and the search for ways to uncover unconscious or suppressed thoughts. Projection techniques require respondents to describe what they perceive in a visual stimulus, such as an inkblot. Their responses "project" traits of their personality, or thoughts,[8] and the technique is closely connected with Freud's work on paranoia.[9]

Projection techniques were first used for market research in the 1940s[10] and a famous study was published in 1950.[11] The study used two almost identical shopping lists as the stimuli (one list included "instant coffee" and the other "noninstant coffee"). Housewives were asked to describe the characteristics of a typical shopper for each of the two lists. Respondents believed that the shopping list with instant coffee was from a "lazy" and "sloppy" housewife, whereas the other one with noninstant coffee was believed to be from a "thrifty" and "good" housewife.[12] Today, projection techniques are used by marketing research agencies to investigate purchasing behavior, consumers' reactions to packaging, and to identify emotional reactions to products and brands. However, it should be recognized that projection is often applied in an unstructured way and its value in market research has been seriously questioned.[13]

Most market research interviews rely on the verbal answers given by respondents but it has been claimed that two-thirds of all social meaning is exchanged nonverbally.[14] The *Zaltman Metaphor Elicitation Technique* (ZMET) is an interview technique that analyzes the way people use metaphors, something that is frequent in everyday speech.[15] ZMET elicits metaphors through nondirect questions and probes subconscious thoughts and behaviors.[16] In 1995, it became the first market research tool to be patented in the U.S.[17] and it has been said that it "really does touch a part of consumers you cannot get to with any other technique I've ever seen."[18]

Surveys and interviews have developed significantly and sophisticated approaches are now available to determine the sample and to design the questions. When used in combination with other methods, surveys and interviews are indispensable tools for market researchers.

APPLYING THE TECHNIQUE

To apply survey technique successfully, the *preparation stage* is essential. This stage includes determining the aims of the research and designing the questions. Many mistakes are made in preparing surveys and so we will place considerable emphasis on preparation. When preparation is complete, the full *administration* starts with a *pilot* test, to ensure that the *survey instrument* (the *questionnaire*, or the *interview guideline*) is effective before full data collection starts. During the *analysis stage* the researcher first checks that the survey has generated reliable answers to all of the research questions and then determines what has been learnt about the sample population.

Preparation

Correct survey preparation covers five areas:

1. Clarifying aims of the research by reviewing what is already known, and identifying gaps in our knowledge.
2. Selecting the appropriate method(s) for data collection.
3. Deciding the content of the survey, and formulating the questions.
4. Designing the *layout* of the questionnaire.
5. Determining the sampling strategy, including defining the *population*, and selecting the *sampling frame* (the people who will be interviewed or surveyed).

Clarifying the Research Aims

Before conducting a survey for academic research, great emphasis is placed on *the literature* (what has been previously published) and this guides the researcher to the research questions. This process takes a considerable amount of time. In contrast, companies will want to design their surveys quickly but it is still essential to check what has previously been published. For example, business case studies, trade journals, market research reports and the like should be reviewed—they can give ideas on both the market to be studied and the questions to ask. Many companies skip this step, because they are not aware of what has been published. With the Internet, searching for relevant information is easy, although, of course, some market reports may need to be purchased.

Selecting the Data Collection Method

In designing the survey, the researcher has to decide on how to collect the data. Interviews and questionnaires are the two methods and both can be administered in several ways.

Interviews can be conducted face-to-face, via video (such as Skype), or by telephone. Experienced interviewers are able to pick up a great number of cues in face-to-face interviews including *extralinguistic signals* (the tone of the voice) and *body language* (nonverbal communication, which is often culture specific). If the interview is conducted in the customer's (or user's) own environment—*contextual interviews* (see Chapter 4)—the researcher can ask questions based on the physical environment. Conducting interviews per video is a fast, cost effective way to reach geographically dispersed respondents and body language may also be (partly) observed.

In face-to-face, video, and telephone interviews, the *rhetorical funnel* guides the questioning. This "starts with a broad question and progressively narrows down to the important specific point or points."[19] This approach allows the interviewer to react *ad hoc* to responses and ask respondents to expand on their answers. Such probing questions should be prepared in advance as *semi-structured questions*. Respondents are typically prepared to spend more time in direct interviews—up to 60 minutes maximum (compared with completing a questionnaire, which should not take longer than 15–30 minutes). It can be valuable to interview managers who process expert knowledge of the topic being investigated.[20] Managers may ask whether, instead of several individual interviews, a group of managers can be interviewed together to save time. However, the respondents do not save time, as the interview is still 60 minutes per interviewee. As long as the goal of the study is not to explore team dynamics, we recommend individual interviews because peer pressure and groupthink are eliminated.[21] A word of warning on interviews—researchers need to be trained to ask questions in a neutral, nonbiasing way and to become good listeners.

Questionnaires are mainly administered through the post or the Internet. Text message surveys on mobile phones are popular in Asia but have the limitation that only a few questions can be asked. Response rates for postal surveys are notoriously low but incentives, providing return envelopes, sending reminders, and so on can help.[21] Internet surveys often generate higher response rates but whether those who respond are typical consumers needs to be considered. One way to persuade potential respondents to take part in a study is to personally administer the survey. This method is commonly applied in shopping centers or airport waiting areas, where researchers approach travelers with questionnaires on clipboards: this is often called shopping mall research. The advantage of personally administered surveys is they check whether the respondent

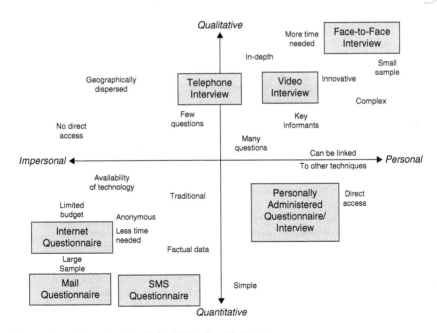

Figure 2.1 Choosing the Data Collection Method

is representative of the target population by asking qualifying questions such as: "Are you a member of a frequent flyer program?" Furthermore, open issues can be clarified immediately. When a questionnaire is personally administered, respondents get the impression they are being interviewed but the questions strictly follow the questionnaire, with the researcher recording the answers and ensuring the data are complete. (When multiple interviewers are used they must be trained to ensure consistency.)

Figure 2.1 indicates the main factors to consider in choosing the data collection method: administration of data collection is the horizontal axis (*impersonal* to *personal*) and the dominant nature of the data being collected is the vertical axis (*qualitative* to *quantitative*). The types of survey are illustrated by gray shading, whereas the contexts are given in a small black font. Although every type of survey can be applied in almost every context, the figure indicates the survey types that work particularly well within a given setting. If, for example, only a few survey questions need to be asked to a geographically dispersed sample, telephone interviewing lends itself as a suitable approach. However, time, resources, and access permitting, face-to-face interviews may be more appropriate.

Selecting the Categories of Questions

There are three categories of survey questions as shown in Table 2.1: *demographic*, *attitudinal*, and *behavioral*. Some surveys collect only one category (for example, demographics when a supermarket cashier asks for the customer's postcode), but most surveys include all three categories so that attitudinal and behavioral information can be analyzed in combination with demographics (see Box Case 2.1).

Table 2.1   Categories of Survey Questions

Categories	Explanation	Example Question	Aim of Questions
Demographics	The personal background of respondents.	What is your marital status?	• Analyzing segments in terms of age, gender, level of education, social class, and so on. • To check whether respondent is representative of the target population.
Attitudinal	Respondents' personal perceptions and opinions on different topics.	What is your opinion on…?	• Understanding perceptions on products, services, shopping experiences, and so on.
Behavioral	Data on the frequency and way in which particular actions are performed.	How often do you…?	• Measuring product usage, shopping frequency, number of hospital visits, number of holidays spent abroad per year, and so on.

Box Case 2.1

Mexican Medications—Demographics, Attitudes and Behaviors[23]

A significant number of U.S. residents go to Mexico to buy their medications and American healthcare researchers conducted a survey in 2001 to shed some light on this development. The survey was a self-administered questionnaire including three categories: "demographics" (8 questions; for example, age, health insurance), "behavioral data" (14 questions; including "How many medications did you purchase?", "How often do you purchase medication in Mexico?"), and "attitudinal information" (2 questions; for example, "Did you purchase your medication in Mexico because: (Check all that apply) You don't have insurance, Don't want to see your doctor, They are less expensive, and so on.)."

During the course of one week, 103 purchasers were approached in a Mexican pharmacy and 100 agreed to participate in the survey. Based on the results, the researchers determined the age of customers (18–81, average 50), their gender (66 percent women), and their citizenship (95 percent U.S.). Behavioral data identified the products that were purchased and the medical conditions of the respondents. The results showed that the main reasons for purchasing medications in Mexico were the lower prices (mentioned by 66.7 percent of respondents), respondents' lack of insurance (mentioned by 17.1 percent), and not wanting to see a doctor (mentioned by 12.4 percent of respondents).

Formulating Questions

The final part of preparation is formulating the questions. This involves choosing the *type of questions*, the *wording*, and the *sequence of questions*.

There are three possible types of questions: *closed-ended*, *semistructured*, and *open-ended* questions. *Closed questions* are used to collect respondents' perceptions, providing them with alternative answers, or offering a *Likert* (numerical) scale for responses. Figure 2.2 shows two closed questions and respondents can indicate their "agreement" or "disagreement," or they can respond with "Don't Know" (or "Neither Nor" on the Likert-Scale). If the Likert-Scale has an odd number of options (for example, "1" to "5"), respondents can use the mid-scale option as a "safe" response that is often synonymous with "Don't Know." Therefore, researchers often prefer an even number of options, which forces respondents to either "agree" or "disagree." The number of points that should be provided on the Likert-Scale depends on the level of knowledge of the respondents. For instance, in a study of car performance, enthusiasts may find a 1–5 scale too granular, whereas other respondents who regard cars as just a means of transport will find the five-point scale appropriate.

Respondents can also be given the option to select from several alternative answers and this is an ideal way to explore preferences. Researchers must carefully select the options, as inappropriate ones will frustrate respondents and lead to incorrect answers. Figure 2.3 shows several examples of "multiple-choice"

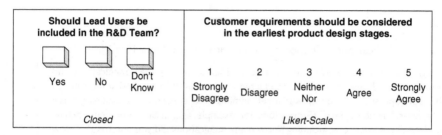

Figure 2.2   Questions Indicating Agreement or Disagreement

Which source adds the most innovativeness to a product design project?	Rank the six sources in terms of the level of innovativeness they add to a product design project.
(please tick the most appropriate box)	(1 being highest level of innovativeness; 6 being the lowest level)
OR	OR
Which sources add the most innovativeness to a product design project?	Rate the six sources in terms of the level of innovativeness they add to a product design project.
(please select 3 sources)	(1= adding the highest level of innovativeness; 5 = adding nothing to the level)
☐ In-house technical functions	☐ In-house technical functions
☐ In-house marketing department	☐ In-house marketing department
☐ External marketing agency	☐ External marketing agency
☐ Suppliers	☐ Suppliers
☐ Customers	☐ Customers
☐ Published sources	☐ Published sources
☐ Others (please specify)_____	
Multiple-Choice	*Ranking or Rating*

Figure 2.3   Questions Offering Alternative Answers

questions and "ranking" and "rating" questions. For the question in the left column, respondents can tick the most appropriate answers with the "Others (please specify)" option allowing them to give an answer that the research team might not be aware of. For the question in the right column, respondents can rank the sources from "1" to "6" (but rankings are difficult to analyze, as will be explained later).

If researchers are unsure of the possible responses, or if maximum flexibility is required, then open-ended questions are appropriate, as illustrated by Figure 2.4 (Box case 2.2 gives examples of open-ended questions used by

	Is capturing the "voice of the customer" in the earliest stages of the product design project really important - why?
What Coffee Machine do you own? (Name of Manufacturer and Model)	_____
	_____
Manufacturer _____ Model:_____	_____
	_____
Fixed and Narrow Scope	*Free and Wide Scope*

Figure 2.4 Open-ended Questions

Bentley Motors). Open-ended questions can offer respondents a "fixed and narrow scope," as shown on the left in Figure 2.4, or a "free and wide scope," as on the right. Offering a wide scope allows respondents to express their views, and original data are collected.[24] The drawback of open-ended questions is that respondents may be reluctant to write detailed answers or may be unable to articulate their views clearly. In addition, because the answers are not standardized, researchers need to reserve sufficient time for coding and analysis (to be discussed later).

Surveys normally include various types of questions and researchers need to avoid the many mistakes that are often made.[25] The most common mistakes are ambiguous terms, the use of jargon, biased response options, double-barreled questions, double-negative questions, incorrect assumptions (in questions and answers), inadequate response options, leading questions, overly long questions, questions which risk recall bias, offensive questions, overlapping categories, terms that are easily misheard (in surveys that are personally administered), and questions that are not applicable to all respondents. To make these clear, Table 2.2 shows examples "poor questions" that we collected in recent years from real questionnaires: a survey of small businesses by a trade association; a survey by a fitness club of its 800 members; and a large-scale survey by a driving association. The effort wasted on these surveys should act as a reminder of the importance of correctly worded questions.

Once the wording of the individual questions has been optimized, they need to be placed in an appropriate order because the sequence of questions impacts responses.[26] General questions set the context and are normally at the beginning. Certain questions may influence the answers to later ones (the *carryover effect*) and so care must be taken. Most surveys start with demographic questions to ease respondents into the survey process. Most respondents appreciate this but sometimes it can be better to start with interesting questions and keep the demographics to the end. As the sequence of questions has an impact on the answers to a survey, we recommend employing the *split-ballot technique*. Two versions of the survey, with a different order of questions should be pretested to double-check whether the order influences responses.

> **Box Case 2.2**
>
> ### Bentley Motors Limited—Keeping the Personal Touch[27]
>
> *Bentley Motors Limited* has manufactured luxury cars in Britain since 1919 and its cars are known for their combination of power, style, and comfort. About 900 cars were sold in 2000 and the marketing department knew many of their customers by name without having to access the company's database. In the past ten years sales have increased rapidly and, with considerably more Bentley owners than ever before, there could be a risk that the personal touch with the customer base could be lost.
>
> The Bentley brand has a very strong heritage and is deeply rooted in tradition and the company's values. However, Bentley's approach to market research is anything but traditional. Kiran Parmar, responsible for global research and concept planning, explains, "it is critically important for Bentley to understand how the brand and products are perceived in the wider market place. My main objective is to funnel the 'voice of the customer' into our product development process."
>
> A large number of customers and potential customers visit the manufacturing plant in Crewe, England each year and, for Parmar, this is an excellent opportunity to sound out the market. "Through research," says Parmar, "we are able not only to get close to our existing customers but also to potential new ones. We need to understand their desires, needs and values and so this is why most of our in-house research is qualitative." If, for instance, design needs to have feedback on the type of leather they want to use for an interior, Parmar and his colleagues generate a list of key questions. They show visitors various types of leather and ask questions such as, "how important is the feel of the leather to you?", or "what does luxury leather feel like?" These open-ended questions allow customers to express their thoughts freely and "although we are conducting a survey, we make it feel like a conversation to the customer and we show that we truly value their views." The many visitors to the factory personally experience the passion behind the Bentley brand and their "collective voice" is captured for new product development.
>
> Over the last few years, new Bentley models have really captured customers' imagination and generated annual sales of over 10,000 cars. But the company is keeping the intimate dialog with its customers alive.

Layout

Once the most appropriate order of the questions has been decided upon, the layout needs to be designed. Layout is the visual design of a questionnaire, which should help to make it easier for the respondent to answer and minimize inaccurate answers. Good layout prevents confusion of the sort shown in Figure 2.5 (from a national survey of shopping behavior). For example, Question 21 makes it difficult to see where to tick, the question does not define the size of the bottle, and it does not offer the option to answer "4 bottles in 1 month." Both Questions 17 and 21 have poor and confusing scaling. For example, "0 □ 0" and "4 □ 4+" in Question 17 have the response options mixed with coding (in bold) that the researchers will use in their analysis. These make sense to the researcher

Table 2.2 Poorly Worded Questions

	Question	Allowed Answers	Assessment of Mistake(s)	Common Mistake(s)	Suggestion for Improvement
1)	As a small business owner, how have your business activities changed during the past year?	1. Increased a lot; 2. Increased somewhat; 3. Increased a little; 4. Decreased.	a) Term "business activities" is unclear	a) Ambiguity of terms/use of jargon	a) Define terms
			b) Researcher assumes that business activities have changed	b) Incorrect assumptions	b) Include "Unchanged" option
			c) "Past year" is undefined; it could mean financial year, calendar year, budget year	c) Ambiguity of terms	c) Define term
			d) The answers are biased toward "increasing"	d) Biased set of response options	d) Balance the positive and negative alternatives

Continued

Table 2.2 Continued

	Question	Allowed Answers	Assessment of Mistake(s)	Common Mistake(s)	Suggestion for Improvement
2)	*If you went to the fittress studio yesterday, did you drink a sports drink?*	1. Yes; 2. No.	a) Somebody who did not go to the fitness studio yesterday cannot answer that question	a) Question not applicable to all respondents	a) Ask qualifying question and include skip-to instructions (for example, "Did you go to the fitness studio yesterday? If not, please go to Question 3").
			b) Time when sports drink is taken is undefined (any time before, during, or after the visit?)	b) Ambiguity of point in time	b) Define time period
3)	*When did you last drive a car while you were drunk?*	1. This week; 2. This month; 3. This year.	a) Respondent might feel too embarrassed to answer the question	a) Question is offensive	a) Try to avoid asking offensive questions as respondent might altogether lose interest in completing the survey
			b) Researcher assumes that respondent is frequently drunk driving	b) Missing alternative answer	b) Include "never" option
			c) Researcher asks two questions into one ("consuming alcohol" and "driving a car")	c) Question is double-barreled	c) Consider splitting question into two
			d) Options ill-defined as No. 2 includes No. 1; furthermore, No. 3 includes No. 1 and 2.	d) Overlapping categories	d) Define categories as distinct options

17 How many years No Claims do you have?
You: **0**   0 **1**   1 **2**   2 **3**   3 **4**   4+ **5**   Unsure
Partner: **0**   0 **1**   1 **2**   2 **3**   3 **4**   4+ **5**   Unsure

21 How many bottles of the following does your household purchase on average in 1 month?

Gin	**1**	Less than 1 **2**	1 **3**	2 **4**	3 **5**	4+
Whisky	**1**	Less than 1 **2**	1 **3**	2 **4**	3 **5**	4+
Vodka	**1**	Less than 1 **2**	1 **3**	2 **4**	3 **5**	4+

Figure 2.5   Poor and Confusing Survey Layout

but are utterly confusing for respondents. Layout should be tested to check[28]: the visual appearance (for example, appropriate font type and size, color, spacing, consistent format) and the logical structure (for example, numbering of questions, clear instructions). The appearance of the questionnaire must fit the context and, for example, surveys for use with teenagers will require appropriate designs.

Sampling

The last step in preparing a survey is choosing the sample. In most cases researchers will survey only a subset of the population. This subset is called the *sampling frame* and there are many approaches to selecting it that are covered in books devoted to sampling and statistics.[29] Leading companies decide on a sampling strategy to fit their research goals (see Box Case 2.3). Regardless of the sampling approach chosen pilot tests need to be conducted. We will give an overview of the key sampling techniques.

Probability sampling involves random selection of the sampling frame from the population. For example, in a survey of mail order customers, 10 percent of people in the company's database could be selected by a computer randomly. *Systematic random sampling* refers to a systematic reoccurring element (such as selecting every tenth person from an alphabetically ordered list of customers). In *stratified random sampling*, the population is divided into homogeneous subgroups (so-called *strata*; for example, customers by postcode or gender) and an equal number of people are selected from each of these. *Cluster sampling* refers to defining boundaries or adopting natural boundaries within the population. For instance, boundaries may refer to geographical areas and a manufacturer might select a sample of customers from major U.S. cities (this is called an *area sample*).

Nonprobability sampling is not based on the concept of probability[30] and the sample will probably not be representative of the entire population. Hence, results cannot be generalized and this is why quantitative researchers refrain from nonprobability sampling. If generalization is not an issue, nonprobability sampling can be a valid choice (see Chapter 4 for an explanation of nonprobability sampling in ethnographic market research). A *convenience sample*, as the name implies, is based on ease of selection but should be used with caution, as friends and colleagues may not be totally objective in their answers. Some research is conducted with a *purposive sample*, where the most appropriate respondents who fulfill particular criteria are chosen, for example, conducting a survey at an airport and asking a certain type of traveler about his or her holiday preferences. With the *snowball sampling*, the researcher surveys a small number of respondents first and then uses them as informants to recommend additional respondents. This approach is useful when the researcher is unclear about the segment to be investigated.

Box Case 2.3

Telefónica O2 Czech Republic—Really Listening to the Customer[31]

*Telefónica O2 Czech Republic—or TO2 for short—*is a leading telecoms provider based in Prague, which competes directly with Vodafone and T-Mobile in the mobile market, and with GTS Novera and České Radiokomunikace in the fixed line sector. It offers a comprehensive range of voice and data services and currently operates more than seven million fixed and mobile connections. TO2 has received numerous awards such as "Recognised for Excellence" by the European Foundation for Quality Management (2006) and as a "Health-Supporting Business" by the Czech government (2008). In a highly competitive business environment, TO2 has always needed to be highly responsive to customers' needs to stay ahead of the competition. Tomáš Hejkal heads the team responsible for TO2's Business Customer Experience and explains "we couldn't have made an impression in the telecommunication market without engaging with the customer." Many companies are keen to listen to the customer but do not develop the sort of expertise that TO2 has.

Tomáš' team constantly monitors the market from two different angles. The first angle to monitor customer satisfaction levels with telecom providers on a regular basis. To do this TO2 may hire a market research agency, or run surveys through their own hotline. In either case, TO2 develops a script so that the research agents ask specific questions and Tomáš explains, "we ask the customer about his satisfaction with TO2, whether we fulfil their expectations, and we also would like to know how we match up compared to an 'ideal operator' and the competition." The results from a random sample are used to calculate TO2's "Customer Satisfaction Index (CSI)." Stratified samples allow TO2 to know the different satisfaction levels with their various services, such the installation of services, customer care lines, and the service provided by representatives in stores. Good customer satisfaction data allows TO2 to identify areas of its business that need attention but as Tomáš points out, "the survey only gives us numbers to identify the areas that need to be improved. But the survey doesn't help us put the finger on what we need to do if CSI for one service drops."

The second angle of survey market research goes beyond CSI and depending on the service area that requires improvement, Tomáš will design telephone and face-to-face surveys with more open-ended questions and used with purposive samples (respondents who are knowledgeable about the specific service being investigated). "By exploring the difference between expectations and perceptions, we are able to present a set of customer requirements to our service development team. Following up every idea might not make sense, but generating a deep understanding of our customers is an exciting task. It is also a task that we don't want to outsource," says Tomáš. The capability to really understand customers is well and truely regarded as a core competency at TO2.

Administration

Before starting full data collection, researchers need to run *pilot tests* to ensure that the data collection method, the questions, their order, and the layout are appropriate. Analyzing the results of the pilot often leads to changes in some aspects of the actual survey.

It is important to select a pilot sample that is similar to that which will be used for the actual survey. It helps tremendously if pilot respondents are willing to discuss their experience with the questionnaire or survey, immediately after completion. This generates useful ideas about the wording, the sequence of questions, and layout. Since actual data are collected, researchers can analyze the pilot answers and ensure these address the aims of the project. We also recommend measuring the time taken to answer questionnaires or conduct interviews, so that the duration and costs of the study can be planned.

At the full data collection stage, questionnaires will need to be distributed to the respondents, or appointments with interviewees arranged. Provided that it is ethical (in the context of the research) and respondents agree, interviews should be audio-recorded, so that researchers do not need to take extensive notes. Interviews can be used for example to identify perceptions (see Box Case 2.4) but it is important that they are conducted in an environment familiar to the respondents but loud surroundings (for example, a café or a place of work) should be avoided. It is essential to test the recording equipment and check the microphone before an interview. We recommend transcribing and analyzing the interview as soon as possible.

Box Case 2.4

Deutsche Telekom AG—Learning to Listen in Order to Entertain[32]

In 2007, Deutsche Telekom AG launched a package called "Entertain." It is a TV service, which uses the infrastructure of the Internet to offer a large range of digital channels, recording functions, a video store, interactive applications, and so on. From the start, management set the aggressive target of winning one million customers by the end of 2009.

Thomas Müller leads Deutsche Telekom's market research department and was involved in the product definition. "We could have simply added more TV channels, however, interviews quickly showed that customers didn't find this attractive." So, Deutsche Telekom aimed to identify the features that customers value, what influences their purchase decisions, and the perceived barriers to Internet-TV. To obtain clear answers, the market research team used interviews with mainly open-ended questions. The results were communicated to the Entertain product development team: customers would like to be flexible when they watched TV and without any of the existing barriers of set times or technologies. "Customers told us they would like to be their own 'TV director' and so we made the whole package including recording and access as flexible as possible," Thomas concludes. Through the focus on identifying customer perceptions, the Entertain package has been very successful. It met its sales target and in January 2010, management set the next stretch target: one million additional customers by the end of 2011. To identify how to get there, Thomas and his team have started the next phase of market research.

ANALYZING THE RESULTS

In analysis phase, we distinguish between qualitative and quantitative data. Qualitative data are normally generated by open-ended questions posed for nonstatistical purposes, such as obtaining insights into a new area. An example would be exploratory research looking at customers' needs in an emerging segment. Quantitative data are collected from closed, multiple-choice questions, for example, an investigation of customer satisfaction levels throughout the world. For both qualitative and quantitative data there are excellent books providing detailed explanations of analysis methods.[33] Therefore we will only give an overview of the key concepts.

Analyzing Responses to Quantitative Questions

It is key for researchers "to recognize is that not all quantitative data are the same."[34] There are four types of measurement scales which produce data that need to be analyzed differently.[35] It should be noted that more sophisticated statistical tests and procedures can be applied to data collected by the interval and ratio scales in the following list:

1. *Nominal scales.* In these, numbers are assigned nominally to responses for identification and analysis. For example, responses to a "Male/Female" question may be denominated "0" and "1" respectively. But, if the gender of 40 respondents is male and 70 are female, it is not possible to compute a gender average. Nominal data are nonmetric and the only value that should be computed is the frequency count. Another example of a nominal value would be "Existing customers" versus "Potential customers."
2. *Ordinal scales* produce ranking data in which the numbers reflect only the order of objects, such as a consumer's ranking of top five drinks. Rankings are used extensively but are difficult to deal with statistically. This is because we do not know whether the difference between the rankings "1" and "2" is the same as, for example, between "4" and "5." Consequently, ordinal scales generate nonmetric data and an *arithmetic mean* (often simply called the *average*) should not be calculated.
3. *Interval scales.* Here the "distances" between the points on the measurement scale are the same (for example, temperature or any Likert-scales). As a consequence, "31" degrees is one degree warmer than "30," just as "21" is one degree warmer than "20." However, "20" is not twice as warm as "10," because "0" ("zero") on the Celsius scale is not absolute zero. With interval measurements, it is possible to compute the *mode* (the most frequently occurring value in a set of values), the *median* (the middle value in a set of values), and the arithmetic mean, normally referred to as the *average*. If, for instance, the temperatures on four given days were 20 degrees Celsius, 25 degrees, 28 degrees, and 25 degrees, the arithmetic mean is 24.50 degrees Celsius (in this case, the mode and median are both 25 degrees). (The mode and the median are useful measures of the central tendency of a set of values that do not fit into a normal distribution.)

4. *Ratio scales.* These are similar to interval scales in that the "distances" between scale points are the same but, in addition, the "0" ("zero") value is meaningful in that it represents the complete absence of the phenomenon being measured. Examples of ratio measurements include time and distance: for example, 100 cm is exactly twice as long as 50 cm. Similarly, if we ask respondents to tell us how many visits they made to a supermarket in the last month, "zero" means "have not visited the supermarket in the last month." Six visits are twice as many as "three" and thus, we are dealing with metric data.

Quantitative data can be analyzed by *descriptive statistics* or more complex approaches. Descriptive statistics identify the mid point of a distribution (by giving the *average*, or another suitable measure of *central tendency*). *Standard deviations* and similar measures describe the spread of measurements, whereas *skew* describes the symmetry and *kurtosis* the shape of the distribution curve. Descriptive statistics give us insights into the range of answers on a single variable, for example, the average age of respondents, or the percentage preferring a particular food. However, they do not provide insights into the relationships between different variables.

A complex and wide range of inferential statistics allow us to conduct more detailed analysis of our data, such as the relationships between variables (for example, Do older respondents prefer particular types of products?). They can also help us to identify trends. The main statistical approaches that can be applied to survey and interview data are (for clear explanations of these we recommend the textbook by Professors Geoff Norman and David Streiner[36]):

- *Analysis of variance.* Such tests allow us to determine whether the differences between two or more groups in our data (for example, market segments) are significant. In these methods the independent variables are nominal (for example, gender) and are used to explain differences in the dependent variables (for example, demand for a particular product).
- *Regression and correlation.* These are used when both the dependent and independent variables are interval measurements. *Factor analysis,* for example, allows us to look at the relationships between a wide range of variables and extract a smaller number of factors (each being a combination of variables) which explain the data.
- *Nonparametric statistics.* These tests allow us to deal with nominal and ordinal data.

Analyzing Responses to Qualitative Questions

Open-ended questions produce a wide range of answers that researchers need to *code*. Figure 2.6 shows a purchasing manager's response to: "Please describe your relationship you have with your suppliers." The respondent's answer includes the concepts "quality" and "price." Product quality is "conform to what has been agreed before…an objective measure." The meaning of the price code is "compared to the market average, some suppliers are expensive and other suppliers

> "Quality is absolutely key in our relationship with suppliers,…, products have to conform to what has been agreed before; I mean, if the quality is low, the scrap rate is high and we won't accept it. Quality is an objective measure that can be compared across suppliers. The other point that can be compared is 'price'. Compared to the market average, some suppliers are expensive and other suppliers offer their products reasonably priced. For us, knowing the average market price is important and we compare the offers against it. Of course, we don't just look for the best prices. But we check the quality of the cheapest suppliers first, before evaluating the expensive ones."
>
> (Purchasing Manager, Electronics)

Figure 2.6   Analyzing Qualitative Answers

offer their products reasonably priced." Reading further "if…the scrap rate is high…we won't accept it" represents a suitable quote that may exemplify the importance of product quality in the business report later. "We check the quality of the cheapest suppliers first, before evaluating the expensive ones" illustrates the order in which suppliers are evaluated. In such a way the answers to open-ended questions identify important factors (codes) and suitable quotes which give insights. The most common software program for analyzing the codes of multiple respondents is *NVIVO* (distributed by QSR International). Qualitative data also result from ethnographic methods and in Chapter 4 we will explain the coding procedure in more detail.

LIMITATIONS OF SURVEYS AND INTERVIEWS

Surveys and interviews are essential techniques but it is important to recognize that:

1. Surveys are overused and so potential respondents are often tired of completing questionnaires or being interviewed.
2. Extreme care is needed to ensure that the questions are clear and unambiguous.
3. The order in which questionnaires are answered cannot be guaranteed because respondents may skim over questions before starting to answer.
4. Researchers have to understand the concepts they are investigating and what they are trying to measure. Otherwise they will not be able to provide the appropriate responses for the respondent to choose from.
5. In case of Internet questionnaires, respondents must have access to the required technology in order to complete the survey (thus certain segments such as retired people may be excluded).

6. In many cases, it will not be obvious who has actually completed the questionnaire.
7. Market researchers often focus on quantity rather than quality, with superficial insights across a large population (rather than deep insights).
8. In answering direct questions, respondents may not be able to articulate their opinions, views, and emotions. For this reason, surveys and direct interviews are not good at identifying hidden needs.
9. In responding to a questionnaire, respondents cannot explain their answers, even if they want to.

VARIATIONS ON INTERVIEWS

The main problem with traditional surveys and interviews is that they rely on direct questions. Respondents often find it hard to respond to direct questions, for example, to give their views on product requirements, or the limitations of current services and products. Subconscious ideas influence consumers' views and two methods can probe these thoughts: *projection techniques* and *ZMET*.

Projection Techniques

Overview

Projection is the term used for a variety of techniques that encourage interviewees to respond to stimuli such as pictures, incomplete sentences, or being asked to respond as they think someone else would. Respondents may be asked to describe their reaction to a visual stimulus—such as Sigmund Freud's famous use of an inkblot. The psychoanalytic *concept of projection* assumes that respondents unconsciously project aspects of their personalities in their responses to stimuli.[37] When applied to market research, projective techniques "uncover deep-rooted thoughts that may not arise as a result of direct questioning."[38] Many companies are unaware of the potential of the projective techniques because of the limited number of published examples.

Applying the Technique

Individuals reveal their subconscious thoughts when they react to different types of stimuli. Stimuli are often ambiguous, in the hope that respondents will project their own meanings and significance, and declare their innermost motives and feelings, which can be interpreted by trained psychologists.[39] In market research the stimuli can vary widely but are usually directly related to a product or brand. The most common types of stimuli are:

- *Pictures.* What people see in pictures reveals something about their personality. For example, if respondents are shown pictures and asked to comment. For instance, a picture of a man and a woman sitting together in a Starbucks coffee shop and a picture of a person sitting alone might be used. How do respondents interpret the scenes? Are respondents positive or negative? Responses can give insights into interviewees' perceptions of Starbucks and reveal more than a direct question such as: Do you like Starbucks? The picture (stimulus) can be carefully selected to match the goals of the market research (which could be to understand how consumers perceive visiting Starbucks alone compared with visiting with a partner or friend).

- *Word association*: Participants are asked to name the first words that come immediately to mind after being shown or told a word. For instance, "vacuum cleaner" may trigger the association "Monday cleaning" for a housewife, indicating the role of regular cleaning. Word associations are deeply routed in personality and values.

- *Sentence completion*. Here, respondents are presented with various incomplete sentences and asked to complete them. For example: "If only this product was..." or "If my children were younger, my washing powder should have..."

- The *Thematic Apperception Test* (TAT) asks individuals to write a story. Based on this story, researchers identify the common themes in what people intuitively express.

- *Role-playing*. Participants are asked to play the part of someone else in a particular situation in order to uncover perceptions of lifestyles, values, and the like.

- *Taste*. In market research on food and beverages, product tasting can also be used.[40]

Analysis of Projection

Reading transcripts of the interviews can identify key themes in respondents' answers.[41] Analysis involves a lot of subjective judgments but it is claimed that trained researchers can reach a high degree of consistency in scoring stories across the participants. Others stress that projection needs expert analysis and so cannot be widely applied. Almost no guidance is available on how to ensure the analysis of projection is valid and reliable[42] but it is advisable to follow the key principles of analyzing qualitative data, such as coding. Triangulation (cross-checking) of the results is also important and can be achieved through focus group discussions[43] (see Chapter 3).

Box Case 2.5

Scottish Schoolchildren—How Do They View the Internet?[44]

Market research with young people is notoriously difficult. Not only are there ethical and access issues to consider but also older adolescents' views are very hard to determine accurately. It can be difficult to gain their cooperation and sometimes they

▶▶

may give deliberately inaccurate responses. To overcome these potential problems, one study of Scottish children's views on the Internet used projective techniques.

A government-funded university researcher was able to negotiate access to a number of schools and to gain the support of teachers. Data were collected in three ways: adolescents were given cameras and asked to make "photo diaries"; small group discussions were held at the schools; and the adolescents were asked to make drawings of the factors they perceived to be positive and negative about the Internet. The researcher interpreted the photographs and the drawings that adolescents had made and claimed that the results gave more insights than would have been achieved with direct questions.

Unfortunately, in the research direct questions were not posed to a parallel group and so it is difficult to tell whether the projection technique was effective. In this research, as so often with projection, the researchers who use it are very enthusiastic but they fail to produce reliable evidence that the techniques work better than the alternatives, and that their conclusions are reliable.[45]

Advantages and Limitations

Projection can help respondents express opinions that they would otherwise be unable to. For example, projection can help uncover the attributes that are associated with different brands, or help children to respond (see Box case 2.5 on Scottish schoolchildren). Two additional advantages are worth noting: projection can elicit more honest answers (for example, on prospective purchasing behavior); and projection can help identify respondents' underlying evaluation criteria.

Projection is frequently viewed with skepticism and suspicion. Some critics even go as far as describing projection techniques as valueless as the interpretation of dreams.[46] The criticism is that the ability to tap into consumers' unconscious thoughts has not been verified[47] and the findings are dependent on the researcher. These disadvantages can be countered with a rigorous research design, experience of working with the technique, and through triangulation. If this is achieved, projection can usefully complement the other techniques described in this book.

ZMET

Overview

Harvard Professor Gerald Zaltman, the inventor of ZMET, claims that consumers cannot easily express what they are thinking, partly because their thoughts may not be clear and partly because much of communication is nonverbal.[48] Paradoxically, the great majority of market research relies heavily on verbal replies. ZMET focuses on metaphors, because these are central to cognition and people use many metaphors.[49] By paying attention to the metaphors used by customers, companies can learn more about their thoughts, emotions, and the inner maps that people subconsciously use to structure their experiences.[50] ZMET draws on a variety of disciplines including cognitive neuroscience, psychology, semiotics, and linguistics. It focuses on explaining the "why" behind the "what" of consumer behavior and uses a multidisciplinary approach to improve the results or regular qualitative research. Latent customer needs cannot be articulated without methods like ZMET.[51]

Applying the Technique

First, the research question needs to be carefully defined. For example: "What do you think of a particular brand or company?"; "How do you use a product?"; "How do you feel about a product concept?" Normally 20–25 participants are interviewed in ZMET studies and each is asked to collect a minimum of 12 images representing their thoughts and feelings about the research topic. Participants usually have about ten days prior to the interview to collect images from any source they want. Generally it is advisable to exclude direct obvious links between the research topic and the images collected. For example, if the research topic is cars, it is advisable to exclude cars as images, because this might limit the use of metaphors. Figure 2.7 illustrates an example of an introductory letter for participants.

ZMET one-to-one interviews last about two hours (see Box case 2.6). Most participants spend a lot of thinking time about their images and become deeply involved in the topic. They begin by telling how each image relates to the research topic. Then, storytelling, repertory grid (see Chapter 6), and laddering

Figure 2.7   Example of an Introduction Letter for ZMET Participants

Source: Based on ideas in the literature and from conference participants

techniques are used to elicit further ideas. Techniques such as asking the inter-viewee which images are "missing," having them sort the "most representative pictures" help uncover respondents' mental maps.[52] Finally, participants discuss the images, create a collage, and record a short text about its meaning.

Analysis of ZMET

All interviews are tape-recorded and transcribed and in the end transcripts and collages are analyzed for recurring themes, or repeated consumer statements like "simple to operate," "too difficult to buy" and so on. Detailed and repeated reading of interview transcripts also helps to identify core constructs and insights into the thoughts of feelings of interviews and how they are associated.

During the content analysis, ZMET researchers also look for the use of meta-phors and nonliteral language used by consumers. The analysis of these meta-phors can shed light on the question how consumers structure and frame their thoughts on a specific topic.

Box Case 2.6

Mobile Financial Services—Barriers to Adoption[53]

From the beginning of 2000, the 3G mobile telephone capability was constantly men-tioned in the press because of the possibilities that the new technology would bring for consumers. One of these was mobile banking but it was not clear how consumers would perceive this. A group of university researchers made an early investigation of this potential market, by interviewing eight mobile phone users. The interviews lasted one-and-a-half hours and ZMET technique was used, with the interviewees being encouraged to share their perceptions through storytelling, discussing images, and the like (although the researchers provide no real details).

The research identified that the respondents, although they were selected as people likely to adopt new technology, perceived several risks with mobile banking, such as banking being too complex to accomplish on the move. However, the small conve-nience sample and the way the results are reported without much evidence presented does not inspire confidence in the results. Similarly, it is not clear that similar insights would not have emerged from direct interviews.

Advantages and Limitations

ZMET has an impressive list of users including Coca-Cola, DuPont, Eastman Kodak, and General Motors but it has certain limitations. First, special training is needed to conduct a ZMET procedure. Second, it is labor-intensive and third, the results are not generalizable to the public at large. Nowadays, ZMET is being applied in new ways, for example, "in situ"[54] where the ZMET interview takes place in the consumer's home, office, car, or whatever personal environ-ment is appropriate for the research topic. During an in situ ZMET, participants do not collect images, but instead personal objects that represent their thoughts and feelings. Thus, ZMET is starting to use some of the ideas of contextual interviewing (see Chapter 4).

SUMMARY

Surveys and interviews are the classic tools for market research. Survey and interview methods have become more sophisticated over the years but good preparation, application, and a thorough analysis are essential. This chapter explained the following:

- The purpose of surveys and interviews must be clear and the questions must be relevant. There are different types of questions and the right type must be selected. For example, open-ended questions are used to capture the views of respondents in an unrestricted manner, whereas closed multiple responses identify which are the most important factors.
- Many mistakes need to be avoided at the preparation stage: ambiguous terms, jargon, leading and loaded questions, and so on.
- Surveys have a number of limitations, largely due to researchers focusing on quantity rather than quality.
- Projection techniques and ZMET represent useful variations on interviews, as they shed light on values and motivations that underlie behavior.
- In combination with other techniques, surveys and interviews are important tools for market research to put substance on qualitative impressions in a rigorous approach.

In Chapter 3, we will describe how focus groups are used and can generate insights for new product development.

MANAGEMENT RECOMMENDATIONS

- Surveys and interviews are essential tools for market research but they need to be planned carefully.
- Take the time and, if necessary, advice required to ensure that the survey questions, order, and layout are prepared and pilot tested.
- Many organizations are poor at surveying and interviewing. So the companies that develop the capability have a competitive advantage in new product development.
- Remember surveys used in isolation are unlikely to uncover hidden needs! Use them in combination with the techniques described in later chapters.

RECOMMENDED READING

1. Oppenheim, A. N. (1992) *Questionnaire Design, Interviewing and Attitude Measurement*. New edition. London, Printer Publishers. [This book is the classic on survey design. Very practical and with excellent examples throughout.]
2. Schuman, H. and Presser, S. (1996) *Questions & Answers in Attitude Surveys*. London, Sage. [A very systematic approach to survey design including

various types of survey questions, wording questions, and issues with
interviewing.]

3. Dillman, D. A., Smyth, J. D. and Christian, L. M. (2009) *Internet, Mail,
   and Mixed-mode Surveys: The Tailored Design Method.* 3rd edition. New Jersey,
   John Wiley & Sons. [An excellent book on survey design; online surveys,
   maximizing response, and so on.]

3 FOCUS GROUPS (AND VARIATIONS)

> Focus groups have potentially enormous value, but not the way most companies use them.[1]

INTRODUCTION

Most companies which want to listen to the *voice of the customer* rely either on surveys and one-to-one interviews or *focus groups*. The term focus groups derives from the term *focused group discussion*[2]: groups of people with sufficient know-how, or a group of current and/or potential customers engage in a relatively unstructured discussion on a selected topic related to a product or service. Members of focus groups are usually individually recruited, based either on their personal experience of the topic of interest, or simply their willingness to participate in the focus group.

Focus groups are a form of qualitative research and are characterized by a setting in which participants are free to interact with each other. In the world of marketing, focus groups are seen as an important tool for acquiring feedback on different aspects of new products.[3] They allow companies to check reactions to product names,[4] packaging, and product function before a product is launched to the wider public.

The term focus group is often used to describe group interviews, although there is a significant difference: in group interviews, the researcher asks questions to several people and gets answers from each individual member of the group. In focus groups, researchers encourage group interaction; participants may talk to each other and answer each others' questions more than the questions put forward by the moderator.[5] While studying the interaction within the group, insights into how each individual is influenced by others' viewpoints can also be gained. Therefore, focus groups are often described as "steered conversations."

In this chapter we will:

- Illustrate the history and development of focus groups.
- Explain the practical aspects of how focus groups should be planned and conducted effectively.

- Discuss the typical variations of focus groups.
- Examine the methods for analyzing focus group data.
- Elaborate on the benefits and drawbacks of the focus group methodology.

HISTORY OF FOCUS GROUPS

Focus groups can be traced back to the Second World War and to the work of social scientists in the 1930s and 1940s. Especially in the U.S., the technique was used to understand how the population reacted to radio broadcasts and speeches intended to maintain morale. In addition, focus groups were used to understand how aircrews reacted in emergency situations and how aircraft controls could be better designed. Although this was not market research, it paved a way to understand how people express their thoughts within a group discussion, compared with their individual viewpoints.

The term *focus group* itself is reported to stem from one of the most influential sociologists of the twentieth century, Robert K. Merton,[6] who first used the term in 1956.[7] The technique was slowly adopted in social science research, but was rapidly applied to market research. In the 1950s and 1960s, focus groups were used to study consumer attitudes, reactions to advertisements, TV programs, and movies; and perceptions of new products and services. By the 1980s and 1990s, focus groups were widely used not only for consumer goods but also in social research, and in the fields of media and cultural studies. A study in 1990 showed that in that year alone, about 110,000 focus groups were conducted in the U.S. Nowadays, it is estimated that about 200,000 focus groups are carried out in the U.S. each year.[8]

Over the years, the methodology of focus groups has become more sophisticated and also they are now used for a broader range of applications. They are often used to determine the "brand characteristics" of politicians, to determine voters' opinions on potential policy, and for investigating the "image" of consumer brands with specific target groups and many other products and services aspects.

APPLYING THE TECHNIQUE

Overview

Successful focus groups require three relatively simple steps (see Figure 3.1):

- Planning including choosing the participants.
- Conducting the session including moderation.
- Analysis of the results.

In practice, each step involves a number of decisions that need to be made carefully to avoid jeopardizing the quality of the results. In order to clearly explain the decisions to be made at each stage, we will use a hypothetical example of a multinational company *WashCo* conducting focus group research on

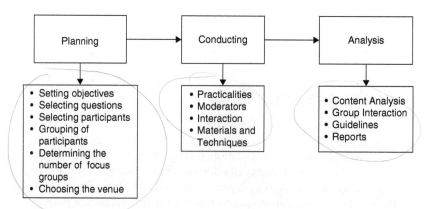

Figure 3.1 Three Important Steps of Focus Group Research

washing powder products. *WashCo* wants to identify customer needs to feed into their product development process and also to test some new product ideas. We will refer to this example throughout this chapter.

Planning of Focus Groups

Setting Objectives

The first step in preparing a focus group should be to establish the *objectives*. Focus groups are a "multi-purpose tool,"[9] but it is important to define the purpose of a focus group in advance. Figure 3.2 illustrates the range of typical objectives of focus groups—ranging from understanding users, designing new concepts, to evaluating potential designs (see Box Case 3.1 on how focus group objectives are established). For example, does *WashCo* want to find out if a completely new washing powder is acceptable to the focus group participants? Or does it want to focus on the packaging, the smell, the price, or the new TV commercial? Or does *WashCo* want to compare the new washing powder with those of the competitors? The objectives need to be formally defined in order to select the right questions to be asked in the focus group.

As illustrated in Figure 3.2, focus groups can be used at various stages within the product development process. In the early stages they can give an understanding of consumer perceptions and behaviors and can also identify the problems that result in specific customer needs; in the middle stages they can help refine ideas or gather feedback on prototypes or ask for new product concepts and designs; and in the later stages, they can shed light on how to launch a new product or service and how various marketing techniques could influence the buying decisions. In all stages, focus groups can be used to establish important frameworks for further research, that is, at each stage new relevant questions can be discovered that are worth following up in subsequent focus groups. The aims of the focus groups at these three stages are completely different and this directly influences the discussion questions that are selected.

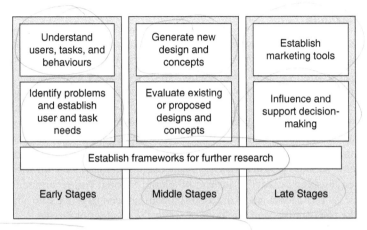

Understand users, tasks, and behaviours	Generate new design and concepts	Establish marketing tools
Identify problems and establish user and task needs	Evaluate existing or proposed designs and concepts	Influence and support decision-making
Establish frameworks for further research		
Early Stages	Middle Stages	Late Stages

Figure 3.2   Multiple Objectives of Focus Groups

Box Case 3.1

Weatherchem—The Spice of Life in India[10]

Weatherchem, a U.S.-based marketing research agency, conducted focus group research in February 2009. The research concentrated on the use of spices and seasoning in India and had the following objectives:

- To identify the most common types of spices used.
- To determine the factors which influence how purchases of spices and seasonings are made.
- To understand the types of packaging available in India.
- To determine what the Indian consumer considers the ideal packaging to be.

A focus group was held in Madras (now known as Chennai) and eight women who cooked more than once a day and who were also the primary grocery shoppers for their households were recruited.

Before the study, Weatherchem assumed that consumers in India would be very price sensitive. The results, however, showed a completely different picture. The price and the brand of the spice were not critical in the purchasing decision; it was freshness, aroma, and quality that were the decisive factors. The women also expressed a strong desire for the spice to be visible through the packaging to determine the quality. The discussion showed that, due to the temperature and humidity in Chennai, it is common practice to repack spices at home, storing them in plastic Tupperware to maintain freshness and to make dispensing easier for cooking. The focus group participants were asked to try out a new "flapper clap" dispenser and were so excited with this that they all stated they would be willing to pay up to 20 U.S. cents more for packaging with this cap. This was a surprise, considering the amount of spices used in a typical Indian household and the average salary of an Indian employee. (But market researchers should always be aware that opinions about purchasing behavior expressed in focus groups may not match actual purchasing! See also Box Case 3.5).

Selecting Questions

Once the focus group objectives have been defined, the *questions* to match each of them can be formulated.[11] It is advisable to use a maximum of five to six questions, because focus groups with consumers should not last more than about 1–1.5 hours, so that the participants remain active from start to finish.[12] Many of the guidelines recommended for designing questions for interviews (see Chapter 2) apply equally to focus groups. For example, open-ended questions are preferable to stimulate broad discussions.

Referring to our *WashCo* example, a possible question could be: "What would convince you to change your brand of washing powder?" (instead of asking: "Would you buy our new washing powder?"). Or: "How could you convince your friends to try out a new washing powder?" (instead of asking: "Would you recommend it to your friends?"). To uncover latent needs, it is recommended to probe into where users would like to save time, and could enjoy using the product or service.[13]

Focus groups should be based on a preestablished but flexible structure: either a semistructured questionnaire or a topic guide which lists the areas of interest that need to be explored. Similar to normal interview guidelines, the topic guide should allow for unforeseen areas of interest that arise during the discussion to be explored (see Box Case 3.2. for unforeseen results in a focus group).

Box Case 3.2

Ravensburger Spieleverlag—Cultural Preferences for Board Games[14]

Ravensburger Spieleverlag GmbH, European market leader for puzzles and board games, has several international subsidiaries. Product development is based at the headquarters in Germany, but a certain level of local adaptation is crucial to meet national tastes and traditions. Ravensburger frequently uses focus groups, for example, to decide which kind of TV advertisement is ideal for which country. In the past, focus groups were often used to check the "gut feelings" of product managers based in the subsidiaries, for example, in Spain and England.

The objective of one focus group in Spain was to find out which TV advertisement for a children's game was preferred by a group of mothers with young children. During the discussion, it was stated several times, that the box size of all children's games in the selection were considered as "too small." Mothers were asked to elaborate on "too small" and they explained that children's games are often bought as presents. The "bigger the present, the better" emerged in the discussion, even if only the box is bigger and the contents the same. This insight was in sharp contrast to German consumers who do not accept larger boxes with little content and complain about having to pay for *Luft* (air).

In England, a focus group research was about a TV advertisement of a popular Ravensburger game. Up until then the game was packaged in a regular box with house-style graphic design. During the focus group, mothers were surprised to see what the game was like in the TV spot. In the discussion they said they would like to see a comparatively large photograph of a family or several children playing the game on the box cover. This packaging change was then introduced in the UK and several other countries. Before this, the cover design had been mainly influenced by German consumers who usually turn the box over to read the summary on the back before deciding to buy or not. English mothers, on the other hand, said they did not want to invest much time in the buying decision and wanted to see a playing scene on the front of the box.

Selecting and Recruiting Participants

When *selecting* and *recruiting* participants, care needs to be taken to recruit a representative sample of the target group. In the consumer goods industry, participants are often selected randomly. For example, people in a shopping mall might be asked if they are interested in participating. Alternatively, research agencies use telephone or mail surveys to select and recruit participants. Recruitment questionnaires are comparatively short and aim to find out if the person has the desired know-how, or belongs to the target group relevant for the research by asking "filter questions." It is often important to have participants with a certain level of knowledge or personal interest in a product or service and so random selection may not always be the best approach. Initial participants of focus groups can also be asked to nominate other people who could participate—this is *snowball sampling*.

If, for example, *WashCo* wanted to test consumers' willingness to change the brand of washing powder, it is essential to select participants who actually decide which washing powder is bought for the household (this could be housewives or singles). A focus group recruitment questionnaire is illustrated in Figure 3.3. However, if *WashCo* was interested in how the smell of a new washing powder might be received by the general population, a random local sample would be sufficient, as everyone is likely to have an opinion on the preferred smell of their clothing. If the product is to be sold internationally, cultural aspects need to be considered as well.

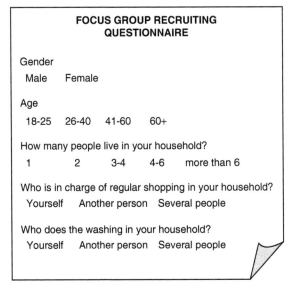

**FOCUS GROUP RECRUITING
QUESTIONNAIRE**

Gender
  Male   Female

Age
  18-25   26-40   41-60   60+

How many people live in your household?
  1   2   3-4   4-6   more than 6

Who is in charge of regular shopping in your household?
  Yourself   Another person   Several people

Who does the washing in your household?
  Yourself   Another person   Several people

Figure 3.3   Example of a Focus Group Recruiting Questionnaire

Recruitment decisions are also influenced by social and demographic factors. If you need to conduct a focus group with adults working full time, they cannot be recruited in a shopping center at 10 am. Similarly, recruiting participants from an affluent area will give different results than with people from poorer areas of the same town. It is also important to check that recruits are not regular focus group participants. Some people actively "apply" to participate in focus groups on a regular basis for the payments they may receive, but they are not always representative.

Independent of the recruiting guidelines, the number of participants selected typically ranges from six to ten. For complex topics, the participants are likely to know more about the topic and a smaller group allows each individual to discuss more. Therefore, focus groups with three to four participants are mainly used when the research objectives necessitate intense discussion with the moderator, or when sensitive topics such as contraception are investigated.[15]

Grouping of Participants

When multiple focus groups are planned, the composition of the individual groups, that is, the *grouping of participants,* is also important. Participants are often grouped according to age, gender, education, or occupation, or whether they have particular experience or specific knowledge. In our example, groups of housewives, students, single households, or groups of unemployed, middle class, and high income consumers could be asked about the washing powder and the results might illustrate which target group is mainly attracted to the new product.

Another point to consider is whether participants know each other. If they do, the discussion will start quicker but the group is likely to take many assumptions for granted and some interesting points may not surface. People in groups who do not know each other might be inhibited or shy, but also will not have any preexisting issues with the group. Also, participants should be sufficiently diverse to support the generation of creative ideas, but also sufficiently similar for their "shared view" to be identified.[16]

Determining the Number of Focus Groups

A key question is how many focus groups should be conducted in order to generate valuable results. The general guideline is that the *number of focus groups* should range between 8 and 10. Fewer may fail to identify a full range of customer needs whereas more might be a waste of time because the later focus groups produce no new insights. The best approach is to follow the *theoretical saturation*[17] concept, that is, to cease data collection when the researcher feels that the last one or two focus groups have identified nothing new. (Instead of ceasing data collection, the latter groups could be used to investigate wider issues.) In our example, once the discussion around the smell of the washing powder resulted in sufficient data for product management, the remaining focus group could discuss the product brand.

In practice, only 2–3 groups are often used due to time and budget restraints. Of course, this short-cut will have ramifications for the quality and the validity of the data.

Choosing the Venue

Choosing the *venue* for a focus group is dependent on the participants selected. If the participants know each other, it is best to choose a place where the group feels naturally at ease. If strangers are recruited for a focus group, neutral sites such as a meeting room in a shopping mall or a hotel conference room are suitable locations. Professional research agencies often have rooms with two-way mirrors, which are explained to the participants at the beginning of the discussion. For example, in London the company *All Global Viewing* has five focus group studios with two-way mirrors.[18] Two-way mirrors enable executives to follow the focus group session without distracting the discussion by their presence. For example, the moderator would mention to the focus group participants that two product managers from the washing powder company are observing from behind the mirror. Microphones are recommended for bigger rooms with many participants, because this helps the quality of the discussion and also increases the quality of voice recordings.

Overall, the venue should be chosen so that participants will be relaxed and will not be interrupted. The room itself should be comfortable and well ventilated. The chairs should be placed so that all members can see each other and a round table is more conducive to discussions than a square one. Name tags should be provided so that the participants can address each other by name. Refreshments are essential, especially if the discussion is expected to last for more than an hour.

Conducting Focus Groups

Practicalities

Even if more than one moderator is present, it is virtually impossible to write down exactly what is said, who said it, and how it was expressed. Therefore it is crucial that the whole focus group discussion is properly recorded using digital video (preferred) and/or audio equipment. It is not advisable to break the discussion to take notes as this is disruptive. However, it is vital to ask the group for permission to record the discussion and to promise (and ensure) anonymity. Another reason why focus group discussions should be recorded is that the aim is to identify shared views from the discussions. As the emphasis is on shared meaning, who said what is less important. However, the individuals that acted as opinion leader(s) or dominated the discussion, and those who did not actively participate should be noted by the facilitator (or observers).

Another practicality is how a focus group should be launched by the moderator. The general rule is that for a focus group session lasting about

30 minutes, an additional 10 minutes are needed to create an appropriate atmosphere for effective discussion. This may sound long but it reflects the importance of the atmosphere and the time it takes for participants to feel sufficiently relaxed. The moderator should start the session by introducing themselves and their co-moderator, if appropriate. Then, the participants' permission to record the session should be obtained. The agenda and main objectives should be explained and then the discussion can be initiated by the first question.

At the end of the focus group, it is important to reward the participants in some way. In our example, a free sample of the washing powder or other products from the company would be ideal as a "thank you." When company representatives are invited to focus group sessions, it is common to invite them to a meal afterwards. Many marketing research agencies pay participants to take part in focus groups and typically between 20 and 30 euros is paid per hour. This practice does carry the risk that participants lose their "neutral stance" and are less willing to critique the products or services of the company paying them.

Moderators

The role of the *moderator* is vital, because "the task of the group interviewer—frequently called the moderator or facilitator-is not to conduct interviews simultaneously but to facilitate a comprehensive exchange of views in which all participants are able to speak their minds and to respond to the ideas of others."[19] Some companies have their product managers moderate focus groups because they have product knowledge readily available and to save costs. In-house moderators are experts in the field under question, but might have strong preconceived ideas, especially if the product is close to launch or is the product manager's "own baby." Professionally trained moderators from market research agencies are likely to be more objective and experienced.

Moderators need skills, which can only be acquired in practice.[20] A moderator must be a good listener, a motivator, emphatic, nonjudgmental, and able to adapt to the situation. He or she should show a genuine interest in the research topic, a natural interest in people, combined with a high degree of curiosity and the eagerness to discover new insights. They need to balance requirement for minimal intervention (thus allowing the discussion to flow freely) with the task to keep the discussion focused on salient issues. While irrelevant discussion is unproductive, some apparently tangential points may lead to interesting insights. Similarly, moderators need to intervene when interesting points are quickly dropped by the group or not followed up.[21]

To support the moderator, it is ideal if a second researcher can take notes. In *serial moderating technique* (SMT) several moderators lead the main sections (for example, questions) of the discussion in succession.[22] The advantage of SMT is that participants are exposed to different moderating styles (which can increase creativity), and there is less pressure than there is on a single moderator (who is responsible for leading all of the discussions).

Managing Interaction

One of the most challenging tasks of the moderator is to ensure sufficient *group interaction*[23] and that everyone participates. As focus groups are normally a one-off occurrence, it is useful to have a few ground rules for participants to keep them focused, maintain the momentum, and achieve closure on questions. The moderator needs to make sure that each question is understood before it is discussed. Each participant should be able to reflect and maybe even take notes. Group interaction is often not given enough emphasis even though it is highly important. Differences in opinion between participants can help individuals to review their opinions and this can lead to interesting insights.[24] As a general rule, a moderator should pause for five seconds after a participant talks before beginning to talk. This five-second pause gives other participants a chance to jump in. Probes, such as "Would you explain this further?" or "Can you give me an example?" should be used to stimulate respondents to explain further. On the other hand, moderators should avoid nodding their head and short verbal responses such as "ok," "yes," "uh huh," "correct," "that's good," and so on.

Group dynamics need to be carefully "managed." A typical issue for moderators is participants who try to dominate the session, either because they are opinionated, knowledgeable about the topic, or because they show no respect for the moderator. This can only be handled by stopping the discussion and repeating the ground rules to the participants. If a participant continues to dominate, the group should be confronted with the problem and asked for ideas about how wider participation can be achieved. Specific actions should also be taken to deal with shy participants or ones who ramble. These different characteristics need to be carefully observed by the moderator and appropriate actions need to be taken.

Materials and Techniques

In order to support group interaction and discussion, companies use a variety of *materials* and *techniques*. The materials that are normally used in focus groups are examples of the actual products being discussed. In our *WashCo* example, participants were given several prototypes of the washing powder in order to look at the packaging, smell the fragrance, or try out the dispensing mechanism. Another option might be to demonstrate a new product, for example, in the case of a machine or a piece of equipment. Sometimes visual data such as storyboards (for example, to test TV commercials), photographs, advertisements, websites, or other drawings and paintings are used. In other cases audio, music, or radio programs are used. Groups can also be asked to conduct particular tasks, such as the preparation of an instant coffee (see Box Case 3.3). Other approaches include asking the participants to do a drawing or painting of their view of a product (this applies projection techniques that were explained in Chapter 2). Focus groups can also include regular brainstorming or methods such as sentence completion or sorting words. In addition, the comparison of different designs or prototypes can be collected in a *repertory grid* (see Chapter 6).

FOCUS GROUP DATA CAPTURE PRO-FORMA

Study Title:

Date:

Moderator Name:

Pro-forma Completed by:

Group Detail:

No. Participants:

Start Time:

End Time:

Participant Demographics: *enter column headings as appropriate*

Participants' Positions:

Draw diagram of table and note participant seating positions.

Discussion Question 1	
Data/Quotes/Observations *(Note down relevant quotes and enter time in right hand column)*	Time
Discussion Question 2	
Data/Quote/Observations *(Note down relevant quotes and enter time in right hand column)*	Time
Discussion Question 3	
Data/Quotes/Observations *(Note down relevant quotes and enter time in right hand column)*	Time
Additional Comments and Reflections	
Consider comments on strongest individual opinion and group dynamics.	

Figure 3.4 Form for Capturing Observers' Analysis and Reflections

Note: This form was developed by Researcher Helen Bruce, Cranfield School of Management in 2010. Used with permission.

Observers' Notes

Immediately after the focus group discussion, it is vital to make written notes of everything that might not be captured on the audio recording. Figure 3.4 gives a suitable form which we developed recently for capturing observers' notes and their reflections. Note that this form goes further than the typical analysis of focus group sessions, in that it requires the observer to reflect on what they have seen. In this way, an element of the way ethnographic market research is analyzed—*reflexivity* (see Chapters 4 and 5)—has been added. The form also gives space to record the seating of the participants and the most important observations of the session such as comments on individual members' contributions and surprises that emerged during the discussion, and so on. Other vital aspects, like tone and nuances in the use of language should be noted.

Box Case 3.3

Maxwell House—Understanding International Coffee Tastes[25]

The brand Maxwell House belongs to the U.S. giant Kraft Food Inc and this instant coffee is well-known in many countries. Before the coffee was sold internationally, a lot of effort was invested in finding out how the product needed to be "tweaked" to match different national tastes. Focus groups were conducted in the setting of a kitchen. People of different nationalities were asked to prepare a cup of instant coffee, with the instructions on the jar stating that the strength of the coffee depends on the number of spoons of instant coffee used. Most focus group participants wanted exactly one teaspoonful of instant coffee to give them the strength they preferred. Consequently, national variants of Maxwell House are now based on "one heaped teaspoonful." In the UK this results in a medium strength coffee, in China the resulting coffee is much stronger.

ANALYZING THE RESULTS

The analysis of focus groups research has to be careful and systematic. Focus group discussion transcripts are more difficult and time-consuming to produce than normal one-to-one interviews. Each speaker needs to be identified, which is often only possible after listening to the audio recording several times or more easily through watching the video. Another complication is that very often two people might talk at the same time and so high-quality microphones are needed to ensure that none of the discussion is lost. If the moderator leaves the room, to talk to colleagues "behind the mirror," participants often continue to discuss in hushed voices. With good microphones "clandestine" insights can result. We saw this in real focus groups conducted by an American company in London in 2010.

Content Analysis

The analysis of a focus group discussion is based on the transcripts and the moderator's or other observers' notes. Depending on the objective of the focus group, *content analysis* using a coding scheme comparable to any other qualitative data is recommended[26] as illustrated in Figure 3.5. (More details on coding qualitative data can be found in Chapters 4 and 5.) In focus groups discussing the TV advertising slot for the new washing powder, codings could include adverbs such as "inspiring," "old-fashioned," "corny," and so on. Some of the codes can be prepared in advance, though in most cases it is likely to be an emerging coding scheme that is used. The more transcripts that are coded, the more codes are added up to the point were no new insights are gained. On Figure 3.5 it should be noted that the terms which are coded have been highlighted (sometimes they are converted into capital letters to make them stand out). It is important to remember that the unit of analysis when analyzing focus group discussions is always the focus group itself and not single participants. Consequently, content analysis should also be done across the different focus groups. At *WashCo*, for example, one could compare the descriptions of the washing powder smell of mothers with those of single office workers.

...

Moderator: "Which smell are you looking for when buying a washing powder?"

Respondent 1: "I never thought of that, because I buy the same washing powder for years now, just because I am used to it. I would not even know how to describe the smell exactly."

Respondent 2: "Surely you must know if it smells like a flower, like lemon, like fresh air or whatever. I mean you smell it when you dispense it, when you take the clothes out, when you iron the clothes, so many times. That is why I can say I prefer an airy, breezy smell if I have the choice."

Respondent 3: "Yes, sometimes the fresh smell sort of frees your head and gives you this light feeling. Like a walk in a summer rain."

Respondent 4: "Very romantic description. It makes me think of the TV advert from years ago where a woman put the washing out on a extremely long line which went right across a huge field with cows on it and all the washing was white and you could almost smell the fresh air when watching the advert."

Respondent 1: "(laughs), oh yes I remember, because as a child I always thought the clothes must smell like cow-pooh when I saw the advert. But coming back to the question, I think I can describe my ideal smell now. It would be the smell from taking a walk by the sea in the morning when the sun is just about to rise. When the day is about to begin, the air is crisp and clear, and only the sea salt can be tasted in the air when you walk by the sea."

....

Figure 3.5   Example Text and Coding of a Focus Group Transcript

Content analysis based on such codes is comparatively straightforward and can answer questions on product features or personal preferences.

Another important part of analyzing focus group transcripts is to look for interesting quotes, metaphors, and stories. These are useful in understanding the subtle aspects of consumer preferences, for supporting the findings from the coding, and can be a useful communication tool in reporting the results of focus groups.

Group Interaction

The most challenging part of the analysis is assessing how the group interacted and how attitudes and perceptions, priorities, and preferences evolved within the group, compared with individuals' views. If the first participant describes the smell of washing powder as: "very sweet" and the second participant says "like a flower," how does this influence the others? The language used is also important to reflect on. Does everyone use the same language, or are there important differences? Are there certain norms, values, or cultural understandings constructed within the group which were different at the end? For example, does one mother convince a second mother in a focus group that it is important to use ecological washing powder which may also be healthier for the children's skin? What are the social processes taking place if some of the participants' opinions change? On some occasions, no clear consensus is developed within a focus group. Such occasions identify topics for further investigation, because they give hints of differences in users' requirements, the evolving market segments, and so on. In such cases, it is neither appropriate nor recommended to try and achieve group consensus.

In the analysis, it is important to note how people talked about a topic, the language they used, their tone of voice, and body language used. These give important clues on participants' perceptions. Transcripts are essential, but for

---

The main points to consider in analysis are
1) Look for statements that were repeated by different participants in one or across focus groups.
2) Look for statements about which participants disagreed or had no strong opinion on, in one or across focus groups.
3) Look for statements that were expressed by participants in only one particular focus group, but not in any of the others.
4) Look for emotions emerging in the discussions. What does the emotion of a participant on participants signify?
5) Look at the conversation as a process and highlight the points where something interesting happened, for example when and why the opinion of a participant or the whole group changed.

Figure 3.6   Checklist for Analyzing Focus Groups
Source: Based on ideas from: Eriksson, P. and Kovalainen, A., *Qualitative Methods in Business Research*. London: Sage; and Marshall, C. and Rossman, G. (2006). *Designing Qualitative Research*. 4th edition. London: Sage, p. 115.

the analysis it is absolutely vital to also report issues such as emotions, tensions, or conflicts within the group (transcripts can include comments on the tone of voice, observers can note the body language and inclinations of tone). The analysis should also look out for pauses, because they can give insights: perhaps the participant is unsure, or embarrassed. This can give market researchers a deeper understanding of the aspects of a product that consumers cannot easily discuss in public. Figure 3.6 gives a checklist of the key points to consider during analysis.

Reporting Format

Focus groups results are usually reported in one of the following four ways:[27]

1. *Thematic reports* describe in detail one or more focus groups. For example, a description on how the packaging of a new washing powder was described by students, housewives, and office workers and how the results compare with each other.
2. *Chronological reports* put more emphasis on the group interaction. For example, they highlight how the washing powder packaging was described before a competitor product was presented to the group as a comparison and afterwards.
3. *Narrative reports* select interesting stories constructed by the groups which could be relevant. For example, if a focus group starts to compare the smell of a washing powder with a walk by the sea, this might give ideas for the product name.
4. *Ethnographic reports* focus on insights from specific incidents from different focus groups. For example, that all students pour the washing powder out of the box directly, whereas mothers and office workers use the dispenser. (Note that the term "Ethnographic reports" for focus groups is an oxymoron. Chapter 4 explains how true ethnographic market research goes much deeper.)

No matter which coding scheme and which type of report is chosen, a typical focus group report gives a list of the product features and attributes required by current or potential customers. An example of how focus group results led to particular product features is given in Box Case 3.4.

Box Case 3.4

Dr. Oetker—Home-made by Mother[28]

Dr. Oetker is a traditional German company which was started in 1902 as a manufacturer of baking powder. Based their success over the years, a range of products range was developed including convenience foods such as frozen pizzas, or ready-made puddings and deserts. The company mentions on its website how a focus group session many years ago led to unexpected results and new product features

▶▶

At the time, Dr. Oetker was surprised that a new cake mixture was not selling as well as expected, despite the fact that the new recipe was regarded as very good by consumers who were asked to taste the baked item. Focus groups were conducted with housewives and it was found that the target group of housewives did not feel at ease with the fact that they had nothing to add to the product. Many of the focus group participants worked part-time or had several young children, and said this was why they would be tempted to buy cake mixtures. However, they felt they would not want to serve these as "home-made cake" if they had done nothing to add to the recipe. Although they liked the end product, they felt bad buying it, because their reputation as a housewife and a good mother was at stake. As a result, the product was changed so that housewives needed to add an egg and the product was a great success and led to several similar additions to the range.

VARIATIONS ON FOCUS GROUPS

Various forms of focus groups have evolved over the past few years. The decision on which variant should be used depends mainly on the research objectives and the sensitivity of the topic being discussed. We will discuss five variants to give an insight into how focus groups have developed. The variants are as follows:

- *Two-way focus groups.* Here there are two groups of participants: one group conducts regular focus group discussions, while the other group observes the discussion. Afterwards, the second group discusses what they have heard and gives their conclusions on the interaction within the first group. The advantage of this approach is that ideas from one group are double-checked by the second group. Furthermore, a deeper understanding of issues can be achieved if series of groups discuss these subsequently.[29]
- *Sequential focus groups.* The first focus group defines questions and topics that the second one will work on. This can lead to interesting results, because the discussion is focusing explicitly on consumer topics without any bias from moderators, researchers, or marketing managers.
- *Teleconference focus groups.* Due to the difficulty of bringing together ideal participants, sometimes teleconferencing is used, where participants get a toll-free number to dial in with a special password. While this approach is cheaper, it has the disadvantage that nonverbal aspects of the discussion cannot be analyzed. Therefore, teleconference focus groups can only be recommended in special circumstances when it is the only way to bring groups together,[30] such as busy experts from different countries.
- *Online focus groups.*[31] In certain markets, for example, in the software or PC games industry, online focus groups are preferred, where all participants are connected online. This form of focus group is ideal for participants with a high affinity to computers and/or for lead users of particular products.

Verbal communication does not take place, but online discussions (for example, chat rooms) can be analyzed. Research has shown that virtual groups yield results that are almost identical to face-to-face interviews.[32]

- *Nominal groups.*[33] In order to prevent the potential domination of a focus group by one member, or members becoming bored, moderators of nominal groups ask the participants to write their thoughts on paper and to reveal them afterwards one after the other. New ideas can also be recorded during the presentation and in the end the group agrees around which ideas the actual focus group shall be conducted. Ideally, this first individual brainstorming step can lead to a higher level of creativity, for example, ideas for new products.

ADVANTAGES AND LIMITATIONS

Advantages

1. It is easier to recruit participants who are otherwise reluctant to be interviewed, or feel they do not have enough expertise.
2. Focus groups are easy to handle, relatively low cost, and they can increase sample size by talking to several people at once. Their value is the subject of some controversy[34] but, when conducted professionally, they offer a number of advantages to market researchers[35].
3. Compared with individual interviews, focus groups can be more comfortable for participants, because they feel like they are treated as experts on a particular topic and there is less individual pressure than in an in-depth interview. Participants can take more time to consider their responses than in interviews.[36]
4. Group discussion can bring the best out of participants. During the process, individual views are often challenged, so that the end result is claimed to be a more realistic account of how people think. Focus groups generate a wider range of information than traditional in-depth interviews.
5. One of the main advantages of focus groups is that they allow researchers to quickly develop an understanding about why people feel the way they do.[37] Individuals in focus groups listen to others' answers, modify their own views, or alternatively may voice disagreement and so on.
6. Many participants describe the discussion in hindsight as "fun" and an "enlightening experience." The processes taking place during the discussion, where the participants can jointly create a chain of thought, are often stimulating.

Box Case 3.5

Coca-Cola—A Simple Matter of Taste?[38]

In 1985 the management of Coca-Cola decided to change the Coke flavor due to massive competition from Pepsi-Cola. Before the launch of the new flavor, a number of focus groups and surveys were conducted, where a majority of participants stated

▶▶

they liked the new flavor, and only a few said they would rather stick to the classic Coke. When the new product was launched, the New Coke was accepted by many consumers. But a significant minority protested loudly about the change of flavor. Coca-Cola headquarters received more than 400,000 angry letters and phone calls with complaints and even Fidel Castro, a well-known Coke drinker, complained. People who preferred the traditional taste stocked up whereas sales of the new flavor fell.

Less than three months after the introduction of the New Coke, the return of the original formula was announced on public TV channels. By the end of the same year, Coke Classic was outselling New Coke and Pepsi by far and Coke's sales had increased at more than twice the rate of Pepsi's. A number of academics and market research professionals have analyzed what went wrong with the focus groups. Most agree that it was because only one question was asked: "Which flavor do you like better." They should have also been asked: "How would you feel if we replaced the current flavor with the new one?"

There are several lessons: market research is not always able to measure the strength of the emotional attachment consumers have to a specific product or brand; although New Coke failed, it ultimately attracted a lot of publicity and the brand popularity (of Classic) rose.

Limitations

1. Focus groups are extremely popular and have high face validity but they have significant limitations, especially when they are used by inexperienced market researchers. The data are hard to analyze—because of the sheer volume of data as well as the difficulty in following the patterns of group interaction.
2. Although focus groups are extremely popular, an "astonishing 80 percent of all new products or services fail within six months or fall significantly short of projections."[39]
3. The members of a focus group are unlikely to be representative of the target population.
4. A difficulty with focus groups is their validity. For example, *observer dependency*,[40] the balance between free discussion and moderator-led questions, or the sequence of questions can influence the results. Even moderators who are professionally trained and highly experienced are not totally detached observers and always act as participants in one way or another.[41] Also, the selection of participants, the type of questions asked, how they are phrased, and by whom can all influence the validity of results.[42]
5. The issues with participants can sometimes outweigh the advantages of focus groups. It can be quite difficult to bring together the ideal focus group because of distance and cost and the quality of recruiting is fundamental to the success of focus groups.
6. Some participants may not be willing to air their views in a group setting and the situation might be intimidating for particularly shy people.

Especially for sensitive topics, participants may feel uncomfortable disclosing details of their private life in a group setting. Social pressures can limit the responses gained or, in the best case, a lot of time is needed to make sure that everybody is comfortable in participating in the discussion. In addition, participants tend to say what is expected of them in a group environment instead of stating what they actually think and do. For example, if you ask "how often do you change your underwear?" you might not get an honest answer from all participants.

7. Participants often face difficulty in articulating how they feel about a brand or a TV advertisement and sometimes mimic the responses of a dominant person in the focus group.[43]

8. When focus groups are used to test the reaction to the features of a new product, they have several drawbacks. In some circumstances, participants might not tell the truth, or do not react as they would in a real-life situation (see Box Case 3.5. for an example).

9. Particularly creative ideas may be suppressed in the group discussion.

10. If a prototype is presented to a focus group, participants are outside their normal environment and so their behavior may be unrepresentative of real purchasing decisions (see Box Case 3.6 for an alternative approach which proved to be successful). Focus groups have even been criticized as being useless for market research into new products, because participants have limited knowledge of possibilities and thus lack the ability to generate creative ideas.[44]

Box Case 3.6

Target—Understanding Students' Dormitory Life[45]

Target, the U.S.-based discount retailer, wanted to launch a product line aimed at college students and their market research agency Jump Associates decided to use a new approach to focus groups. The firm sponsored a series of game nights at universities, inviting freshmen as well as students with one year's experience of a dorm. To get teens to talk about dorm life, Jump devised a board game that involved issues associated with going to college. The game naturally led to informal conversations and discussions on college life. Researchers observed and a video camera recorded the proceedings.

The research was a success. Target launched a "dorm product line," with, for example, the "bath in a box" set, which included an extra-large bath towel which enabled students to appropriately cover themselves on the way to and from the shower.

SUMMARY

This chapter has shown that:

- Focus groups are one of the most popular methods of market research because they are easy to organize and (superficially) easy to analyze.

- The planning stage of focus groups is very important. Care has to be taken to define a clear objective, careful selection of participants and moderator(s), well chosen questions, as well as choosing the ideal venue for the focus group session.
- The focus group idea is easy to understand, but difficult to conduct in practice due to the complex task of grouping the participants, managing the group interaction, and the role and responsibility of the moderator. Analysis of focus group data is difficult due to the quantity and quality of the data gathered. It needs to address the content of the discussion as well as the interaction within the conversation which also includes nonverbal aspects and subjective observations by the moderator(s).
- The aim of focus groups can be to develop new product ideas or test them. No matter which aim underlies the discussion, results should always be combined with other market research techniques, because focus groups are always subject to a limited validity.

MANAGEMENT RECOMMENDATIONS

- Review whether your focus groups are well prepared and conducted. Also, consider if you are overusing the technique.
- Reflect on the way you use customers, experts, and other lead users for the innovation process in your company. How can the expertise from these groups best be integrated into the product development and design process and at which step is a focus group approach useful for the testing of prototypes?
- Use new approaches to participant selection for focus groups. New products are not necessarily easy to discuss with existing customers. Instead, new customer groups or a new mixture of focus group participants might come up with real creative innovations or might be more suitable to voice their attitudes toward a new product idea.
- Think about the best way to combine focus groups with other techniques for market research. Compare the results from focus groups with implicit techniques like repertory grid or conjoint analysis to get an ideal combination of results.

RECOMMENDED READING

1. Morgan, D. L., *The Focus Group Guidebook*. London: Sage, 1998. [Detailed introduction into the focus group technique including history, examples, cost issues, and what you can expect in terms of results.]
2. Langford, D. J. and McDonaugh, D., *Focus Groups: Supporting Effective Product Development*. New York: CRC Press, 2003. [Specifically examines focus groups and their application in design-related product development projects.]
3. Krueger, R., *Focus Groups*, London: Sage. 4th edition. 2009. [Very good hands-on guide to focus groups. Author has a lot of previous experience with focus groups, which is noticeable throughout the book.]
4. Fern, E. F., *Advanced Focus Group Research*. London: Sage, 2001. [Targeted at people with prior knowledge of focus group technique. Good discussion of limitations and also the future of focus group research.]

Part 2
New Methods of
Market Research

4 ETHNOGRAPHIC MARKET RESEARCH

> Rather than asking people to comment about what they usually do or say ...
> ethnographers prefer to observe them doing it.[1]

INTRODUCTION

Most marketing executives regularly visit customers and they will often observe them using products. However, casual observation and informal discussions with customers are unlikely to lead to breakthrough products. Also, such visits cannot be compared with the thoroughness of *ethnographic market research*, which has two main elements: *systematic observation* and *contextual interviewing*. There is nothing casual about the way ethnographers study tribal cultures and so, in this chapter, we will stress the need to plan and conduct observation in a similarly meticulous way. "Systematic observation is a research method in which events are selected, recorded, coded into meaningful events, and interpreted by non-participants."[2] This definition contains several elements that differentiate systematic observation. First, what is observed is selected, which means that the times at which we observe customers interacting with products need be chosen carefully. Second, coding implies that data are categorized in a painstaking way to reveal underlying meanings and issues. Finally, the definition's reference to nonparticipants implies that the interpretation is made objectively.

The expression *voice of the customer* has become closely associated with new product development. It is often used by companies that believe they have a deep understanding of their customers, as they have listened to what they have said. But, as we stress throughout this book, direct questions in isolation do not provide an adequate understanding of customers; customers may not be able to articulate their needs; and what consumers say in focus groups may not match real behavior. The science of ethnography has a long tradition of not simply accepting what people say, in explaining their customs and culture. Ethnographers juxtaposition what they are told with what they see. Therefore, as market researchers, we must develop the ethnographer's healthy suspicion that what they are told is not the whole story.

Systematic observation is nearly always combined with contextual interviewing (an interview conducted in the interviewee's own environment) and so both are covered in this chapter. The preparation and experience that is needed for ethnographic market research should not be underestimated,[3] and this is the reason that some companies are hiring ethnographers. However, ethnographers who do not have a good understanding of new product development may not be able to make useful contributions. We know of an innovative company that was very disappointed in the results of a project where academic ethnographers (who did not have any industrial experience) were invited to contribute to NPD. It is important to adapt ideas from ethnography in an appropriate way and, therefore, we will present approaches that are based on theory but have been tried and tested in an NPD context.

In this chapter we will:

- Discuss the history of ethnography and how the technique has been applied to market research.
- Give an overview of the key constituents of the method.
- Explain how ethnographic market research can be planned and conducted effectively.
- Cover the main approaches to analyzing data—this is particularly important as ethnographic market research produces large volumes of qualitative data and many market researchers are unfamiliar with the best ways to deal with this.

HISTORY OF ETHNOGRAPHIC MARKET RESEARCH

Ethnography is the social science that provides the theoretical and practical basis of systematic observation and contextual interviewing. Therefore, we will explain the origins of ethnography and how it has been adapted for use in a product development context. Ethnographic market research, in particular the interpretation of the results, requires experience and so it should come as no surprise that nearly all the pioneers had received a formal training in social science before choosing to work on new product development.

In this chapter we will use the terms *ethnography* and *anthropology* extensively. Anthropology is "the study of the origins and customs of mankind" and it includes *physical anthropology*, the study of the evolution of mankind from apes, and *cultural anthropology*, the study of different cultures. Ethnography is "the scientific description of peoples and cultures" (definitions from the Oxford English Dictionary). Ethnography can be thought of as the underlying methodology used in cultural anthropology. Although the term *anthropological expeditions*[4] is sometimes used to describe trips to observe customers in their own environment, ethnographic market research is a more appropriate term.

Ethnography Emerges

The origins of ethnography go back to colonial times when British, French and other academics became interested in the cultures of the countries in their empires.[5] It may seem bizarre to us today but the first researchers did not observe at first hand the cultures that they were studying! Instead they employed colonial administrators to go out on their behalf and ask questions about culture. Academics even went as far as publishing a guidebook in 1874, which specified standard questions to be asked. Today, the approaches used in early cultural studies are often referred to using expressions such as the "armchair method" and "veranda anthropologists." With the value of hindsight, the early researchers have been strongly criticized for the way in which they were totally detached from what they were studying. Such detachment led early figures in anthropology such as James Frazer (author of the classic *The Golden Bough*)[6] to misinterpret customs and beliefs, as he interpreted them without a sufficient understanding of context.

In contrast to these early researchers, explorers, military officers, and administrators were directly in "the field" and they often reported their contacts with different peoples. Although many of these reports gave little more than superficial descriptions, some have been said to contain "interesting, often shrewd observations."[7] However, most colonial officials struggled to understand the cultures in which they came in contact—for example, British officials in Africa were exasperated by the lack of a clear hierarchy in some tribes.

In 1922, the cultural anthropologist Bronislaw Malinowski took what was for the time a radically different approach, when he lived for a year with islanders to collect the data for his famous study of Western Pacific culture.[8] Around this time other researchers were starting to immerse themselves in studies of African cultures, with a number of notable studies of the peoples of the Sudan, including E. E. Evans-Prichard's classic study *The Nuer*.[9] This was based on 15 years of work investigating the all-pervading role that cattle play in the life of the Nuer people and their de-centralized political system—which had left colonial officials confounded.

An important development that impacted ethnography was the "Chicago School" of sociology. From the 1920s, sociologists from Chicago went out into marginal sections of society (*subcultures*) to understand behavior from the perspective of the "underdog." This led to studies of city life, such as a famous ethnographic investigation of the language and culture of "street corner" society. The depression in the 1930s and the subsequent hardships faced by many sections of U.S. society (as, for example, described in John Steinbeck's 1930 classic novel, *The Grapes of Wrath*) stimulated a wide interest in understanding different sections of society.

The wave of anthropological and sociological studies which started in the 1920s not only gave insights into numerous urban and native cultures but also helped develop the methodology. Thus by the middle of the twentieth century, ethnography had become well established. Its key aspects were the *immersion* of the researcher in the group being studied; a focus on learning their language, dialect, or jargon; producing detailed *field notes*; and regular reflection on the part of the researcher of what they had learnt from their observations.

The second half of the twentieth century saw further enhancements in the way data were analyzed and the ever greater influence of technology. For example, today we take for granted the availability of technology, which has led to *video ethnography*, where events are recorded for later analysis, potentially by multiple researchers. Software for the analysis of qualitative data has also had an impact on ethnography.

Ethnography Impacts Product Design

At the end of the nineteenth century, the management of production processes became focused on *ergonomics* (the study of work and its environment), and *human factors* (the study of how objects can be made easier to use by considering human characteristics). These studies led to production workers being systematically observed and were a catalyst for the adoption of ideas from the social sciences into business.

The "scientific management" approach of Frederick Taylor stems from the 1890s. It was a philosophy of breaking complex production operations into stages, and studying how workers could complete their allocated tasks most efficiently, for example, by considering the best ways in which objects could be positioned or moved.[10] Scientific management had a strong influence over the way Henry Ford designed his production operations and led him to say, "nothing is particularly hard if you divide it into small jobs." For management to understand how to optimize the work allotted to a particular stage, observation was necessary. But in contrast to the sphere of interest of anthropologists, scientific management focused on the task and not on the people conducting it. It was to be some years before the social aspects of production situations were to become recognized.

The work of Taylor formed the basis for the famous 1939 Hawthorne study, named after the U.S. factory in which it was conducted. The study was led by the psychologist Elton Mayo and the anthropologist Lloyd Warner and looked at how the physical environment of a factory influenced output. However, they also "found that there was a behavioural aspect to productivity that had not been studied previously."[11] The recognition that the way people work together has a major impact on productivity was a break with previous thinking, and generated the momentum for more sophisticated methods of observation to be adopted.

At the same time as production methods were being studied, engineers were looking at how products could be better designed to match human factors, both physical and psychological. In 1900 a German engineer Karl Kromer working in the U.S. tried to design products ergonomically.[12] In an informal way, such thinking goes back centuries. Human factor analysis developed particularly during the Second World War, with the designers of aircraft and other equipment striving to minimize the chance of incorrect operation. In addition, ideas from psychology were used in the screening of aircrew and observation was used in the investigation of how operator errors could lead to accidents. Following the War, human factors continued to be an important consideration in product design and the work of Chuck Mauro was widely publicized in the U.S. Mauro was a designer who had also studied psychology and physiology. In the 1970s he developed agricultural equipment for Russia. He based his design on an understanding of Soviet expectations of farming equipment—large multi-purpose machines were *de rigeur,* as opposed to the smaller specialized devices favored in the West. Later, with his own human factors company, Mauro became famous for designing the NASA control room and the trading floor of the New York Stock Exchange.

In the U.S., a small group of individuals, all of whom had an affinity for anthropological methods and thinking, were at the forefront of pulling ideas from social science into the new product development arena.[13] People such as Jane Fulton Suri championed *discovery research,* going out to observe and speak to customers and consumers in their own settings. "Discovery research is an open-ended exploratory effort to learn about consumer culture. It is useful for developing original product and service ideas or finding new applications for existing and emerging technologies."[14] Ron Sears, who had trained as an experimental psychologist studying the behavior of rats, switched in 1979 to identifying why customers found photocopiers hard to operate. Similarly, at Rank-Xerox's Palo Alto Research Center, cultural anthropologist Lucy Suchman led the group which from 1979 looked at the behavioral aspects of product design, and lobbied for easier-to-use products. Liz Sanders worked at one of the influential consultancy firms and from the 1980s introduced ideas from ethnography—looking, for example, for the differences between what people say and what they do—and using *projection techniques* from psychology (techniques to help people express their unconscious needs).

Ethnographic market research is now used in NPD in three main ways: discovery research, human factors, and usability testing. However, the recognition that the behavioral sciences can help us understand how customers interact with products and services has been slow to spread. The majority of companies do not know the value of systematic observation and contextual interviewing. For example, a study by IBM of 13 "forward-thinking companies" found that only half of them use systematic observation techniques to understand their customers.[15] And the adoption of ethnographic methods into market research has been hindered by the tendency of market researchers to rely on quantitative data.[16] Although such data can give insights into, for example, the size of market segments or buying intentions, they do not uncover cultural aspects. Another reason for the slow adoption of ethnographic methods is that they have not been taught in university courses on marketing.[17]

Business leaders are slowly becoming aware that the experiences consumers undergo with products and services are multiple. "These experiences concern not only physical products, but also retail spaces, brands, company histories, and identities … And, these experiences require interpretation."[18] To provide such interpretation, ethnographic market research is an ideal approach. Over the past 15 years, a handful of product design consultancies have built their reputation on their use of ethnographic and creative approaches in new product development, and the most famous of these is IDEO, which was established in California (and now employs Fulton Suri). In addition, some leading companies such as Nokia are developing their in-house capabilities (see Box Case 4.1).

The latest change in ethnographic market research is that consumers are increasingly interacting via the web, for example, in user groups. Researchers are realizing that the conventional techniques of ethnography need to be adapted for use on the web and the terms *webnography*[19] or *netnography*[20] are being applied. Online studies offer easy access to consumers and product users and a wide array of data can be collected, such as textual data (from emails and chat rooms) and visual data (from websites and social networking pages). These can be supplemented by online interviews. No doubt webnography will develop quickly in the next few years and ethnographers will develop novel ways to identify the cultural elements of online groups.

Box Case 4.1

Nokia—Going to the Gemba[21]

One of the world's leading manufacturers of mobile telephones, Nokia, has recognized the importance of observation in understanding customer culture. The UK operation that is responsible for developing some of the company's products was aware that the Japanese market has different characteristics. Rather than employing a market research company, management decided that it was important for members of the new product development team to see the issues firsthand. Therefore, sales, marketing, R&D, and managers were all paired up with Japanese colleagues. These pairs observed Japanese people using mobile phones in public places and gathered opinions, which meant that issues such as the delicacy of approaching people on the street had to be considered.

In Japanese quality management, the word *Gemba* means "where things actually occur; it is raw, untainted information"[22] and it is used to stress that managers must spend sufficient time on the production floor, if they are to learn how to improve production efficiency. Nokia's use of the term *Gemba* is analogous to the way anthropologists talk of *the field*.

Sending new product development employees into the *Gemba* to conduct the market research had the advantage of widening commitment but most of the employees were not experienced in market research. Therefore, Nokia produced a "Training Guide" for the team: this consisted of an introduction to the objectives of the research; an explanation of the importance of the Gemba, guidelines for observation; guidelines for approaching and interviewing people; and obtaining volunteers for focus groups. Following the procedures in the Guide, Nokia employees collected photographs of

▶▶

the locations where they made their observations; the answers to a semistructured questionnaire (a contextual interview). and short field notes following a set format.

The Nokia case demonstrates three important issues. First, the importance of having market research conducted by the NPD team and not just by a market research company. Second, the need to provide clear guidelines for the team involved, to ensure that observations are conducted systematically and consistently. Third, the reluctance of Japanese people to voice their opinions to strangers shows that cultural issues need to be addressed.

From the information that Nokia have published, it appears that the primary limitation of their research was that those involved had no previous experience of systematic observation. Although the Training Guide was prepared, it is difficult to learn systematic observation without practice. Inexperienced researchers can learn much more from working with skilled observers who are coding video tapes of consumer behavior. An important part of any ethnographic research project can be the training of the team. Often the best way is to have the most experienced researchers make the first visits and use the data collected as an intricate part of training of the rest of the team.

OVERVIEW OF ETHNOGRAPHIC MARKET RESEARCH

Ethnography has developed over the past 80 years into a robust and reliable approach, provided it is applied correctly. Systematic observation can be used to assess customers' issues and can be contrasted with what they say about products and services. An advantage of observation is that it is direct and so does not rely on customers' or consumers' reported perceptions, such as those derived in surveys.[23] Observation focuses on the locations in which customers' problems occur, that is directly, in their own environment where they are also more likely to respond to questions frankly.

Key Assumptions

The seven key assumptions of ethnography, which are most important to NPD related market research, are the following:

1. Studies should be conducted in *the field*, where people—the *actors* or *respondents*—are in their natural environment.
2. The researchers should *immerse* themselves in the social setting that is being studied and strive to understand situations through the eyes of the participants, using their language and jargon.
3. Observers can adopt various roles—from a *nonparticipant observer* all the way through to becoming a *full participant*.
4. Systematic observation is a crucial aspect of ethnography but it is not the only data collection technique used—"Ethnographic 'fieldwork' is not a homogeneous method, but involves a variety of techniques of data collection."[24]

A range of data should be collected and the overall *ethnographic record* will typically consist of the researchers' field notes, recordings (audio or video), photographs, interview transcripts, and so on.

5. The aim of ethnography is to understand the underlying culture of the groups of people being studied, by producing what is called a *thick description* of social behavior.[25] This understanding will give insights into the types of products and services required.

6. Respondents' statements and explanations should not be taken at face value—"What respondents report about their behaviour is often, for a variety of reasons, not entirely consistent with what is observed by the researcher"[26] (see Box Case 4.2).

7. *Reflexivity* is important—researchers need to regularly reflect on what they have seen and heard and what can be learnt from this.

Box Case 4.2

Astra Zeneca—Studying Noncompliance[27]

Pharmaceutical companies have been relatively slow to adopt ethnographic market research but Astra Zeneca has recognized the value that such methods can bring to understanding the problems that people face with their illnesses and medications. In fact, there is a developing field of *medical anthropology* that is focused on the study of how medicine is practiced, how doctors interact with patients, patients' understanding of their situation, and the way patients deal with their illnesses. Ethnographic market research has also been used to discover the reasons for patient noncompliance—why patients do not take their medications in the prescribed quantities, at the correct times, or in the correct way. Noncompliance is a major problem in healthcare in many countries.

Astra Zeneca focused on identifying when and how diabetic patients took their insulin at home. A market research company conducted 15 interviews in patients' homes, using a semistructured questionnaire and observing patients preparing for and taking their medications. The study gave insights into the problems associated with patients' physical deterioration, the influence of diet and exercise on their condition, a disconnect between patients' and physicians' thinking, and the problems of multiple treatments. All of these factors were found to influence compliance and subsequently were considered in the preparation of better educational material for patients. In addition, new material was produced for doctors on how medications are typically administered and how patients can be better briefed.

When Is It Appropriate?

Ethnographic market research has mainly been used for consumer products (B2C products) but it is also pertinent in B2B and service situations. It is appropriate for discovering opportunities for new products and services and it is therefore an important tool to enable radical innovation. In addition, it can be used to understand the sales process, to study how products are really used, and to throw light onto consumer culture (for example, identifying new ways to segment the market).

Ethnographic market research may not be appropriate when incremental product innovation is the priority, or where the time available negates the possibility of researchers becoming sufficiently immersed in the study at hand. It is also not appropriate for organizations that want to follow a pre-defined strategy, or are convinced that they already know their customers intimately. Put another way, ethnographic market research requires companies to have an open-minded attitude and the ability to accept the ambiguity that always exists at the start of such research projects (the results are always difficult to predict).[28]

PLANNING ETHNOGRAPHIC MARKET RESEARCH

Using fully blown ethnographic techniques in market research is seldom appropriate, as they can be time-consuming and expensive.[29] Therefore, the discussions in this section are based on the tenets of ethnography but the approaches that we will recommend have adapted to make them appropriate for the NPD context. It should also be noted that it is difficult to decide everything about ethnographic market research in advance and so planning and conducting fieldwork is always an iterative process.

To allow readers to develop a clearer understanding of how an ethnographic market research project can be planned and conducted our discussion will cover the following:

- Understanding the field.
- Choosing the type of observation.
- Gaining access and making introductions.
- Sampling strategy: what and when to observe.
- Data collection and recording.

Understanding the Field—The Grand Tour

Before detailed data collection can commence, it is important to understand *the field* of interest. A product manager conducting research is likely to be totally focused on their particular product or service but too narrow a focus may lead to aspects being missed, which give insights into behavior and the need for products or services. Ethnographers speak of taking a *grand tour of the field*[30]; an initial visit aimed at generating an overview. For market research at a supermarket, this could involve looking at the location, the car parks, the entry and exit points, and neighboring shops before looking at the store itself. A grand tour for a consumer product would be simpler and would involve visiting a consumer's home, looking at where the product was stored, how and when it was used, and other items that are used at the same time, and so on. For example, research on barbeque grills viewed consumers' garages (storage), kitchens (food prepreparation), and gardens (cooking and entertaining).[31]

The aim of the grand tour is to allow the wider context to be understood and to generate ideas for the *sampling strategy*: deciding which areas and events to observe in detail. In addition, the grand tour should help to define which actors to interview and how some of the contextual interview questions can be phrased (and based around the items observed in the physical environment). A useful way to summarize the grand tour is to draw a flow diagram of the main activities observed (see also Figure 5.1).

Where a large number of observations are necessary, then multiple research-ers may be needed to collect the data. In such cases, it is important to train the research team, to avoid systematic errors, such as one observer always being more positive than others.[32] The training that is necessary for the research team can be identified at the end of the grand tour and work can be started on the neces-sary documentation (see Box Case 4.1 on Nokia for details of their "Training Guide").

Choosing the Type of Observation

Observation can take place without those observed being aware of the research-er's status. Such *covert* or *discrete observation* may appear attractive as it avoids the necessity to negotiate access. It is normally only viable for consumer prod-ucts and services that are used in public. For example, mobile telephone usage in public has been observed by both Nokia and Intel. One manufacturer built miniature cameras into cars at shows to observe how customers reacted to new products. However, this is ethically questionable and carries a high risk of the company being "outed." It should be kept in mind that people quickly become aware that they are being observed and often react very negatively when they have blown the cover of the researcher.[33] Obtaining permission in advance is safer and we believe that it leads to better research.

Despite our warnings on the risks of covert observation, it should be noted that regular use has been made of security videos for the purposes of market research. For example, Johnson Controls, an automotive supplier of car interior parts, analyzed car park security videos to identify the problems shoppers have with loading their purchases into the car boot (U.S.: car "trunks"). Asda, a UK supermarket chain, used insights from security videos to gain ideas for optimiz-ing the layout of its stores.[34] Security videos from airports and service environ-ments can be shown at high speed and this can give useful insights into how the flow of passengers can be optimized.

In addition to choosing whether to make their status known, researchers must choose between two main types of observation: *participant observation* and *nonparticipant observation*. Being a full participant over long periods of time can give access to the *backstage of events*[35] and a deeper understanding of culture. Nonparticipation is more normal in ethnographic market research as it is simpler and enables the researcher to concentrate on observing and listening. That said, within a generally nonparticipant role, a market researcher might choose to deepen their understanding by trying certain actions themselves. For example, a researcher studying production line equipment may ask to work for a few hours "on the line." Similarly, a researcher looking at washing machine usage may ask if they can help with a family's weekly wash. Such participation obviously needs to be carefully considered—is it safe, practical, ethical, and culturally acceptable?

Access and Introductions

Gaining access is not necessarily easy and researchers must always be aware that they are typically invading the privacy of those observed and taking up their time. Therefore, care should be taken and ethical issues considered. It is worth taking the time to negotiate good access, that is, the permission to enter the field at the times the researcher selects and to observe and interview key actors, sometimes at length. Without good access, even the best ethnographic tools and techniques will be compromised.

Upon meeting each actor, the researcher should introduce themselves, the aims of the research, the amount of time and type of cooperation required, and thank the person for agreeing to cooperate. Reward or recognition for those who cooperate with the research is worth considering. It is also important to explain that the respondent's privacy will be respected and to build a strong rapport.

Sampling Strategy

Choosing a sampling strategy is about selecting the times at which to collect data, the activities to observe, and the people (actors) to interview. Researchers simply cannot observe everything connected with the topic they are studying, as this would be impractical, unscientific,[36] and will generate huge volumes of data. Even if an ethnographer is living in the field, it is not possible to observe everything of relevance. Instead, the events, actions, behaviors, or episodes to be observed are selected according to criteria that may emerge from the grand tour and which are likely to evolve over the course of the study (see Box Case 4.3). For example, observing and talking to certain actors may identify other actors that the researcher should also interview or observe (so-called *snowball sampling*, where the initial sample leads to a larger one).

Table 4.1 summarizes the different sampling strategies related to time, events, actors, and theory. *Time sampling* focuses on identifying when to conduct field observations and has three associated subcategories. *Continuous sampling* involves prolonged observation and total immersion in the field. It allows a deeper understanding of the culture to be achieved and would be relevant for a company focusing on "teen culture," where a detailed understanding of what types of services and products that young people find interesting requires time. *Time interval sampling* looks for how often particular behaviors occur within a specified period. In ethnographic market research, a common and effective approach is to observe *a day in the life* of the user of a product and this is an

Table 4.1 Sampling Strategies

	Strategy	Subcategory	Explanation	Comments
1)	Time sampling	Continuous	The researcher records every instance of behavior they can observe for the entire duration of the fieldwork.	Expensive, time-consuming, and difficult to gain access. Does allow the researcher to fully immerse themselves in the field but is seldom cost-effective for market research.
		Time-interval sampling	Involves observing over a chosen time period to determine how often particular behaviors or actions take place during a specified time period.	A very appropriate approach for ethnographic market research. Typically applied as a day in the life of key actors.
		Time-point sampling	Involves selecting only those behaviors that occur at a specific time. Researchers enter the field solely to observe these. Can be very similar to event sampling.	Typical strategy for market research. For example, family breakfasts might be observed, to better understand the need for different foods. In using time-point sampling, researchers need to be sure that they are not missing important clues that occur outside the period observed.
2)	Event (or activity) sampling		This involves observing one behavior contingent upon the presence of another behavior.	Needs to be used carefully as focusing too quickly on particular events may lead to important contextual issues being missed.

3)	Sampling of actors	Probabilistic	A random selection from the *sampling frame*—the complete set of actors who could be observed and interviewed. This strategy is aimed at generating a *representative* sample.	Seldom applied in ethnographic market research, as achieving a representative sample is seldom the goal.
		Stratified	Subsections of the sampling frame are sampled proportionally.	This approach is strongly related to probabilistic sampling. It is useful to identify subgroups in ethnographic market research and ensure that people from all of these are included in the sample.
		Purposive	A sample of actors to be observed and interviewed is selected to best meet the aims of the study.	Researchers must be cautious that a purposive sample does not simply become an *opportunistic* one, where the choice is driven by the easiest access.
		Snowball	The advice of the first actors interviewed is sort to identify other people to interview and/or observe.	People who have experience of the field being studied can often give good advice and even provide access to other actors. Researchers do, however, need to make sure that, if required, they are achieving a diverse enough sample.
4)	Theoretical sampling		The identification of repetition in the data can be used to decide when to stop further sampling.	This approach can provide confidence that sufficient data have been collected, even with comparatively small (and therefore nonrepresentative) samples.

Note: Table constructed from the discussion in: Dane, F. C., *Research Methods*. Pacific Grove, CA: Brookes/Cole, 1990 and other sources.

example of time interval sampling. Agilent Technologies, a manufacturer of chemical analysis equipment, observed the working day of laboratory technicians. This showed when and how they used chemical analysis equipment, and how it needed to be more easily connected to other data gathering equipment. The third subcategory is *time-point sampling*—observation to determine what happens at specific times.

Event sampling is a common approach, particularly observing customers as they utilize products and services. Panasonic observed women shaving, food manufacturers have observed family meals, and financial service providers have observed the interaction between their employees and customers at the point of sale. In business situations where events may be at particular times of the day, to all extents and purposes event and time-point sampling are identical.

A very different approach to sampling is to consider the range of people to be observed and/or interviewed and Table 4.1 indicates what researchers need to consider about the *sampling of actors*. The first step is to consider all the people who could be observed or interviewed; this is called the *sampling frame*. For a consumer product this could be a target population, or a particular segment and a random selection from this is used to generate a *representative* or *probabilistic sample*. If there are subsections of the sampling frame that have very different characteristics, then the sample selected is chosen to include an appropriate proportion of each of these groups—so-called *stratified sampling*. This allows an overall sample to be selected that includes all of the characteristics of the market. Achieving a representative sample is one of the central tenets of quantitative market research but it does not normally fit with the aims of exploratory ethnographic market research. However, it *is* useful to identify what the sampling frame consists of, as this will make ethnographic market researchers more aware of the characteristics of the sample they select, especially potential limitations of this selection.

The most common sampling strategies for choosing the people to be observed and interviewed in ethnographic market research are *purposive* and *snowball* sampling. Purposive samples are chosen to best match the aims of the research and their selection begins with the two questions: Who can give insights into the use of a particular product or service? And how can we obtain access? Researchers need to be careful to avoid choosing an *opportunistic sample* (where the friends, family, and direct contacts are chosen) just because this is the easiest way to gain access. Opportunistic samples often have hidden risks (for example, close friends or contacts may try to be overly helpful in a way that brings bias into the research).

The question of when to stop data collection is an important one in ethnographic market research, as the findings will never become representative unless large numbers of people and events are observed. Therefore, a *theoretical sampling*[37] approach is taken. In this, new data are constantly compared with what has already been collected. Do the new data provide disconfirming evidence? Or do they fit a pattern that has already been established? In the latter case the first indications are there that more data will not lead to more insights. How does this work in practice? For example, if a particular activity was being observed, then observations would identify the approaches and behaviors associated with that activity. Initially, each observation would identify different approaches and behaviors but soon a pattern of the different variations on that activity would emerge—a *theory* on the activity. Further observation would provide confirmatory evidence for the theory; in research this is referred to as *theoretical saturation* (see also Figure 6.3, p. 131).

In practice, an evolving mix of sampling strategies is common, rather than a single approach throughout the research. So Table 4.1 is useful as a guide to prompt researchers to consider all aspects of the research that are related to timings, events, actors, and theory in order to develop the most appropriate sampling.

Box Case 4.3

Panasonic—The Lady Shaver[38]

With only 5 percent market share in the U.S., the Japanese company Panasonic was looking to design a breakthrough shaving product for women. A team of female ethnographers was hired and this group took the time to arrange access to women at home, to systematically observe and discuss shaving with them. It quickly emerged that some women viewed shaving as tiresome and consequently hurried when shaving, whereas others were meticulous and unhurried. The ethnographers hypothesized that young, urban women formed the bulk of the latter category and the sampling strategy was accordingly focused on this group.

Over several weeks, the researchers observed women shaving and gained significant insights for Panasonic. Japanese people associate high gloss with high quality and so previous Panasonic shavers were highly finished. Contextual interviewing showed that such a finish was perceived by American women to be slippery and therefore easy to drop. This led Panasonic to adopt a rubberized surface, which also was found to underline the waterproof nature of the new product. Observations revealed that women shaved faster than the engineers had previously believed and this influenced the design of the shaving head. Shaving behind the knees and around the ankles was perceived by women to be particularly difficult and so an ergonomic design was developed. Finally, the ethnographers observed that space for the charging unit of a shaver was very limited in a typical bathroom. Therefore, the new product's charger was designed to fit neatly into a power socket and to support the shaver itself.

The Panasonic case shows how ethnography provided ideas for better product features, which helped the new product to be more successful. In addition, it illustrates the iterative nature of planning and conducting such market research. Before the research started, American women's attitudes to shaving were unknown. Once the two dominant attitudes became clear, the sampling strategy was modified to give extra insight into young, urban women's views and this group become the target segment in the advertising. The advertising was also based on the subtle understanding of perceptions of shaving developed over the course of the research.

Data Collection—The Ethnographic Record

The ability to collect multiple types of data is one of the strengths of ethnographic market research[39]—"a characteristic of good ethnography is its *inclusion of both qualitative and quantitative data.*"[40] The full range of data collected is termed the *complete ethnographic record,* which is illustrated in Figure 4.1.

A comprehensive ethnographic record consists of field notes of what was heard and seen, interview transcripts, tape recordings, photographs, video recordings, copies of documents from the field. Other constituents of the ethnographic record can be artifacts and the results of multiple methods. In anthropology, physical examples of a tribe's symbols might be collected (this was common practice in early studies but is now practiced with caution as some contemporary tribal leaders have protested and called for the return of artifacts collected by researchers in the past). In market research, artifacts that might be collected could be old toothbrushes (in research looking at dental hygiene), and magazines (when looking at teenagers' access to news media). Other data include *physical traces*—the term applied to supporting evidence that can be collected from the environment. Looking for physical traces is analogous to the way detectives discretely look for physical evidence of crime. In market research on food products, a physical trace could be that although a consumer claimed that they used a coffee machine daily, it could be seen that the water container was totally dry, indicating that the machine was used less often than claimed. Researchers investigating eating habits may check the "use by" dates on items in the homes of the people they are observing.

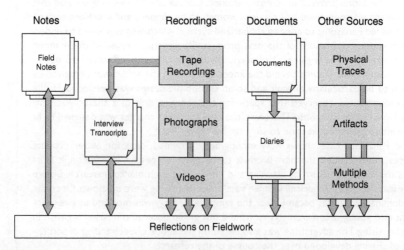

Figure 4.1   The Complete Ethnographic Record for Market Research

---

Field Notes

Research Project: Middle-Aged Insurance Purchasers
Case: # 171
Location: Interviewees' home: living room and home office.
Actors: Customers (couple who have not previously purchased from VirginMoney). 54-year-old accountant and wife (52-year-old teacher).

Field Observations:
- First part of interview was in the living room of a middle-class large detached house.
- Three graduation photographs of children displayed on sideboard.
- Man had comprehensive files of the family's financial products and a program on his PC for comparing investments.
- With his accountancy background, the husband appeared to be the decision-maker but he complained, "*some of these products are just too complicated for me to explain and, if my wife doesn't understand them, then it doesn't seen a good idea—as she will have to deal with the administration if I die first*" (see interview transcript).

Initial Reflections
- Status of children's education appears to have a major impact on whether parents are interested in extra life insurance.

Remember!
- Notes should cover: space; actor(s); activities; object(s) and physical traces; events; time sequences; goals; feelings; and explanatory variables.

Figure 4.2   Field Notes for Market Research

Source: Based on the format given by Rust, L., "Observations: Parents and Children Shopping Together: A New Approach to the Qualitative Analysis of Observational Data," *Journal of Advertising Research*, Vol. 33, No. 4, July/August 1993, pp. 65–70.

Field Notes

Good field notes are the cornerstone of ethnographic data collection. Notes on the events observed, the settings and interaction seen should be taken as soon as possible after the event.[41] Figure 4.2 shows how field notes should be taken, with headings for the location of the observations and the actors observed and interviewed, the key observations and *initial reflections*. At the bottom of the form is a reminder of the items that should be covered in field notes,[42] such as the space in which the observation takes place, the objects seen, and so on. It is useful to have blank field notes forms printed on postcard-sized cards, as these are easy to fill out in the field.

The field notes shown in Figure 4.2 are from research about middle-aged people's opinions on financial products. The research took place in family homes and a contextual interview probed when and how couples consider buying additional insurance. The advantage of conducting the research in their homes included visual clues of factors that influence decisions (for example, graduation photographs and files of financial information are noted), and frank statements on how complex financial products are perceived to be.

It should be noted that the field notes "form" includes a place for researchers to write their reflections. For example, a researcher investigating purchasing of food, chocolates, and drinks at petrol stations would quickly recognize that the extent of nonfuel purchasing depends on the time of day. More observations over time would lead to subtle insights on the culture of nonfuel purchases at petrol stations. One of the aims of reflection is to identify *exploratory variables;* factors that could explain events or actions and which need to be looked at carefully in future data collection.

Contextual Interviews

Contextual interviews form a fundamental part of ethnographic data. It always helps to prepare a number of semistructured questions in advance. Clear unambiguous questions need to be designed, following the recommendations given

Table 4.2   Key Questions Related to an Activity

	Underlying Research Questions	Questions to Ask
1)	What is the purpose of the activity?	• When do you use this product or service? • Why do you use this product or service? • How does this product or service help you do your work? • Who else benefits from this?
2)	What needs to be conducted in advance?	• Can you tell me what you need to prepare in advance?
3)	What procedures are used?	• Can you explain to me how you use this product or service? • What makes the activity easier (or harder) to complete? • Are there different ways of doing this?
4)	What are the time and space requirements?	• How long does this typically take? • Can you do this somewhere else? • What are these [other devices or artifacts observed]?
5)	What are the personnel requirements?	• Who do you need to help you do this? • What skills do they require?
6)	What is the nature of the social organization?	• Who else uses this product or service? • What is the relationship between these people?
7)	What are the occasions for performing the activity?	• When do you need to do this? • How often? • Who else uses this product or service?
8)	What happens after you have completed the activity?	• What must happen? • What needs to be verified? • What concludes the activity?

Note: Table based on a variety of sources including: Rosenthal, R. and Rosnow, R. L., *Essentials of Behavioural Research: Methods and Data Analysis.* 2nd edition. New York: McGraw-Hill, 1991; and Bettencourt, L. A. and Ulwick, A. W., "The Customer-Centred Innovation Map," *Harvard Business Review,* Vol. 86, No. 5, May 2008, pp. 109–114.

in Chapter 2. Building rapport is essential in contextual interviewing, in order to "bring out" respondents' views. Therefore, using appropriate jargon might be useful but researchers should be cautious; just using jargon might not lead to them being accepted by the members of a particular subculture.

Table 4.2 gives an idea of the sort of questions that need to be developed for use in contextual interviews linked to observing an activity, such as products or services in use (see Box Case 4.4). The second column identifies eight research questions connected with an activity. The third column gives examples of the questions that would be asked in the contextual interviews themselves. It is best to prepare questions in advance, but in contextual interviewing, extra or modified questions may be asked, depending on what is observed. It is important to ask questions in an appropriate way. Adopting the role of a somewhat naïve outsider can help, as can using a natural language. In conducting interviews, researchers should avoid making assumptions and should plan that the answers to the questions can be triangulated with other data. For example, interviewees can be asked how long an activity takes and their perception can be triangulated against actual time taken (but researchers should be careful to time activities discretely).

Box Case 4.4

Lucci Orlandini Design—Designing for the Disabled[43]

Lucci Orlandini Design is an Italian company, founded in 1968 by Roberto Lucci and Paolo Orlandini and based north of Milan. The company has designed over 500 products including household appliances, furniture, and lighting for many well-known brands and has won several design awards. Their credo is to create designs that are "simple to manufacture and simple to use."

In December 2002, one of the Europe's largest kitchen manufacturers, Snaidero, asked them to design a kitchen that was suitable for disabled citizens, of which there are almost 40 million in Europe. "We were experienced at designing kitchens but with this project, we were entering new territory," Lucci recalls. They quickly realized that it would be impossible to design a kitchen that covered all disabilities and so with Snaidero they decided to focus on several conditions including paraplegia, amputations, vision impairment, and Alzheimer's disease. "People with these disabilities share similar needs and are looking for greater independence and safety in the kitchen and being able to move around in a wheelchair. We really wanted to design something great for them! But the kitchen needed to be versatile, so that it could also be used by friends and relatives who are not disabled," Lucci explains.

The two designers decided to conduct research themselves. This took them to the Niguarda Hospital in Milan. "First we had a look at the kitchens that were used in the hospital. Of course, hospital staff were using them but having kitchens at hand allowed us to invite patients to the scene and to get their impressions first hand" says Lucci. Patients were asked to conduct everyday tasks and were observed. For example, it

▶▶

was seen that people in a wheelchair could not get close enough to a sink to wash dishes. The height of the worktops was also an issue. "Imagine yourself in the wheelchair; wouldn't it be good, if you had a worktop not just in front of you but also to your right and to your left? Remember, you can turn around in a given space but you can't move around a lot. We had a curved worktop in mind, but we simply didn't know whether it would work," Orlandini states. So, simple mock-ups were built and users in wheelchairs were invited to test them. The designers knew that curved units would be more expensive to produce and during the interviews had learned that many disabled people live on low incomes and kitchens had to be affordable. "Paolo and I saw that the project was becoming more complex, the more we listened to the user," says Lucci.

A full prototype with real appliances was made at the Snaidero plant and the team had it tested at the Gervusutta Hospital in Udine. "We focused on the ergonomics and designed 'wrap-around' worktops that allowed disabled people to reach the whole worktop surface." The prototype went through several iterations before the final product, Skyline Lab, was introduced in 2004. The product has been very successful and has won several design awards including the Well-Tech Award and the Dedalo Minosse International Award. More importantly, the design has been extremely well received by disabled users. Lucci puts this success down to, "Conducting primary research and involving users—without them we wouldn't have come up with this particular design."

It is also good practice to use the physical environment as a cue for questions. For example, in a B2C environment, research into the use of electric toothbrushes might take other electrical devices as a cue for questions such as: "Can you tell me how you find the design of your shaver's charging unit?" In a B2B context, researchers working for Bosch used manufacturing equipment as the subject of discussion, asking such questions as, "Could you please explain how this equipment works? And which are the things that cause you most problems?"

To ensure that none of the questions are forgotten, it is useful to have them printed on the back of the field notes form.

Recordings

In addition to written notes, video recordings, audio recording, and still photography are all useful ways of data recording. Interviews are often recorded using audio devices, as these are more convenient and less intrusive than a video camera.

Digital video cameras are now so cheap that they enable all events that are interesting for market researchers to be recorded: for example, typical sales situations; using products; interacting with service providers; and so on. However, video cameras can be intrusive and market researchers need to consider whether they will have a negative influence on the observations. Still photography is less intrusive and may be a useful alternative. The ethical aspects of filming will need to be considered and this is an absolute must when children are the focus of the researchers, in order to encourage actors to give a "running commentary."

It is useful to motivate the actors by asking them to explain what they are doing, as they do it and there is some evidence that having people describe what they are doing as they do it accesses their tacit knowledge. It should be noted that asking actors to give step-by-step explanations could change the way they approach the task and so some researchers have recommended that it be avoided. Our experience is positive, provided a suitable rapport with the actors has been established. In any event, good listening skills and appropriate body language are essential on the part of the researchers.

There are two main ways to approach video recordings—either to record long sequences observing whatever action occurs, or to be focused and record shorter selected action. The latter tends to be the more effective approach, as long recordings are difficult and time-consuming to analyze. So it is particularly important to have a clear sampling strategy for video ethnography.

Special cameras are available that record eye movements and the changes in the size of consumers' pupils as they, for example, examine product literature. However, such devices are normally only used for very specific observations in a laboratory setting. For example, one experiment used eye movement detectors to look at how the layout of a menu influenced diners' choices.[44]

Documents

Researchers need to actively check whether actors have documents that are of relevance to the study. For example, in a study of the usage consumer electronics, it would be useful to check whether those interviewed still have the operating manuals for the equipment they own. Inspection of these could provide physical evidence of whether these have been read (for example, worn pages or "dog ears").

Diaries and Other Data Sources

Having actors keep diaries can also provide useful information.[45] Researchers should provide actors with a set of categories that need to be covered in diary entries. These categories will be strongly related to the coding system adopted but researchers should stress that actors are encouraged to add any comments, reflections, or thoughts that occur to them. Diaries have the advantage that they bring a longitudinal aspect and self-reflection but extra motivation must be provided if the actors need to make regular and comprehensive entries.

Physical traces, artifacts, and multiple methods (for example, repertory grid interviews) should all be considered in defining the scope of the ethnographic record. A wide range of data sources can give both additional perspectives and enable triangulation.

Reflections

The *reflections on fieldwork* shown in Figure 4.1 are not primary data as such. Rather, they are part of data analysis that is integrated into the overall ethnographic record (and acts a stimulus for deeper understanding). The *initial reflections* on the field notes are the first step in which the researcher considers what has been observed, and heard. After a number of field visits, a review of the initial reflections enables the researcher to reflect deeper. These are normally intuitions, perceived anomalies, patterns, trends, sources of confusion, and the like.

Researchers should regularly update their reflections as the research progresses. Reflections help identify further events that need to be observed, limitations of the current approach, and emerging hypotheses—for example, issues that appear to be common amongst the actors or situations observed. It is useful to have a bound notebook for the reflections and much of the ethnographic record (and having squared rather than just lined paper makes it easier to draw diagrams quickly). As indicated in Figure 4.1, the researcher should base their reflection on what can be learnt from all of the different sources of data, including the initial reflections on each of the field notes forms.

ANALYZING THE RESULTS

One of the challenges in understanding how ethnographic market research is conducted and analyzed is that the two are intertwined, rather than consisting of independent stages. Therefore, researchers should carefully consider how they will analyze data *before* data collection starts. Similarly, as soon as data are available, preliminary analysis should start as this will lead to insights that may enhance the way further data are collected. Data analysis is *inductive* (reasoning from observed examples that a general theory exists), as opposed to being *deductive* (where explanations of data are based on reasoning from existing insights, or theories).

Figure 4.3 gives a conceptual overview of three key aspects of ethnographic market research that take place in parallel—*data collection, reflexivity,* and *analysis*. Data collection starts with the grand tour, the results of which influence both the initial data collection procedures and the first part of the analysis, initial coding. As the first data are collected, researchers need to reflect on what they have learnt and this will also influence the coding and possibly the way in which further data are collected. Insights from the initial coding typically lead to enhanced data collection, such as a wider range of data sources, modified sampling, and so on. The collection of enhanced data leads to further reflection and then the full analysis. Between data collection and analysis there may be a number of iterations and there will typically be extensive triangulation between the different data sources. It should be noted that Figure 4.3 is a representation of how data collection, reflexivity, and analysis are conducted but every project will be a variation on this theme.

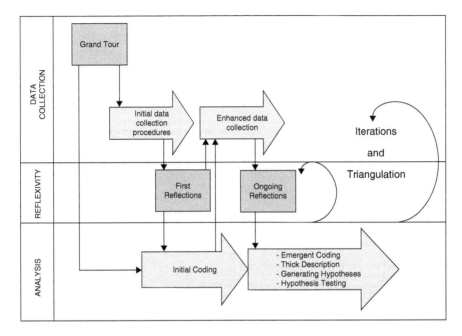

Figure 4.3   Conceptual View of Ethnographic Data Collection and Analysis

The analysis of ethnographic data is a process of successive focusing; from a broad investigative focus (looking at many actions and events, and keeping a broad line of enquiry), to a focused one. The four main stages of analysis are as follows:[46]

1. Data coding.
2. Generating a thick description.
3. Generating hypotheses.
4. Hypothesis testing.

Data Coding

Coding is the process of sorting observations into categories and is the first step in attaching meaning to what was observed. Coding should be applied to interview transcripts, video recordings, and other sources of data. Once each data source has been coded, triangulation between them leads to a better understanding and more valid results. It is recommended to prepare an *initial coding scheme* before starting observation and coding must be seen as an iterative process. The initial coding scheme is closely linked to the research question: what is the market researcher looking to understand? The coding scheme identifies what the researcher should watch for and therefore helps prevent oversights. This is particularly important, as the clues to unarticulated needs are often nonverbal.

During the course of actual data collection, it is almost inevitable that extra issues will be observed that will need to be included in the *emergent coding scheme*.

For example, market researchers interested in the use of toothpaste might use the following initial coding scheme—the demographics of the actors; the make of toothpaste in the bathrooms; the way the actors use their toothbrushes; the time they take to clean their teeth; and the availability of dental floss and mouth wash. Upon embarking on data collection, researchers would quickly recognize that a host of other points should be coded: for example, the other

Table 4.3   Generic Coding Scheme for Systematic Observation

	Data Categories	Points to Look For (Codings)	Observed?	Timings	Notes
1)	Triggers for acquiring the product or service	• Why, when, and how?			
2)	Triggers for product or service usage	• Who, what, where, when, why, how?			
3)	The environment in which the product is used, or the service consumed	• Physical layout/objects • Actors • Activities/events • Time sequence			
4)	Interactions with user's environment	• Physical interactions • Proxemic distances • Social interactions			
5)	Product or service usage	• Doing things right • Doing things wrong • Wasted time (*nonvalue adding time*) • Misuse • *Workarounds˙* • Confusion • Dangerous situations (for example, physical danger or risk of loss of data)			
6)	Intangible aspects and unarticulated needs.	• Emotions • Frustration and wasted time • Fears and anxiety • Linguistic signals • Extra-linguistic signals • Nonverbal signals (for example, body language) • Spatial signals			
7)	User customization	• User modifications of the product • User modifications of the (normal) process			

Note: * Fulton Suri, J., *Thoughtless Acts*. San Francisco: Chronical Books, 2005.

Source: Compiled by the authors from a variety of references including: Leonard-Barton, D. *Wellsprings of Knowledge: Building and Sustaining the Sources of Innovation*. Boston, MASS: Harvard Business School Press, Boston, 1995.

types of personal hygiene products available; the number of people sharing the bathroom; the time spent each day on personal hygiene, and so on. This richer data set will provide deeper insights into the consumers being studied. Data are typically gathered on all the behaviors related to the topic, rather than just those directly related to the product or service being investigated. Fieldwork nearly always widens the range of contextual data that is collected.

Table 4.3 gives a generic coding scheme for observation studies and has seven categories of data; from the *triggers for acquiring the product or service*, up to *user customization*. The table gives points to look for and the additional columns can be annotated with the timings of when these are observed, and additional notes. The seven coding categories force the observer to look at not only how a product or service fits into the user's overall environment but also to look for signals that indicate unarticulated needs. For example, the triggers for using a vacuum cleaner could be weekly cleaning, or something spilled. The latter trigger brings specific requirements such as ease-of-access and ease-of-handling, which will influence product design. (The Black & Decker Company created the well-known hand-held "Dustbuster" vacuum cleaners to address this need.)

As indicated by Table 4.3, frustration with services or products can indicate that a current design does not meet the user's main needs. However, the signs may not be obvious. A good observer will look for subtle signs such as *extra-linguistic* signals (for example, the speed and emphasis in speech), *nonverbal* signs such as body language, and *spatial signals* (for example, the proximity of a user to others or objects). Another clue to unarticulated needs can be that users have modified or customized the equipment to better meet their needs. For service products, the equivalent of such a modification is that the consumer may alter their behavior to make up for limitations of the existing service. Such changes in behavior are often subtle and the consumer may be unaware of them. Due to the difficulty of observing and coding at different levels simultaneously, the best solution is to make video recordings, which can be viewed off-line by a number of people all looking for the different codes and further clues. The disadvantage of video recording is that it may influence the user's actions or embarrass the people being interviewed.

Moving images can also be analyzed to determine time sequences. For example, the various steps such as collecting dirty washing and sorting it, that lead up to the use of a washing machine. *Proxemic distances* can also be checked. These are the distances between key actors, or their distance from key objects. Time sequence analysis can be summarized as a flow diagram, annotated with typical times. Such diagrams can be interpreted to identify *nonvalue adding time,* that is, time that does not help the actors achieve their aims. Although nonvalue adding time is essentially *wasted time,* researchers should be careful when using the latter term with actors, as many users of products and services will be unaware of the time that they are wasting. A good example of this is the QBNet chain of men's hairdressers in Japan that has eliminated most of the nonvalue adding time from its service by, for example, by having colored, highly visible lights outside its shops which indicate whether there is a queue (a "green" lights indicates that there is no queue). This means that customers do not park their cars only to find that there is too long a wait for a hair cut.

Another approach to analyzing observational data is to identify several typical scenarios of how products or services are used, with associated problems and issues. Simple drawings and storyboards can be used to summarize these, including triggers for use and the problems encountered. Storyboards are useful tools to support communication with both users and with the whole of the NPD team. Often customers have to modify products to *workaround* their limitations, and this can give excellent ideas for product enhancements.

Generating a Thick Description

After each of the different data sources has been coded, the researcher faces the challenge of distilling this information into a thick description (remember that in this context "thick" indicates that the description should provide insights into the actors' culture). Writing the description is a challenging process that, where possible, should be conducted by two or more researchers in parallel. Just as the researcher or research team has immersed themselves in the field, they now need to immerse themselves in the data. What do we mean by this? Researchers first need to review the data and their reflections. Then, it is good practice to look for relationships and contradictions in the data. A good analogy to this stage is learning to become effective at proofreading. An experienced proofreader will only need to read a text once, and can simultaneously identify mistakes in grammar, clarity, style, and so on. For a beginner, it is better to read a text several times looking at a different aspect each time. Similarly, a neophyte ethnographic researcher should review the complete ethnographic record several times, looking separately for relationships in the data, contradictions, and then cultural understanding.

Relationships in the Data

Looking for patterns in the data provide insights into actors' feelings, motivations, or problems. Are particular behaviors associated with a particular event, or do they precede it for example? For example, Miele (see Box Case 9.1) observed that the parents of children with allergies cleaned their children's rooms meticulously, often several times a week. However, such parents did not recognize that they were wasting time by cleaning more than was necessary. Cleaning had become a ritual, which gave parents peace of mind that their child's room was as clean is it possibly could be (as they had no means of "measuring" cleanliness). Miele's product gives that peace of mind and saves time. Recognizing the ritual nature of cleaning could also be used to generate a powerful marketing message.

As the complete ethnographic record will include a wide range of data sources, the researcher must be prepared to triangulate the contradictions found in the verbal data with several other data sources. For example, verbal data should be compared with video footage, documentary evidence, and so on.

Contradictions in the Data

In addition to relationships, researchers need to look for contradictions and Table 4.4 indicates what these can be. Transcripts need to be reviewed for *disjunctures*, where actors' explanations of behavior do not fit with what was observed. Explanations should not be taken at face value and ethnographers often generate important insights from disjunctures. For example, researchers found that sport fishermen claimed that the color and design of fishing equipment was unimportant to them. However, they were observed to carefully select engines for their boats which matched the overall color scheme.[47]

Another source of insights is to identify when actors make *over generalizations*, or add *gloss*. What do we mean by these terms? Actors will often oversimplify their explanations of events and activities. Similarly, actors may put a gloss on their explanations—a positive interpretation or "spin" on something they have done. Users will often explain how they use equipment in a positive way and omit to explain how often they make mistakes. Mothers have been found to claim that their children choose healthy for breakfast but this was different to what was observed.[48] Readers will only need to honestly reflect on how they explain things to friends and colleagues, to understand that adding a gloss is a common and, for some people, almost a subconscious mechanism. The final type of contradiction to look for in verbal data is a *claim of idiosyncrasy*, where actors think or claim that their behavior is special, or unusual (whereas their type of behavior is common in the group of actors being studied).

Table 4.4 Looking of Contradictions in Data

	Issue	Meaning	Suggestions
1)	Disjunctures	Actor(s)' explanations actions do not fit with observed actions.	• Compare each element of an explanation of behavior with each element of observed behavior.
2)	Over generalizations	Actor(s)' explanations of activities and events.	• Check claims actors make about their explanations. • Listen for expressions such as "this always …", "everyone knows …" and so on.
3)	Gloss	In order to enhance how they are perceived, actors explain actions in a positive way, omitting any reference to their own limitations. Gloss is the equivalent of "spin" in politics.	• Look for positive slants that appear in explanations such as "this is quite easy …", "it didn't take long to learn …" or similar statements. • Body language and speech inclination can give an indication that an actor is adding gloss.
4)	Claims of idiosyncrasy	Actors claim or even believe that something about their action or behavior is unusual, or special.	• Listen for expressions such as "I know this is unusual…," or "nobody else would do it this way …" and so on. • Compare actions and behaviors across actors to see if they are similar.

Note: Table constructed from the discussions in: Arnould, E. J. and Wallendorf, M., "Market-Oriented Ethnography: Interpretation Building and Marketing Strategy Formulation," *Journal of Marketing Research*, Vol. XXXI, November 1994.

Developing a Cultural Understanding

Market researchers must strive to understand culture through the eyes and understanding of the actors, including the role and meaning of symbols and symbolic acts; and the use of language including dialect and jargon.[49] In this part of the analysis, researchers need to question whether their own culture causes them to take things for granted and miss underlying meanings.[50] "Culture refers to learned, socially acquired traditions and the lifestyle of a group of people, including patterned, repetitive ways of thinking, feeling and acting."[51] It can take many forms, from national or ethnic cultures, through to the culture of small groups of customers. It should be noted that "we cannot observe people's thoughts and feelings"[52] and so generating a cultural understanding is not a simple process (see for example Box Case 4.5).

In work on organizational culture,[53] it is useful to look for specific pointers, including the *stories* that are told in organizations, the *routines and rituals* used, and the *symbols* of organizations. Taking these suggestions and combining them with others from the literature, it can be recommended that researchers look for the following eight points in order to gain insights into culture:

1. *Relationships, organization, and power structures.* How is the group being studied organized, formally or otherwise? What are the power structures?
2. *Stories.* What stories are typically told by members of the group and what do they mean?
3. *Symbols.* What are the symbols that appear to be used by a group? (These can be linked to dress codes, equipment, decorations, and so on.)
4. *Routines and rituals.* What are the routines that the group constantly conduct? Are they of a ritual nature?
5. *Language, slang, and jargon.* How do the members of the group use language? Do they have a specific slang or vocabulary?
6. *Attitudes and opinions.* What are the typical opinions and attitudes that are expressed by group members?
7. *Emotions and feelings.* Do members of the group show their emotions or feelings, and on what occasions?
8. *Beliefs and values.* What are the underlying beliefs and values of the group?

The identification of some or all of the above pointers will help unveil culture. A key further step is to "identify the *central problem* [or *problems*] facing the group being studied."[54] This is done by taking each of the above eight elements and asking: *what does this tell us about the central problem(s) facing the group?* Later, the question can be asked: *what types of products or services can help the group address this problem?*

A good example of the process of understanding culture is a food manufacturer's investigation of the preparation of a Thanksgiving meal in the U.S. The research question for the food manufacturer was: *what opportunities are there for new products?* Families were observed preparing the Thanksgiving meal, and contextual interviews were conducted with mothers (who were deeply involved in the preparations).[55] From the observations, the stories told (such as recipes being attributed to "grandma ...") and other indicators of culture were identified. As the study progressed, the researchers started to understand the ritual nature of the preparation of the meal, it became clear that mothers wanted to prepare something special and were loathe to use fast easy-to-use ingredients. So, the central problem facing mothers was identified: they did not have much time but were expected (and themselves wanted) to serve a special meal consisting of "home cooking" (as grandma would have cooked). Once they had recognized this, food manufacturers knew that products for Thanksgiving that were perceived as "convenient" or "instant" would never be successful. So the cultural aspects identified were useful to identify the type of products that would be needed and accepted.

Box Case 4.5

Sainsbury's—Doing the Ethnographic Egyptian[56]

Sainsbury's is a leading UK supermarket retailer, well-known for the quality of its food and its long tradition of good service, which started in 1869. Similar to a number of other successful retailers, Sainsbury's decided to expand internationally at the end of the 1990s and one of the countries it chose was Egypt. It might be thought obvious that the national culture will strongly impact how a foreign investor's operations, in this case retail services, are perceived and so should be recognized by management as a fundamentally important point to focus on. However, this was not the case in this foray into the Egyptian food market.

In Egypt, food retail has always been the arena of small, relatively inefficient, small independent mostly family-owned retailers. Sainsbury's assumed that through its size, efficiency, and attractive supermarkets with good service it could steal a lead on the market. The management decisions were made and during 2000, 106 supermarkets and local stores were opened. The fast roll-out was part of the management strategy to bring better organized stores to Egypt but management had overlooked some of the cultural elements. Several decisions were made which were later regretted. First, the massive marketing push led to a bitter backlash from local retailers, who gained support by claiming that Sainsbury's was trying to dominate the market. Second, the decision to offer UK cuts of meat rather than traditional Egyptian ones was not accepted by customers. Third, offering samples of food for customers to try did not work as all the samples were typically taken by the first customer to see them. As the story unfolded, Sainsbury's cooperated with an ethnographic study which used the analysis of metaphors to identify the key cultural aspects that needed to be considered. This study found that Egypt's history of occupation meant that foreign retail chains were viewed skeptically, and although the wider choice and value was appreciated by customers, a whole host of changes in Sainsbury's stores and service would be needed to woo Egyptian customers into becoming regular shoppers. The ethnographic study gave deep insights but it came too late—all 106 Egyptian stores were closed by Sainsbury's after 14 months.

"Sainsbury's knew what is needed but did not know how to do it" is how one Egyptian couple who were interviewed put it. Interestingly, Sainsbury's are by no means alone in this, as several other famous retail names have faced similar issues in international markets—for example, Wal-Mart struggled in Chile, and Marks & Spencer's was not successful in Canada and Germany.

Writing the First Thick Description

It is a good discipline to write a 2–3 page summary of what was observed, and what can be concluded from the relationships in the data, the contradictions, and the pointers to culture. The description can be considered to be a *thick description*, if it gives insights into the culture of the group of actors observed, the central problems and issues they face, and the way they both perceive and deal with these.

Generating Hypotheses

As researchers immerse themselves in the data, they will start to become aware of patterns, such as the way behaviors are linked to activities and, from these reflections, generate hypotheses. It is useful to start by looking at the occurrence of events in the data (these are normally coded E_1, E_2, E_n) compared with behaviors (these are normally coded B_1, B_2, B_n). Comparison of the frequency and the occurrence of the different codes will show when particular behaviors precede, accompany, or follow particular events. Looking for the relationship between events and behaviors may sound complex but in practice researchers will learn to spot such links quickly.

An example of behavior that precedes an activity is the way rock climbers meticulously check their equipment before starting a climb. This involves hanging the various pieces of their equipment in a specific order on their climbing harnesses, to ensure that they are easily accessible when climbing becomes demanding. Observing a climber conducting this ritual would lead a market researcher to hypothesize about how often such behavior occurs, its role, and its meaning. Looking at the steps taken in preparation could lead the manufacturers of climbing equipment to improve their products.

A research project that looked at the influence children have on their parents' purchasing behavior in supermarkets provides an excellent example of how hypotheses are generated and tested.[57] Researchers observed parents shopping with their children but did not have preconceived ideas on what they would discover. As such, the research took a *grounded theory* approach—the explanation of the data emerged from the data themselves. For each of the 200 families observed, field notes were taken using a similar format to Figure 4.2, and including space for the researcher to estimate the ages of the children, to record children's actions such as pointing to things on the shelves, and parents' purchases. The fact that 200 families were observed shows that ethnographic market research can, when focused on a relatively simple event, generate large data sets. (Statistical tests can even be applied to such data sets—although ethnographic market research is largely qualitative—where appropriate numerical methods can be used.) As the data were analyzed, the hypothesis emerged that parents with smaller children were more likely to be influenced in their purchases than parents with older children.

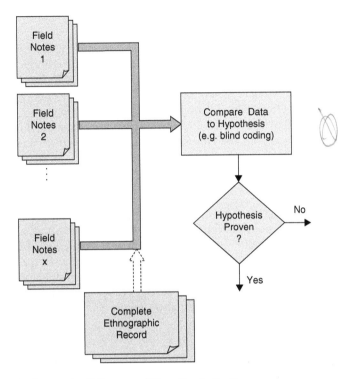

Figure 4.4   Conceptual Diagram of Hypothesis Testing

Testing Hypotheses

Figure 4.4 illustrates the way in which hypothesis testing takes place. To test the hypothesis the field notes can often provide the necessary data but, as indicated on the diagram, sometimes additional data from the complete ethnographic record are needed.

In the supermarket study mentioned above,[58] once the researchers had immersed themselves in the data, it seemed that the parents of younger children were more likely to be influenced. In order to see if this was the case, a dozen sets of field notes were selected at random. This provided partial confirmation of the hypothesis. The next step was to make copies of all 200 sets of field notes with the age estimates removed. Then the 200 sets were checked to see which families were more strongly influenced by their children. Checking the cards for purchasing behavior with the age estimates removed ensured that hypothesis testing was conducted without bias. The 200 cards were then re-annotated with the age estimates—and the hypothesis was confirmed.

SUMMARIZING THE FINDINGS

Throughout this chapter we have stressed the complex, iterative nature of eth-nographic market research and the broad nature of the complete ethnographic record. Companies used summarizing market research quantitatively can be overwhelmed by qualitative data. Therefore, the question arises: how can the results be summarized effectively? Ethnographic data should lead to a final thick description, suitable visual material (for example, video clips), and impli-cations that can be drawn from the cultural insights and the central problem identified.

Final Thick Description

The thick description is likely to have been rewritten several times, as more relationships and contradictions are found, hypotheses are investigated, and as the researchers develop a deeper cultural understanding. A simple but effective way to structure the final thick description is to start with the aims of the mar-ket research, then explain how this led to the sample selected, continue with an explanation of the culture of the main groups of actors observed, and finish with the explanation of their central problem (see also Chapter 5).

Visual Material

Market researchers should bear in mind that their results need to be presented to service or product development teams, and management. So in addition to preparing a written thick description, it is advantageous to prepare a presenta-tion with suitable graphics, such as photographs, diagrams, and short illustra-tive video clips. Collecting material that provides *vivid exemplars* of the way customers and users act, and their subcultures is a useful way to present the findings.[59]

Recognizing Implications

The identification of the central problems facing the group of actors being stud-ied is fundamentally important—it provides companies with the opportunity to generate breakthrough products and services. As the central problems facing customers and users are often subtle and not directly recognized by them, it also means that competitors are unlikely to have these insights. Creativity theory tells us that people can be very creative if they are given direction, and articulating the central problem(s) facing customers gives the right level of guidance. It has also been said that researchers really need to develop an empathy with custom-ers, in order to be able to be "inspired to imagine new and better possibilities for people."[60] This is a good reason for the NPD team to be actively involved in the market research (as illustrated by Box Case 4.1 on Nokia).

Essentially, ethnographic market research identifies the problems that customers and users face, and the cultural aspects of the way they use products and services. Product developers need to use this information and generate creative solutions. How this is best done will be covered in Chapters 9 and 10.

LIMITATIONS TO CONSIDER

Ethnographic market research is very flexible and generates cultural insights that can lead to real breakthrough ideas for products and services. But it is not a panacea for all market research needs and it is appropriate to identify its limitations:

1. Ethnographic market research looks at real situations but actions can be influenced by the presence of the observer.
2. Research is time-consuming and analysis is complex. If poorly applied, ethnographic studies can be "frustrating and expensive."[61]
3. The research needs to be carefully focused, to prevent the results being too general to help new product development teams.[62]
4. Some marketing departments react negatively toward ethnographic methods, seeing them as a threat to their normal work and consequently criticizing them as "unrepresentative."
5. Many ethnographic studies are conducted by market research agencies that provide the results to their clients but are unwilling to provide details of their methodology. If an agency is used, it is important to check that they are willing to teach an NPD team their approaches.[63]
6. Inadequate sampling can lead to errors[64] but it should be noted that the aim in sampling in ethnographic studies is to provide meaningful rather than exhaustive results. Companies can find it hard to accept the validity of such data and therefore need to understand the nature of theoretical sampling, as opposed to the widely understood representative sampling.

SUMMARY

Ethnographic market research is based on the methodologies developed by cultural anthropologists and sociologists over the past hundred years. This chapter has shown that:

- There are a number of key tenets to ethnographic studies that enable them to generate deep understanding of culture, which can lead to breakthrough product ideas.
- Ethnographic studies require careful planning, since vast arrays of data are typically collected. Multiple sources of data are advantageous and data collection takes place in parallel to analysis.
- Analysis of ethnographic data requires reflection on the part of the researchers and is an iterative process.

- The aim of ethnographic market research is to understand the culture and central problem of the group being studied. Once these have been identified, then breakthrough ideas for products and services can be generated.

In Chapter 5 we will look at a detailed example of ethnographic market research, in order for the reader to see exactly how recommendations for selecting, collecting, and analyzing ethnographic market research are applied in practice. This detailed example will vividly show how the insights can lead to breakthrough products and services.

MANAGEMENT RECOMMENDATIONS

- Choose a current new product development project and apply ethnographic market research in parallel to your standard approaches. This should not only identify your customers' hidden needs but also demonstrate how effective ethnographic market research can be (this will be important in gaining acceptance for new approaches within your organization).
- Consider how you can best enhance your organization's capability to conduct ethnographic market research. Treat working with specialists as not only a way to understand specific market needs but also as an opportunity for organizational learning (ensuring that your organization becomes better at understanding customers' real needs).
- Focus your organization on identifying the central problem(s) faced by your customers, clients, and users.

RECOMMENDED READING

1. LeCompte, M. and Schensul, J. J., *Designing and Conducting Ethnographic Research*. Lanham, U.S.: AltaMira Press, 1999. [Excellent and comprehensive explanation of ethnographic methods—an absolute "must."]
2. Mariampolski, H., *Ethnography for Marketers*. Thousand Oaks, CA: Sage, 2006. [Useful book on ethnographic market research, with many examples, but less strong on "how" research can be conducted.]
3. Arnould, E. J. and Wallendorf, M., "Market-Oriented Ethnography: Interpretation Building and Marketing Strategy Formulation," *Journal of Marketing Research*, Vol. XXXI, November 1994. [Useful overview of how ethnographic data can be used in determining marketing strategy.]

5 EXAMPLE: WAREHOUSE EQUIPMENT RESEARCH

> My company believes in the benefits of the anthropological approach to market research, offering it along with traditional research methods.[1]

INTRODUCTION

This chapter describes discovery research into the opportunities for innovative warehouse equipment. It shows how ethnographic market research can be conducted using the approach presented in Chapter 4. The discussion is based on an actual project conducted in 2007 for a major manufacturer, which for reasons of confidentiality we will refer to as *WarehouseEquipCo*.

The main sections of this chapter:

- Explain how the research was planned and conducted.
- Cover how the data were analyzed.
- Discuss the conclusions and implications.

PLANNING AND CONDUCTING THE RESEARCH

Establishing the Aims

This project investigated the role of "mixed pallets" in warehousing. Typically manual handling is used to select goods from different pallets and place them on a separate pallet. Such mixed pallets will have boxes of different sizes and a mixture of products on them, fulfilling an order where a customer wants smaller quantities of certain products. The project was the first time that the sponsoring company had become involved with ethnographic market research and the project aims were defined as follows:

1. To investigate the influence of mixed pallets on the running of a warehouse.
2. To identify the problems associated with preparing mixed pallets which could lead to product opportunities.

Once the aims had been agreed, the sponsor organized access to a "typical" warehouse for the grand tour.

The Grand Tour

The grand tour looked at everything from "goods in" to "goods out." An employee from the warehouse being visited was informed of the research aims and asked: "We haven't visited a warehouse before, so can you please show us around and explain everything that happens from when goods arrive until when they leave?" On the tour it was noted that much of the work was conducted in a "staging area," where pallets were prepared for loading onto lorries. The preparation of mixed pallets and the problems with "picking" (collecting the various boxes needed from around the warehouse) and "stacking" were observed. In the staging area display boards with performance data were observed (for example, the number of shipments). The grand tour enabled the research team to select topics to focus on, warehouse employees to interview, and questions to ask.

To summarize the grand tour, a flow diagram was drawn—Figure 5.1. This documented the five key procedures observed in the warehouse. The diagram was annotated with notes on the actions observed, quotes from employees' explanations, and time required by employees to complete each stage. Photographs and a floor plan were also attached. The bottom of the diagram was used to draw conclusions and, for example, Figure 5.1 shows that it was decided to link the contextual interviews with performance data displayed in the staging area (asking: "How does your current equipment help or hinder you in achieving these targets?").

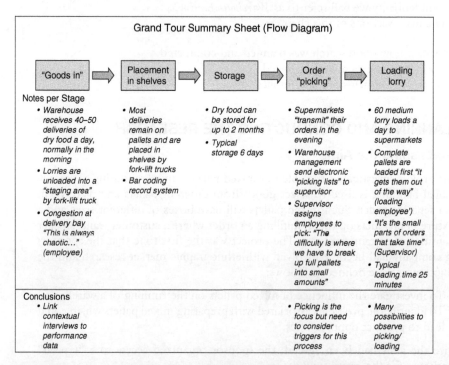

Figure 5.1   Summary Sheet from the Grand Tour Visit (Simplified)

Type of Observation and Access

Covert observation was deemed inappropriate, as it was necessary to obtain warehouse owners' permission for the visits. Nonparticipant observation was chosen as it was felt that if the researchers participated this would modify actions significantly. The size of warehouse was chosen as the main selection criterion rather than the type of goods stored (such as food, pharmaceuticals, or automotive spares). *WarehouseEquipCo.* had many contacts and so was able to arrange access to warehouses of different sizes.

Sampling Strategy

The grand tour was conducted over one working day (time interval sampling). This allowed the frequency and duration of key activities during the day to be identified. For example, 18 mixed pallets were prepared during the day in this "typical" warehouse. It was decided to focus on two activities at each of

Table 5.1   Sampling Strategies as Applied in
the Warehouse Equipment Project

	Strategy	Subcategory	Application in the Warehouse Project
1)	Time sampling	Continuous	Rejected as it would be difficult to obtain permission for such as extended access and it would be too expensive.
		Time-interval sampling	The grand tour was a whole day which helped to identify the key events to be observed on subsequent visits to warehouses.
		Time-point sampling	Not utilized.
2)	Event (or activity) sampling		The preparation of mixed pallets and the loading of HGV were chosen as the key events to be observed and videoed at each warehouse.
3)	Sampling of actors	Probabilistic	Not utilized.
		Stratified	The six warehouses visited were chosen to include small, medium, and large facilities.
		Purposive	The sponsoring company provided the contacts to warehouses but a deliberate mix was chosen; some warehouses that were equipment customers of the company sponsoring the research and some that were not.
		Snowball	Interviewees at each warehouse visited were always asked if they thought there was somebody else that the researchers should talk to—several suggested speaking to HGV drivers.
4)	Theoretical sampling		The number of new issues being identified at each warehouse visited was reviewed, to identify when theoretical saturation was being reached.

the warehouses to be visited: the preparation of mixed pallets, and the loading of heavy goods vehicles (HGVs). Effectively, an event sampling strategy was blended with other elements of strategy, as indicated by Table 5.1 (this is based on the generic guidelines given in the previous chapter—Table 4.1). Snowball sampling was used to identify additional actors to interview. As activities were videoed, employees were asked: "Can you explain how you go about stacking a mixed pallet, please?"

The concept of theoretical sampling is important in ethnographic market research. A useful way to apply this is to count the number of new issues identified on each visit. The first visits identified many new issues but, as more were conducted, each new visit identified fewer new factors (see also Box Case 5.1). The caveat is that the sample should not be too narrow, otherwise the factors identified on each visit might be too similar. For this reason the warehouses visited stocked different types of products.

Box Case 5.1

Smith & Nephew Medical Devices[2]

Smith & Nephew is a major manufacturer of medical devices with 8500 employees and annual revenues exceeding 1.7 billion euros. It has four main product categories: advanced wound management; endoscopy, orthopedics trauma (fracture repair), and orthopedics reconstruction (for example, hip replacements). The company's Research Centre is based adjacent to York University in the UK, and conducts basic research for the product divisions. In addition to developing technology, managers at York are responsible for introducing new approaches into the business. For example, Dr. Ceri Batchelder, a Senior Technology Analyst, and Dr. Neil Stainton, Innovation Manager have worked as a team to drive the adoption of observation, contextual interviewing, and other methods. Together, they have identified a number of points about how ethnographic market research can be successfully applied.

First, they recognize the limitations of the traditional techniques: "In traditional focus groups, participants tend to concentrate on the most obvious characteristics of products. And, our experience is that interview participants with no direct stake in the outcome are generally well-disposed to new ideas, perhaps partly to 'please' or 'give the right answer' to the interviewer," says Stainton. In applying ethnographic methods Stainton has a number of tips. "Theoretical sampling is a useful concept and we have strong evidence that it works. After a series of visits, it becomes surprisingly clear when there Is lIttle added value to further observations. Later visits can be used to focus in on topics of specific interest." At Smith & Nephew good field notes are seen as absolutely essential: "it is virtually impossible to remember all elements of a visit even after a few hours. And it is easy to get confused if carrying out several visits. Field notes should include observations, a summary of discussions, and direct quotes—the latter can be very powerful in presenting findings to a wider audience. Even noting down seemingly irrelevant information can be useful in reviewing the wider picture," says Stainton.

▸▸

Batchelder has observed that real competitive advantage is not attained from the methodologies alone. Organizational issues need to be considered: "The alignment of a number of factors is required to successfully identify and implement hidden needs...it is not just the techniques but also the way technologists and product developers are involved," she says. "We try to involve technologists, product developers, and marketers in the research, as these different perspectives lead to creative ideas on how to solve customers' issues. I think that the new market research methods are most effective when used by cross-functional research teams."

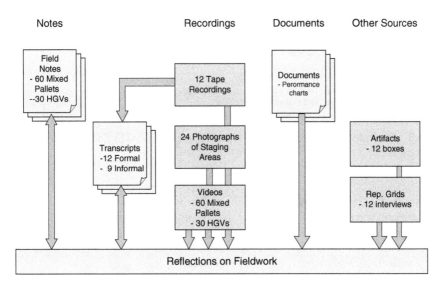

Figure 5.2   Complete Ethnographic Record for the Warehouse Equipment Project

Data Collection

The researchers visited six further warehouses; at each they observed the preparation of ten mixed pallets and the loading of five or more HGVs. Figure 5.2 shows the complete ethnographic record and this structure was used when the data were entered into *Nvivo*, a useful qualitative data analysis package (which expedites data coding and searching).

Field Notes

Field notes were completed by the researchers during and after the visits. Figure 5.3 shows an example—the preparation of Mixed Pallet #3 (at Warehouse "A"). It includes recognition of several points: the way employees know that certain

---

Field Notes

Research Project: Warehouse Discovery Research
Case: Mixed Pallet # 3
Location: Warehouse A
Actors: Supervisor and two employees (late shift).

Field Observations:
- Employees make jokes about certain customers' propensity to make last minute changes—'Oh this is for xxx, so we'll leave it a bit longer rather than doing three times over!'(employee to supervisor).
- Supervisor said that they work on orders serially but in practice the employees start picking 2–3 at a time.
- Stacking the picked items on apallet is awkward and can damage the packaging. Employees use their experience here: 'Yes, the flour packets fit well with the teas…and beans with cereal'(employee loading the last pallet of the order; see interview transcript).
- Not every customer wants a full load—'loading a lorry for several deliveries makes life even harder and wastes our time'(supervisor).

Initial Reflections
- Hypothesis: certain combinations are much harder to stack.
- Picking equipment needs to be able to stack different items effectively, to avoid damage, or movement in transit.

Remember!
- Notes should cover: space; actor(s); activities; object(s) and physical traces; events; time sequences; goals; feelings; and explanatory variables.

Figure 5.3 Example Field Notes from the Warehouse Equipment Project (Mixed Pallet Preparation)

customers change their orders at the last minute (the jokes also gave insights); the need to work on several orders in parallel; and the problems with mixed pallets. The researcher reflected that certain combinations of boxes are hard to stack, something that the employees do from experience. A total of 60 field notes were completed and 30 similar forms summarized the observations of the loading of HGVs.

Interviews

At each warehouse one employee and one supervisor were interviewed and tape recordings were made of these 12 formal interviews. In addition, snowball sampling led to six other employees being interviewed informally. At three warehouses the employees suggested that the researchers also talk to HGV drivers. These conversations were based around an open-ended question ("What are your views on mixed pallets?") and the replies were revealing. For example, one driver said "Mixed pallets are a xxxxxxx pain, they're unstable and I get blamed if there's damage …"

Video Recordings

Video recordings were made of the preparation of 60 mixed pallets and the loading of 30 vehicles. These videos showed the problems with mixed pallets: the time required to pick the required boxes, carry them to the staging area, stack them, and load them into HGVs. In one recording an employee said, "Stacking is like a 3-dimensional puzzle [pause] but without a good solution [interviewee grins]." Mixed pallets were observed to be unstable and shrink-wrap plastic, together with pieces of wood, was used to strengthen them.

Documents

The documents collected included copies of picking lists and shift patterns and Figure 5.4 shows example performance data, consisting of five A4 diagrams that were displayed in the staging area, including the number of shipments (HGVs per month) and customer complaints. Contextual interviews based around the diagrams elicited statements such as, "the complaints are often from the same customers, particularly those who order the most mixed pallets," and "we could reach our goals if we didn't have so many late order changes."

Other Sources

Examples of easy-to-stack and difficult-to-stack packaging were collected (12 in total), measured, and weighed. Some repertory grid interviews (see Box

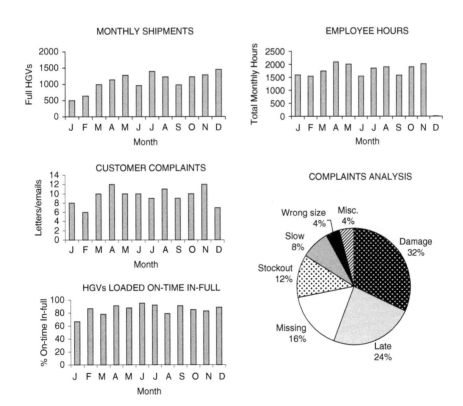

Figure 5.4   Example Performance Charts (from Warehouse C)

Case 5.2) were also conducted to obtain additional data on the problems with mixed pallets.

Box Case 5.2

Repertory Grids from Warehouse Employees

Good ethnographic research uses a range of data collection methods and in the warehouse project, repertory grid technique was used to understand employees' perceptions of mixed pallets. This was contrasted with what was observed and what was said in the contextual interviews.

The advantage of repertory grid technique is that it uses indirect questions to determine what interviewees really think (see Chapter 7 for a detailed description). The interviews showed that warehouse employees perceived mixed pallets in terms of the "physical effort involved"; "the mental effort" (to solve the puzzle of stacking different boxes in a stable way); the amount of mechanical support available; the "experience required"; and the "popularity of the task." Preparing complicated mixed pallets was perceived as mentally demanding but rewarding, as long as there was not pressure to complete the task too quickly.

In the warehouse project, the repertory grids demonstrated how the employees preferred tasks that require experience, and their emotions about what they perceived negatively—"having to work like a robot." Possibly due to the macho culture of most of the warehouses, this aspect did not arise in the contextual interviews or from the observations. Such considerations of users' emotional views are important in product design but pose an interesting dilemma in this context: can a product be designed that provides more automation but still makes the employees' task interesting?

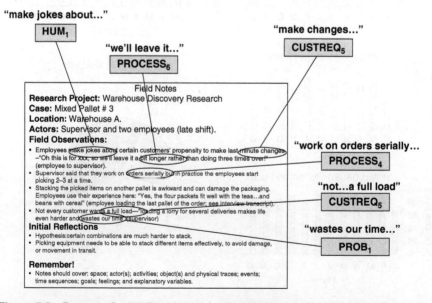

Figure 5.5   Example Coded Field Notes for the Warehouse Equipment Project

Table 5.2   Data Coding Scheme for the Warehouse Equipment Project

Initial Data Codes	Emergent Codes	Meaning of the Codes	Total Codes Assigned to Complete Ethnographic Record
1) $ENVIR_1$		Open staging area	
$ENVIR_2$		Tidy staging area	
$ENVIR_3$		Cluttered staging area	
	$ENVIR_4$	Dirty staging area	
2) $PROCESS_1$		Picking items from shelves	
$PROCESS_2$		Stacking a mixed pallet	
$PROCESS_3$		Loading a vehicle	
$PROCESS_4$		Sequence of working on orders	
$PROCESS_5$		Misuse of equipment	
	$PROCESS_6$	Postponing work	
	$PROCESS_7$	Heaviest boxes placed at bottom	
	$PROCESS_8$	Carrying boxes manually	
	$PROCESS_9$	Employees' own variations on processes	
3) $TIME_1$		Time to pick a mixed pallet	
$TIME_2$		Time to stack a mixed pallet	
$TIME_3$		Time to load a vehicle	
$TIME_4$		Non value-adding time	
	$TIME_5$	"Time for a rest" (employees' expression)	
	$TIME_6$	Overtime	
4) $PROB_1$		Wasted time	
$PROB_2$		Not enough time	
$PROB_3$		Damaged product (boxes)	
$PROB_4$		Problems stacking boxes	
	$PROB_5$	Unstable mixed pallet	
	$PROB_6$	Customer complaints	
	$PROB_7$	Late arrival of vehicles	
5) $EQUIP_1$		Pallets	
$EQUIP_2$		Boxes	
$EQUIP_3$		Fork-lift trucks	
$EQUIP_4$		Scales	
$EQUIP_5$		Tape	
$EQUIP_6$		Shrink-wrap machines	
	$EQUIP_7$	Wooden strengtheners	
6) $CUSTREQ_1$		Order content	
$CUSTREQ_2$		Delivery time	
$CUSTREQ_3$		Order of pallets in HGV	
$CUSTREQ_4$		A mixed pallet	
	$CUSTREQ_5$	Less than a full load	
	$CUSTREQ_6$	Last minute changes to order	

Continued

Table 5.2 Continued

	Initial Data Codes	Emergent Codes	Meaning of the Codes	Total Codes Assigned to Complete Ethnographic Record
7)	BOX$_1$ BOX$_2$	BOX$_3$	Box size Box shape Off-size boxes	
8)	DOC$_1$ DOC$_2$ DOC$_3$ DOC$_4$		Order schedule Picking list Warehouse performance charts Customer letters of complaint	
9)	BEHAV$_1$ BEHAV$_2$ BEHAV$_3$ BEHAV$_4$		Hurried and/or not concentrated Emotion and frustration Body language—positive Body language—negative	
10)		HUMOUR$_1$ HUMOUR$_2$ HUMOUR$_3$	Jokes about customers Jokes about management Jokes about colleagues	
	Total = 36 codes	Total = 17 codes		
	TOTAL = 53 codes			

ANALYSIS OF DATA

Data Coding

The analysis closely followed the iterative process recommended in Chapter 4 (Figure 4.3). After the grand tour, a coding scheme was generated by the researchers together with a warehouse manager. Table 5.2 shows that the brainstorming identified 35 codes in 9 categories, whereas the visits identified 17 emergent codes (for example, PROCESS$_6$, the postponing of work) and one new category (HUMOUR). The final coding scheme consisted of 53 different codes in 10 categories.

Coding of Field Notes

Figure 5.5 shows how the field notes were coded. Each card was entered into *Nvivo* and an appropriate code was added to each statement. For example, customers not requiring a fully loaded HGV (CUSTREQ$_5$) and wasted time (PROB$_1$). Note that codes are normally written in capitals, as this allows them to be differentiated at a glance. The range of codes on any one card gave an indication of the relationships in the data.

Warehouse C Interviewee 2 (Supervisor)

"When I get the order [CUSTREQ$_1$], I look through the picking list [DOC$_2$] to see if it includes what we call 'off-sizes' [BOX$_3$]. These are boxes that don't stack easily, or are hard to combine with others [PROB$_4$]. After the quick check [PROCESS$_9$] I start the manual picking [PROCESS$_1$], using the picking list [DOC$_2$]. Yes, the picking list [DOC$_2$] also acts as a guide through the warehouse as the items are listed by the rows in which they can be found [PROCESS$_1$]. Each of the items is collected [PROCESS$_8$] and when all the items are in the staging area the 'mixed pallet' is stacked [PROCESS$_2$] with the heaviest items at the bottom [PROCESS$_6$]"

Figure 5.6   Example of Data Coding of an Interview Transcript

Table 5.3   Coding Scheme for the Video Recordings of the Preparation of Mixed Pallets

Data Categories	Points to Look For	Appropriate Codes	Observed/ Timing
1) The warehouse environment	• Physical layout/objects • Warehouse employees • Time sequence(s) • Performance data	ENVIR$_{1-4}$; EQUIP$_{1-7}$ PROCESS$_{1-9}$; BEHAV$_{1-4}$ TIME$_{1-6}$ DOC$_3$	
2) Preparing mixed pallets	• Physical interactions • Social interactions	PROCESS$_{1-9}$; ENVIR$_{1-4}$ BEHAV$_{1-4}$; HUMOUR$_{1-4}$	
	• Doing things right • Doing things wrong • Wasted time (*nonvalue adding time*) • Misuse of equipment • Confusion • Awkward situations • Employee modifications to processes	PROCESS$_{1-8}$ PROCESS$_{1-9}$; PROB$_{1-7}$ PROB$_1$; TIME$_4$ PROCESS$_7$ BEHAV$_{1-4}$; PROB$_{1-7}$ PROB$_{1-7}$ PROCESS$_9$	
	• Emotions and frustration • Linguistic signals • Extra-linguistic signals • Body language • Spatial signals	BEHAV$_2$ BEHAV$_2$ BEHAV$_{1-4}$ BEHAV$_{3-4}$ BEHAV$_{1-2}$	

Coding of Interviews

Similar to the field notes, the interview transcripts were entered into *Nvivo* to make the coding faster and to allow relationships in the data to be investigated. Figure 5.6 shows that the same codes as for the field notes were used.

Coding of Video Recordings

Each recording was viewed by several researchers to ensure reliable coding. With many different points to look for and codes to assign, an iterative approach was

Table 5.4   Codes Assigned to the Complete Ethnographic Record

	Data Source	Number of Codes Assigned
1)	Observation of preparing mixed pallets (field notes and videos)	2,475
2)	Observation of loading HGVs (field notes and videos)	612
3)	Formal interviews	239
4)	Informal interviews	93
5)	Documentary evidence	52
6)	Repertory grids	120
7)	Other (photographs and artifacts)	189
		TOTAL = 3,780

Table 5.5   Simple Descriptive Statistics from the Field Notes

	Topic Analyzed	Primary Code	Related Codes/Frequency	
1)	Mixed Pallets	$CUSTREQ_4$	Carrying boxes $PROCESS_8$	13%
			Problems stacking $PROB_4$	73%
			Time to stack $TIME_2$	59%
			Damages $PROB_3$	17%
			Frustration $BEHAV_2$	38%
			Shrink-wrap $EQUIP_6$	93%
			Performance charts DOC	19%
2)	Wasted Time	$PROB_1$	Late changes $CUSTREQ_6$	49%
			Late arrival of HGVs $PROB_7$	55%

used. The coding scheme for the video recordings is shown in Table 5.3 (which was derived from the generic coding scheme in Chapter 4—see Table 4.3). The researchers considered the warehouse environment and also looked for clues on what influenced the preparation of mixed pallets. A similar scheme was used for coding the observations of the loading of vehicles.

Coding of Documents

The documents were coded for their content and for the problems they identified. For example, the customer complaint pie charts (see Figure 5.4) typically showed the causes of customer complaints. The codings were also compared with the answers to contextual interview questions based on the charts. Damaged boxes (products) were an issue ($PROB_3$) and interviews indicated that much of the damage was related to mixed pallets.

Reflections

Throughout the research the team members recorded their reflections. These started with the initial impressions of warehouses as being well organized and running smoothly. Later, it emerged that despite good organization, there were times when loading of pallets and HGVs was hectic. There were also significant problems with mixed pallets, late HGVs, and demanding customers, such as supermarkets. Observing the difficulties with mixed pallets led the researchers to reflect that, although mixed pallets were only a small percentage of the goods shipped, they were a major source of problems.

The complete ethnographic record was found to include a total of 3780 codes, as indicted in Table 5.4. The majority of these codes were from the field notes and videos of mixed pallet loading (1290 and 1185 codes respectively; giving a total of 2475). The other codes were identified as follows: 612 were from the field notes and videos of loading lorries; 239 were from formal interviews and 93 from informal interviews; 52 from the documents; 120 from the repertory grids; and 189 from the other sources (photos, artifacts, and so on). Some readers may think that the time taken to apply coding systematically is inappropriately long. However, it should be stressed that *insights do not come directly from the codes assigned but rather from the process of assigning them* that immerses researchers in the data. (It is also useful to involve different functional groups, such as marketing and R&D, in the coding process as this increases "buy-in" to the results. Chapter 10 covers such organizational issues.) Combined with looking for contradictions and hypothesis generation, systematic coding differentiates good research from casual observation. Some companies pressure researchers to take shortcuts but this compromises the quality of the results.[3]

Relationships in the Data

One of the advantages with using a software package such as *Nvivo* is that codes can be linked. So it is easy to summarize the frequency of codes and to look for relationships. Table 5.5 shows that certain codes often occurred together with other codes. For example, discussions on mixed pallets often mentioned stacking problems (73 percent); the time required (59 percent); damages (17 percent); and so on. By looking at simple descriptive statistics, important relationships in the data could be identified. The initial reflections on the field notes forms for the 60 observed preparations of mixed pallets were checked and from these it emerged that mixed pallets often led to frustration and excessive use of shrink-wrap plastic.

Contradictions in the Data

A number of insights were generated as the data were checked for contradictions. An example disjuncture was one manager saying "mixed pallets are not an issue for us, as it's a small percentage of total pallets," whereas his employees said, "Every urgent order seems to have a mixed pallet." Employees

Project Aims

1) To investigate the influence of mixed pallets on the running of a warehouse.
2) To identify the problems associated with preparing mixed pallets which could lead to product opportunities.

Methodology

A total of 48 hours of on-site data collection were conducted at 5 warehouses (plus one pilot). Multiple sources of data used and a total of over 3500 codes were applied in the analysis.

Findings

Warehousing

- A typical warehouse will be run 24/7 and will make about 1000 shipments per month, with strong seasonality depending on the nature of the products shipped. Employees and management are measured on their ability to load HGVs correctly, on time (within a 15 minute window), and without customer complaints.
- Mixed pallets are only a small percentage of total shipments (5–10 percent) but impact the running of a warehouse significantly. This is because late changes to orders nearly always involve mixed pallets (65 percent of the time) and rushed preparation can lead to damage. It is largely manual work. In the worst case, a partially loaded HGV must be unpacked to get to the pallets that need changing (one employee likened it to the problem of off-loading missing passengers' baggage from an aircraft). Mixed pallets are therefore loaded last but often late order changes are "simply" to break a full pallet into "half-and-half" of two products.
- Complaints are taken very seriously as, for example, supermarkets put extreme pressure on their suppliers. Most complaints (56 percent) are related in some way to problems with mixed pallets. It was found that the time taken to solve orders with mixed pallets can even negatively influence the loading of HGVs which do not require any mixed pallets.
- Automation of the preparation of mixed pallets was perceived by all six warehouse managers as "not worth the investment."
- Interestingly, the problems with mixed pallets were not acknowledged by warehouse management as an issue but the employees actively involved in picking and stacking did recognize the issues. Employees enjoyed preparing mixed pallets when they were not under pressure. The more experienced employees could look at a "picking list" for a mixed pallet and describe the order in which they would start stacking. In each warehouse employees thought this was unique but the generic problems with mixed pallets were solved by the "specialists" in a similar way.

Cultural Issues: The employees within a warehouse are "low-skilled" in the conventional sense but develop a very good knowledge of the products stored and how to efficiently pick customer orders and load these into HGVs quickly. However, there is a high turnover of staff (typically 30 percent). Employees with more experience take a definite pride in dealing with mixed pallets; inexperienced employees under time pressure just rush and become resigned. Unfortunately, they are often prevented from doing a professional job because the preparation of mixed pallets often takes place under time pressure and in response to changes to customer orders. At most warehouses, certain employees are recognized by their peers at being particularly good at solving the "3-dimensional puzzle," through their experience.

Implications

Warehouses need a better system to deal with the following problems:

1) Staff turnover, which means that the expertise with mixed pallets is constantly being lost.
2) New products often have different sizes of packaging and so the preparation of mixed pallets is constantly changing.
3) Stability: using rolls of shrink-wrap and pieces of wood is not very effective.
4) Time pressure: late order changes require mixed pallets.
5) When loading an HGV, there is a need to track the position of specific pallets, so that late customer changes can be dealt with more effectively.
6) Employees want a way to prepare mixed pallets in a more professional way despite the inevitable time pressure.

Figure 5.7 Project Summary Sheet for WarehouseEquipCo. (Edited for Reasons of Confidentiality)

at two warehouses claimed that the mixed pallets they had stacked were stable, although it was observed that the fork-lift truck driver had problems with them. (This is an example of gloss.) Interviewees at several warehouses claimed that their approach to mixed pallets was unique ("nobody else would do it this way"). However, looking at the steps involved showed a large degree of commonality, providing evidence that the idiosyncrasy claimed was false.

SUMMARIZED FINDINGS

Writing the Thick Description

The research collected a large amount of data and *WarehouseEquipmentCo.* requested that the research team prepare a slide presentation. As we discussed in Chapter 4, the ethnographic approach emphasizes that the results should be summarized in what is called a thick description. So, to prepare for the slide presentation, a ten-page thick description of the overall results was produced and then this was précised to one page (see Figure 5.7). To ensure a good trail of evidence, the key points in this summary were used to prepare the slides, with use of the photographs and videos to illustrate the points. (Note that researchers should choose visual material which is supportive and illustrative, rather than choosing the most "interesting video clips" and constructing the summary to match them!)

Implications of the Findings

From the issues identified (Figure 5.7), a number of opportunities were determined by *WarehouseEquipCo.* and are being considered for development into products and services, which will integrate with the company's complete offering. Although the exact details of the products being considered are confidential, it can be said that *WarehouseEquipCo.* has changed its overall strategy. As an "innovative solutions provider" to the logistics industry, it has recognized that it must constantly monitor how warehousing is conducted and the hidden issues. Consequently, it is training cross-functional teams to generate better customer insights, on a regular basis.

CONCLUSIONS

The warehouse project applied the approach that we presented in Chapter 4. Careful consideration was made of the data to collect, the sample, the data collection instruments, and so on. It is important to conduct ethnographic market research in a systematic but appropriate way. We do not propose that "one-size-fits-all when it using ethnography, nor that there is consensus about any one right way to approach a research question, no matter how straightforward or complex."[4] Therefore, the framework we have given is best perceived as a starting structure from which any specific project can be developed: with experience researchers will treat the structure as a theme on which to base variations.

Hidden needs analysis focuses on identifying customers' problems and this project was successful in pinpointing a number of issues in the warehouses. Key was the recognition that mixed pallets are only about 10 percent of shipments but are the cause of a large amount of wasted time, the majority of complaints and, generally, disrupt the efficient running of a warehouse. Using these insights, *WarehouseEquipmentCo.* is now developing a number of devices to make picking and stacking of mixed pallets faster and more stable.

In addition to the specific information gathered about opportunities for new products, the project identified some of the barriers to the adoption of ethnographic market research techniques within *WarehouseEquipCo.* These included an initial skepticism of the marketing department to new methods and the management's surprise that qualitative data were substituting quantitative survey data.

SUMMARY

Our discussion of the *WarehouseEquipCo.* project has demonstrated the complexity of ethnographic market research and has shown that:

- Real market insights emerge from observing, taking systematic notes, and reflecting on what was seen and the coding of the data.
- Although the steps we have defined and the tools we have provided (such as tables and forms) are intended to be used, they should in no way be seen as a rigid framework. Individual projects will call for modified approaches and experience may lead to a changed emphasis.
- In using the ethnographic approach, the systematic nature of the research should not be compromised.

MANAGEMENT RECOMMENDATIONS

- Identify a market segment where your organization has not yet been successful and initiate an ethnographic research project to generate ideas for new products and services.
- Ensure that the research is carried out systematically and that coding is used to avoid bias.
- Scope the research project to gain the right level of insights and ensure that your employees learn as much as possible about the new approaches.
- Aim to learn not only about the market but also how to overcome the barriers in your organization to the adoption of innovative techniques for market research.

6 REPERTORY GRID TECHNIQUE

> [R]epertory grid technique…is an attempt to stand in others' shoes, to see their world as they see it.[1]

INTRODUCTION

Psychology is a science that focuses on understanding the workings of the brain and how people think. In attempting to understand such complex processes, psychologists do not ask direct questions such as "how do you think?" However, in trying to understand their customers, many companies rely solely on direct questions posed through focus groups and surveys. The challenge in understanding customers should not be underestimated—sophisticated approaches are necessary to generate the insights to develop breakthrough product concepts. So it is not surprising that an approach developed for psychology—*repertory grid technique*—has important applications in market research.

Repertory grid is a flexible technique, which can be used to help respondents articulate their views on topics such as their feelings during the purchasing process, or their opinions of products and services. The technique is a structured form of interviewing which leads to a matrix of quantitative data—the repertory grid.

In traditional market research surveys, customers answer questions about *existing* products or services and their future needs. The drawback of this approach is that it leads customers to think in terms of the features of existing products. Customers are mostly unable to imagine or to articulate the possibilities for the future. In contrast, repertory grid interviews help respondents identify the issues they face, rather than channeling their thinking into predefined terminologies and categories. Once customers' real issues have been identified, then creative solutions can be conceived.

In this chapter we will give readers a detailed understanding of the power of repertory grid technique and the knowledge required to design effective interviews. The topics covered are:

- The history of the technique.
- How the technique can be applied.

- Analyzing the results.
- The technique's advantages and limitations.

HISTORY OF REPERTORY GRID TECHNIQUE

The technique was developed in the 1950s by George Kelly, who studied physics and mathematics before becoming a professor of psychology. Kelly was of the opinion that, in trying to make sense of the world, everyone develops "rules" by which they view situations, people, relationships or objects, in fact almost any phenomenon with which we are confronted. The rules by which we make sense of these situations are our *personal constructs*.

The *Theory of Personal Constructs,* developed by Kelly makes a number of points that are relevant to market research. All individuals develop constructs as a way of explaining events. Constructs are constantly revised to match our experience. In relationship to products and services, this means that individuals' constructs change over time and market research needs to be kept up-to-date. Personal Construct Theory says that interviewees typically differ in how they construe events, although from one interview to another there will be many equivalent constructs—these are termed *common constructs*. Finally, social contexts influence individuals' constructs and so different market segments will typically exhibit different sets of common constructs.

Kelly defined a construct as, "a way in which two or more things are alike and at the same time different from one or more things."[2] A repertory grid interview *elicits* (i.e. identifies) an interviewee's personal constructs. Although people constantly update their constructs, they are normally not explicitly aware of this. The process of eliciting constructs often explores an interviewee's views at a level to which they were previously unaware. Consequently, when a grid is completed, interviewees often comment that the interview process has helped clarify their own understanding.

Market researchers in the 1960s were quick to acknowledge the value of the repertory grid technique saying: "in our view, the Repertory Grid represents an approach of such fundamental importance that we regard it as having as much potential...as any technique since the invention of the questionnaire."[3] Strangely, the adoption of the technique in market research has been low and a recent informal poll of market research consultancies in Europe showed that very few offer the technique.[4] Similarly, marketing professionals in both small and large companies are generally unaware of repertory grid. There are several reasons that the technique is not more widely used. First, interviewers require specialist knowledge before they can undertake interviews effectively. Second, the flexibility of the technique means that there are a set of subtle decisions to be made in designing repertory grid interviews. (However, once learnt, the technique is relatively simple and easy to apply). Finally, some researchers have criticized repertory grid technique as not being based on sufficient theory.[5] However, in taking this (overly) academic standpoint, they have overlooked the very practical advantages of the technique.

Box Case 6.1

Tourists Images of Travel Destinations

Tourism is a significant industry for many countries and so it is important to understand the factors that influence tourists in their choice of destinations. There is high potential for using repertory grids in this sector. One advantage that repertory grids bring is they can identify tourists' impressions of travel destinations before they have even visited them. Grid interviews can unearth how people's views are based on what they have read, heard from friends, seen in advertising, or picked up through the media. For example, an investigation of prior perceptions of London's tourist attractions, including galleries and museums, generated better ideas for advertising.[6] Another study looked at perceptions of different seaside resorts.[7] A third study compared countries as holiday destinations and allowed Austrian tourist officials to identify how their country was perceived compared with Switzerland, their main competitor.[8] Finally, another study looked at New Zealanders' preferences in choosing short-break destinations and found important differences between what emerged from the repertory grid interviews with tourists and what was previously known by tourism managers. This study concluded that repertory grid is "an economical technique that has been underused by tourism market researchers."[9]

APPLYING THE TECHNIQUE

Overview

To give an overview of how repertory grid technique can be used to understand customers' needs, we will describe how it was used by the information technology (IT) service provider, Equant. The Equant organization installs and maintains computer networks for businesses (see Box Case 1.3 for more about this company). The company used repertory grid interviews to generate ideas for improving its service offering by interviewing purchasing managers from their clients' organizations. The interviewees were asked to name six services with which they are familiar—we will refer to these as services A, B, C, D, E, and F. The services are what are termed the *elements* of the repertory grid interview and the name of each different service was written on a separate (postcard-sized) card, as shown in Figure 6.1(A). Different types of services were named by interviewees and Table 6.1 shows that one interviewee's selection included facility management, financial auditing, Equant's IT service, and one of Equant's competitors (Service E).

As indicated by Table 6.1, the cards were prenumbered in a random sequence (5, 1, 4, 3, 2, and 6), to enable the selection of random sets of cards. It can be seen that the name of the first service ("A") was written on the card numbered "5," whereas Service B was written on the card numbered "1." After the cards had been annotated with the names of services, the cards were ordered from 1 to 6, thus, effectively mixing them (from the order in which the elements were named). Next, the interviewee was presented with a set of three cards (termed

Table 6.1   The Services (Elements) Chosen by One Interviewee

Service Products
Service A—Facility management (security and cleaning)
Service B—Equant Services (IT Service Provider)
Service C—Data warehousing
Service D—Financial auditing
Service E—Competitor's IT Services
Service F—Employee training seminars

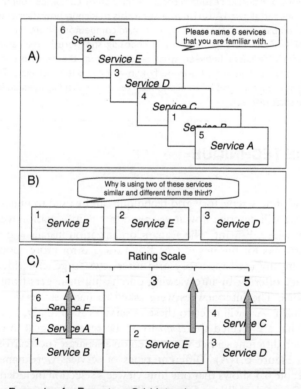

Figure 6.1   Example of a Repertory Grid Interview
A) The Elements of the Test—Services—Written on Cards; B) The First Triad Presented to the Interviewee; C) The Rating of the Services in the First Triad

Source: Reprinted (with enhancements suggested by Koners, U.) by permission of Sage Publications Ltd from Goffin, K., "Repertory Grid Technique." In Partington, D. (ed.) *Essential Skills for Management Research*, London: Sage, 2002. Copyright © (Keith Goffin 2002).

a *triad*). Figure 6.1(B) shows that the first triad consisted of Cards 1, 2, and 3, corresponding to Services B, E, and D respectively. As the triad was presented, the interviewee was asked: *"Why is using two of these services similar and different from the third?"* This question elicited a construct—a service attribute—with the interviewee explaining that two of the service providers were "easy to work with," whereas working with the third was "difficult." Each of the services in the triad was then rated against the first construct using a five-point scale, as shown in Figure 6.1(C). Service B was rated highly (a "1"; "easy to work with"), whereas Service D was given a minimum rating ("5"; "difficult") on this service attribute. The interviewee was then required to rate the three services that were not in the triad (A, C, and F) using the same 1–5 rating scale.

Further triads were then presented to the interviewee and the same question was asked: *"Why is using two of these services similar and different from the third?"* The interviewee was not allowed to repeat constructs and so each new triad elicited a new service attribute. As each attribute was elicited, the interviewee was asked to explain what they meant by, for example, "fast response" and they gave details of the actions they expected. The interviews were recorded and so such explanations were captured and gave insights into managers' perceptions.

Following each construct, the interviewee was required to rate all the services using the five-point rating scale and the ratings form the repertory grid, as shown in Figure 6.2. To more clearly understand the constructs, the respondent was also asked to explain the *construct pole,* which is the end of the scale typically associated with poor performance, and this was entered into the grid (right-hand column).

In Figure 6.2 the six elements—Services B to F—are shown across the top of the grid. Down the side are the service attributes identified during the interview. The asterisks around the ratings in the grid indicate which cards were in the triad that elicited particular attributes. For example, the first attribute was elicited using a triad consisting of Cards 1, 2, and 3 (indicated by the ratings with stars: *1*, *4*, *5*). Looking at the ratings, it can be seen that on the attribute "fast response" Service C (Card 4) is rated mid-scale ("3") but rated as poor ("5") on the attribute "absolutely reliable service (guarantee)." A typical 45–50 minute repertory grid interview will elicit 8–12 constructs. The ratings tell us not only about how the interviewee perceives services from particular companies; but they also give us information on the importance of specific service attributes. For example, the ratings on the attribute "clearly defined service product" are not as widely spread (they only range from "1" to "3") as those for "good value for money" (where the ratings range from "1" to "5"). This shows that this latter attribute differentiates more strongly between the different services chosen as elements.

Repertory grid technique can unveil hidden needs, because these tend to be indicated by low ratings for all elements. In Figure 6.2 it can be seen that none of the services is rated as reliable, or having sufficient guarantees (all the ratings are either "4" or "5").

CONSTRUCTS (SERVICE ATTRIBUTES)	CARD 1 Service B	CARD 2 Service E	CARD 3 Service D	CARD 4 Service C	CARD 5 Service A	CARD 6 Service F	CONSTRUCT POLES
Easy to work with	*1*	*4*	*5*	5	1	1	Difficult
Fast response to problems	1	4	5	*3*	*4*	*4*	Slow
Professional employees	*2*	5	*3*	4	*1*	1	Little knowledge
Clearly defined service product	3	*2*	1	*3*	1	*1*	Poorly defined...
Service is good value for money	*3*	*3*	5	*1*	5	5	Expensive
Absolutely reliable service (guarantee)	5	4	*4*	*5*	5	*5*	Indifferent
Provide performance statistics	2	*4*	*1*	3	*4*	2	No measures
Propose performance improvements	4	5	*2*	*4*	*5*	4	No discussion

Figure 6.2   A Repertory Grid on Service Providers

From the many repertory grid interviews that it conducted, Equant identified opportunities for improving its service offering. One of the factors that helped in this process was that the range of services chosen as elements was not restricted solely to IT service providers (all of whom tend to have similar service offerings).

The Equant example demonstrates how grid technique can be used to identify service opportunities. It can also be used to generate ideas for manufactured products. The Hewlett-Packard Medical Products Group used the technique in the 1990s and recognized the emerging importance of product attributes such as "easy to connect to the patient (set-up)" and "easy-to-clean, or sterilize" in the medical equipment market.[10] An emphasis was placed on these factors in all subsequent new products.

Design Decisions

Designing market research based on repertory grids requires a series of decisions to be made about how the elements will be selected and the constructs elicited. Overall there are six main decisions relating to:

- The appropriate sample of interviewees.
- The choice of elements.
- How to present the elements.
- The way to elicit the constructs.
- The rating system to be used.
- The administration of the interview.

The Sample

Repertory grid interviews are normally used for exploratory research. That is, they are used to identify constructs, which can be used in generating ideas for product and service innovations, or can be used as factors in larger surveys. Consequently, the number of repertory grid interviews conducted tends not to be particularly high.

In choosing a suitable sample there are a number of points to consider. First, personal construct theory tells us that individuals will have personal constructs and so a series of interviews will be required to identify the common constructs of a particular market segment. Experience with repertory grid technique shows that about 30 interviews are sufficient to identify all the constructs from a particular group. This is demonstrated by a piece of research investigating R&D engineers' constructs.[11] As part of this research, six engineers were interviewed at each of five companies. The 30 interviews elicited 272 constructs and comparing these showed they corresponded to 65 distinct constructs. To check that this list of constructs was complete, a Pareto analysis was conducted and Figure 6.3 shows that 27 distinct constructs (corresponding to 54 percent of the total of 65) were identified during the first five interviews and another 12 at the second company (corresponding to a cumulative total of 72 percent of the distinct constructs).

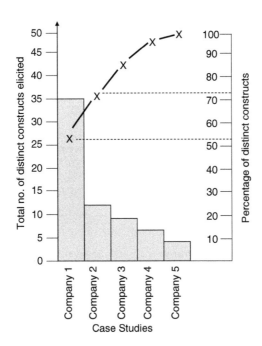

Figure 6.3   Pareto Diagram of the Constructs Elicited from Six Case Studies

Source: Goffin, K. and Koners, U., "Tacit Knowledge, Lessons Learned and New Product Development." Accepted for publication in the *Journal of Product Innovation Management,* Vol. 28, March 2011.

The diagram indicates that 30 interviews were sufficient to identify a comprehensive list of constructs and it can be reliably assumed that further interviews would not have elicited constructs that had not already been identified.

It is appropriate to conduct 20–30 repertory grid interviews within each of the market segments that need to be investigated. Using a Pareto diagram is an effective way of checking that enough interviews have been conducted. The choice of the sample is closely related to the choice of the elements, as we will now discuss.

The Elements

It is important that the type of elements chosen fit with the aims of the investigation. Table 6.2 gives examples of the types of elements used in various pieces of market research, with the aims of the research and the types of interviewees. It can be seen that an insurance company (Example number 1) obtained a deep

Table 6.2 Examples of the Choice of Elements for Market Research (for Service and Manufacturing)

No.	Initiator of the Research	Aim of Research	Elements	Sample (Interviewees)	Comments
1)	Insurance company (*VirginMoney*)	To understand how middle-aged customers perceive insurance products	A range of financial products (e.g. mortgages, pension funds, etc.)	Representative samples of the insurance company's customers and noncustomers	Unveiled the perceptions and worries customers have when choosing complex financial service products and gave ideas for innovative solutions
2)	Airfreight service (*Malaysia Airlines*)	To determine the factors that influence customer satisfaction and the trade-offs customers make between service quality and price	Airfreight services from various airlines	Shipping managers at companies which regularly ship by air from Asia	Enabled the service provider to understand how customers perceived service quality and provided factors that were used in conjoint analysis (see Box Case 6.2)
3)	Small home improvement company (*Fascia Mania*)	To understand house-owners' perceptions of home improvements, including the sales and installation process	Different types of home improvements	Customers and prospective customers of Fascia Mania	Showed how to give customers reassurance during the sales process. Shows that the method can also help small companies (see Box Case 6.3).

Continued

Table 6.2   Continued

No.	Initiator of the Research	Aim of Research	Elements	Sample (Interviewees)	Comments
4)	Manufacturer of pharmaceutical production line equipment (*Bosch Packaging Technology*)	To determine how to design production line equipment to minimize operating problems	Discrete sections of the current production process	Manufacturing managers, engineers and production line operators	Revealed many of the small problems that collectively reduce production efficiency and provided ideas for an innovative new product
5)	Medical equipment manufacturer (*Hewlett-Packard*)	To collect ideas on the trends in requirements for operating theater equipment	A range of medical equipment devices used in operating theaters (not just the type of equipment produced by Hewlett-Packard)	A selection of medical personnel including doctors, theater nurses, and bio-engineers	Showed the importance to medical staff of design issues related to ease-of-maintenance and of staff training
6)	Academic study (but looking at the challenges facing automotive suppliers)	To identify manufacturers' requirements of their suppliers	Automotive suppliers: three of which had a "close" relationship with the manufacturer; three a "distant"; and three an "intermediate" relationship	Purchasing managers at manufacturing companies	Showed that the factors mentioned by most customers are not necessarily the most important ones (see text on Analyzing the Results)
7)	Skin care manufacturer (*Beiersdorf*)	To determine what influences eczema sufferers in their choice of skin care products	Both skin care and personal hygiene products	Eczema sufferers	Showed that consumers require more than a single product (see Box Case 6.4)

Note: Examples collected by the authors from personal experience of using repertory grid technique for market research projects.

understanding of customers' perceptions by conducting repertory grid interviews with various financial products as elements. In contrast, a manufacturer of pharmaceutical production line equipment (Example number 4) used discrete sections of the manufacturing process as elements, since operators did not have experience of working with different types of manufacturing lines. Interestingly, this novel choice of elements elicited detailed constructs that led to the design of an innovative production system (see Box Case 10.1, p. 223).

The examples given in Table 6.2 cover both the manufacturing and service sectors and show that the aims, elements, and interviewees selected must be considered in unison. In choosing the type of elements, it is useful to check a number of points. Elements must be specific and discrete (for example, products, people, or events). If they are not discrete, then the comparisons between the elements in the triads will be confusing to the interviewee. The interviewee must be familiar with at least five elements, in order for there to be enough triads available. Some creativity is required in selecting the type of elements and, if products are selected as elements, then the range should not be restricted to very similar products. This was the case in Hewlett-Packard's (HP) investigation of operating theater equipment (Example number 5), where a broad range of medical equipment was used for the elements and not just the limited range of equipment manufactured by HP. The necessity to choose a broader range of products as elements, which is often driven by the need to have enough triads, works advantageously in another way—since the more varied products lead to more interesting constructs (and give companies insights into related products). In choosing elements, simplicity is also important—clear elements support effective interviewing. Pilot interviews should be made to confirm that the types of elements selected are meaningful to interviewees and fit the purpose of the research. The important point to bear in mind is that respondents must have sufficient experience with all elements so that they are able to make meaningful comparisons.

In one of the original forms of repertory grid technique used in psychology, the *Role Construct Repertory Test*, the interviewee is asked to name elements to fit a number of specified roles, such as "a teacher you liked," "the most intelligent person you know." Specifying roles is a common approach in psychology, and in market research it can be applied, for example, as name "three suppliers that you have close contact with" and "three where you have much less contact" (Example 6 in Table 6.2).

Normally elements are nominated by interviewees; so-called *personal elements*. In some interviews the elements may be defined by the researcher in advance—these are termed *provided elements*. As provided elements are the same for each interviewee, the resulting grids can be more easily compared. However, every interviewee must be familiar with the elements chosen, which can be difficult to achieve. In this case, interviewees may be allowed to choose the elements which they are familiar with from a *pool of provided elements*—this means that different interviewees will have some commonality of elements. In one of the travel market research projects described in Box Case 6.1, "Switzerland" and "Austria" were used as provided elements.

Box Case 6.2

Air Freight Service Quality at Malaysia Airlines[12]

What are the most important factors for companies that regularly ship their products from Asia by airfreight to consider? A researcher from Malaysia Airlines used different airlines' airfreight services as elements for interviews with 19 shipping managers. A total of 44 different constructs related to service quality were elicited and the most important of these were determined. Interestingly, repertory grid technique was combined with conjoint (trade-off) analysis. After the most important constructs had been identified, a subset was used as factors for identifying how shipping managers make trade-offs between price and service quality, in choosing between different airlines. This is a classic example of how combining methods leads to more reliable results— Malaysia Airlines had carefully checked what their customers perceived were the most important factors, before investigating trade-offs. Unfortunately, some companies predefine the factors that they believe are important to customers and use these in conjoint analysis. This seriously limits the validity of the results.

Presentation of the Elements

In order to elicit meaningful constructs, the researcher must decide on the most appropriate way for the elements to be presented to the interviewee. A computer can be used to conduct the whole of a repertory grid interview and this will be discussed under the administration of the test. Usually, however, each element is written on a card and then different triads are presented to the interviewee manually.

The number of different triads that are available depends on the number of elements used, as shown in Table 6.3. Obviously, if the interviewee can only name three elements, then only one triad can be defined and repeated construct elicitation will not be possible. Therefore, five or more elements are needed to produce a sufficient number of triads.

The combination of elements in each triad is important because, if successive triads are too similar, it is harder to elicit meaningful constructs. In the repertory grid shown in Figure 6.2, each triad has at least two different cards in it (and the first two triads are completely different). Academic researchers have found that if only one element is changed between successive triads, then the resulting constructs will be less important.[13] Therefore, it is advisable to change at least two elements between successive triads. As Table 6.3 shows, there will be a large number of possible triads if the number of elements is high. However in a 45–50 minute interview, the interviewee will typically only be presented with about 10–15 different triads.

Normally, elements are presented in threes. However, the *dyad method* uses two elements and this has been reported to be more effective for repertory grid interviewing with children.[14] It can also be used to explore business relationships, that is, the dyads are "Company X in relation to Company Y," "Company X in relation to Company Z," and so on.

Table 6.3   The Number of Possible Triads
for a Given Number of Elements

Number of Elements	Number of Possible Triads
1)	0
2)	0
3)	1
4)	4
5)	10
6)	20
7)	35
8)	56
9)	84
10)	120

Source: Goffin, K., "Repertory Grid Technique." In
Partington, D. (ed.) *Essential Skills for Management Research*,
London: Sage, 2002. Copyright © (Keith Goffin 2002).

Elements are normally written on cards but in the case of provided elements (which are known in advance) pictures or photographs may also be used.[15] Visual stimuli can be useful for comparing products and, for simple products, it may be possible to present the actual products themselves in triads, as opposed to cards. One piece of market research investigated consumers' "ideal cheese" by encouraging them to taste triads of different cheeses![16]

Eliciting Constructs

A key part to eliciting constructs is the question that is posed to the interviewee as each triad is presented. The general form of this question from the work of Kelly is: *"In what way are two of these alike and at the same time different from the third?"* This question must be adapted to a specific research project and this needs to be done without introducing bias. For example, value judgments such as "how are two of these better than the third" should be avoided.

The question used for construct elicitation must be piloted. Selecting the specific wording is a balancing act between guiding interviewees to produce constructs that are relevant and narrowing things down too much. For example, in consumer research on car performance, the interviewee might be presented with triads of provided elements (different car models with names and photographs). The question posed with each triad could be: *"In what way are two of these car models similar and different from the third in terms of performance?"* This type of question focuses the interviewee on performance and avoids trivial answers such as "two of them are blue and the other is red." However, the use of a qualifying phrase, such as *"in terms of...,"* needs to be carefully considered to avoid excluding potentially useful constructs.

The issue of unexpected or trivial answers is a challenging one. Should a researcher reject such constructs? Care is needed as constructs may initially appear unimportant but further questioning may reveal their significance. In general, constructs should not be rejected unless there is supporting evidence that they are outside the scope of the research. Researchers need to develop their interviewing skills to ask suitable questions to probe the meaning of constructs.

There are two types of constructs: *personal* and *provided*. The most common approach in exploratory research is to elicit personal constructs—the interviewees give their constructs in response to triads, with no suggestions from the interviewer. Across a group of people interviewed on a particular topic, there will be many common constructs. Care must be taken in grouping interviewees' personal constructs into categories and identifying common constructs. Interviewees may use similar words to describe quite different concepts and so we will come back to this issue when we discuss how to analyze a series of repertory grids.

Provided constructs, as the name implies, are predefined by the interviewer. The interviewee is simply asked to rate elements against the provided set of constructs. Academic researchers have investigated the relative merits of the different constructs and found that interviewees are better able to express their thoughts using personal constructs. Market researchers may use the first part of an interview to elicit personal constructs and the latter part to obtain the interviewee's views on a number of provided constructs.[17] For example, one such provided construct could be "value for money," when the researcher needs to gather information on every interviewee's perception of this construct, and not just those interviewees who identify it themselves.

Box Case 6.3

Fascia Mania—Understanding Home Owners[18]

Fascia Mania is a small home improvement company based in Birmingham in the UK. Founded by two brothers, Andy and Clyde Scothern, it employs about 30 people who promote, sell, and install home improvements. Their main products are gutters and fascia replacements—fascias are the wooden boards where the top of walls meet the underside of house roofs. Normally fascias require maintenance, cleaning, and painting. Replacements look much better and are low maintenance, as they are made of high-quality white plastic.

Many companies selling house improvements in the UK have a bad reputation and customers often speak of the "cowboy companies," particularly those organizations selling double glazing. Fascia Mania wanted their service offering to be perceived as totally reliable and so they employed a market researcher to utilize repertory grid technique, in combination with contextual interviewing.

Different types of home improvements were chosen as the elements in the repertory grid interviews and the constructs elicited gave insights that were very useful to

▶▶

Fascia Mania. They showed that home owners perceived fascia replacements as the final but important step in making their homes "perfect." There were important implications from this. First, the home owners Fascia Mania's sales people should target were those who already have had replacement windows, a new kitchen, and so on. Second, the negative perception of many home improvement companies led Fascia Mania to place a strong emphasis on reassuring the customer, meeting agreed delivery times, and so on. Overall, the case demonstrates that repertory grid technique can give excellent insights into the sales process as well as product and service requirements.

For market researchers designing their first repertory grid interviews, it is important to practice construct elicitation. Conducting interviews with colleagues can provide good experience before moving to pilot interviews.

Rating the Elements

In the Equant grid, each element was rated on a five-point scale. Other possibilities include ranking elements or using more graduated rating scales.

Although ranking offers a simple way to gauge how interviewees perceive elements, it is an ordinal measurement and it does not, therefore, allow easy statistical analysis—the degree of differentiation between each of the ranked elements may not be the same. Consequently, rankings have significant limitations that make them normally unsuitable for repertory grid technique. It has also been noted that conducting rankings can be tedious for interviewees.[19]

For most situations the five-point rating scale is appropriate; however, more sophisticated interviewees can deal with more complicated scales. For example, an 11-point scale was used to give greater opportunity for differentiation in consumer research.[20] It should be noted that with more points on the scale, more time will be required to rate the elements and this can become annoying for the interviewee. The goal is to select a scale where respondents can make meaningful evaluations.

The *range of convenience* of a construct is an important concept. Every construct has a limited range of applicability and an interviewee may not be able to rate some elements against a particular construct. Researchers should note on the repertory grid where elements fall outside the range of convenience by entering "N/A" for "not applicable."

Administering the Interview

Despite the flexible nature of repertory grid interviewing, the underlying process of every interview consists of:

1. Determining the elements.
2. Eliciting and understanding each construct.

3. Rating the elements against each construct.
4. Terminating the interview.

A fundamental decision is whether to conduct the interview manually or to use a computer package, which allows interviews to be conducted automatically (as a "dialog" between the interviewee and the computer). Here the advantages of one-to-one interviews, such as the researcher being able to ask supplementary questions, should not be underestimated. Therefore, manual interviewing is likely to be the best approach. However, if a wide survey using repertory grid technique is planned, then computer-based interviews may be the only practical option.

In administering the interview, the researcher has three main tasks that must be conducted. These are to elicit and understand the meaning of constructs; to produce a comprehensive grid; and to keep the interviewee's attention. Practice is needed to deal with these tasks professionally, in parallel. Interviewees will have limited patience with a researcher who is slow in selecting triads (for example, sorting the cards), or does not pose meaningful questions to clarify constructs. There are three essential tools for interviewing: the cards; an interview script, and a blank grid (see Appendices 3 and 4).

Table 6.3 showed that with 10 elements there are 120 combinations of triads available. However, many of these triads will be similar and so the most varied triads should be selected. The interviewee is likely to become tired after 45–50 minutes of interviewing and this corresponds to the elicitation of about 8–12 constructs. In market research, where the interviewee is normally a volunteer, a good rule of thumb is to ask for an hour of their time. The repertory grid should be finished within 45 minutes and the remaining 10–15 minutes can be used to ask additional questions and give the interviewee feedback on the research and their grid.

Box Case 6.4

Beiersdorf Skin Care—Perceptions of Eucerin[21]

Beiersdorf AG is a leading German company with a long history of product innovation—it was founded in Hamburg in 1882 and produces a wide range of products, including such famous brands as Nivea. The company has an expertise in skin care products and a focus on "innovation by developing products with ideas that offer our customers better answers to existing problems and new answers to new problems."[22]

Eucerin Dry Skin was formulated to treat dry skin and eczema. The product performed excellently in trials, particularly for consumers with persistent and distressing conditions. The efficacy of the formulation was largely due to its active ingredient, urea. However, the perceived negative association between this compound and urine made it difficult to promote the product on this basis. Eucerin was well received by some users in the UK but it failed to make sufficient headway in the crowded market and so the product manager decided that a better understanding of customers' perceptions was needed.

▶▶

Repertory grid research was conducted with members of focus groups, assembled from sufferers contacted via a self-help association Provided elements were used; these were a range of products that included not only the direct competitors to Eucerin, but also a number of related cosmetic, nonclinical products. After the repertory grid interviews, focus group discussions probed how sufferers perceived the various brands against their criteria.

A large number of constructs were identified from the research. Interestingly, the product-based criteria (such as mode of action and formulation), which product management had thought were the most important, were not prominent. Instead, the most important factors for consumers included "clinicalness" (whether a product was perceived as a cosmetic, or a medicine); "irritant" (the likelihood of creating skin reactions); and "confidence" (the perception that product was really effective and not just "snake oil").

As a result of the research, the marketing of the Eucerin Dry Skin range was enhanced. The product was positioned as an "upmarket" treatment, in terms of efficacy and clinical effectiveness. The active ingredient was emphasized, as it was recognized that this would not be counterproductive (as severe sufferers were often aware that cattle urine is a common treatment for skin problems in Africa).

Within 12 months of the change in the positioning, Eucerin products were enjoying record sales with a near doubling of market share. The range was extended and now includes Eucerin Face Cream and other related products. Overall, the case shows that it is just as important to use innovative market research to optimize the product positioning as it is the product features.

ANALYZING THE RESULTS

Market researchers should note that the analysis covers both *qualitative* data (from the interview transcript) and *quantitative* data (statistical analysis of the ratings). Data analysis should be planned carefully, before interviews are conducted, as it is extremely risky to collect grid data before defining how it will be analyzed.

The Example: Supplier Performance

We used the Equant example to illustrate many aspects of repertory grids. Now, we will use a different example, taken from research investigating relationships between automotive manufacturers and their suppliers. Manufacturing companies in the automotive sector are extremely demanding and so their suppliers must understand exactly what is expected of them. A study of manufacturers' requirements used repertory grid interviews with 39 managers at manufacturing companies.[23] The research showed that repertory grid technique probes deeper than direct questioning and allowed automotive suppliers to identify the areas of their service offering that should be enhanced. As we will see in the following sections, the analysis of a single grid gives insights into how individuals think,

whereas the analysis of a series of grids enables us to identify the key characteristics of a market segment.

Analyzing a Single Grid

Figure 6.4 shows a grid from one of the 39 interviews—it summarizes the perceptions of a purchasing manager who was designated as Respondent 5/9_5.
Nine personal elements were used; the manager was asked to name three suppliers with which their company was in close contact, three with which there was
only loose contact, and three with which there was intermediate contact. These
nine elements are shown across the top of the grid (Suppliers 1 to 9). During
the interview, 12 constructs were identified including "active relationship maintenance" (with a pole "no relationship maintenance") and "additional services."
The constructs were elicited using triads that are indicated by the asterisks in
the grid. A five-point rating scale was used and the grid contains ratings of every
element against all of the constructs. A visual inspection of Figure 6.4 shows
that the ratings against certain constructs are more widely spread than on others. For example, the ratings for "active relationships maintenance" range from
"1" to "5," whereas those for "price" range only from "1" to "3." Some of the
elements are highly rated on nearly all the constructs. For example, Supplier 8
received ratings of "1" on all but one construct.

Once a visual inspection of the grid has been made, it is normal to enter
the grid data into a software package. Software packages offer a wealth of possibilities (included automated interviews) and market researchers should make
themselves familiar with these prior to data collection. It is beyond the scope of
this chapter to review in detail the different software packages available on the
market but *Idiogrid*[24] and *WebgridIII*[25] both provide suitable levels of analysis.
Computer analysis normally provides:

- Statistics for the elements.
- Statistics for the constructs, including intercorrelations.
- The *cognitive map*—a diagrammatical representation of an interviewee's
  perceptions.

Statistics for the Elements

Table 6.4 shows the statistics for the elements. It can be seen that Supplier 8's
best rating was "1," its lowest "5," and an average rating of 1.33. The elements
that have very good ratings on some constructs but poor ones on others can
be recognized by their higher standard deviations. It can be seen that Supplier
1's ratings had a relatively wide spread, with a standard deviation of 1.62. The
supplier with the poorest average rating is Supplier 2 with a standard deviation
of 0.99.

The statistics for the elements allow us to understand how each of the suppliers is perceived. They can, for example, provide insights about how key competitors are viewed and therefore give ideas for marketing strategies.

	Supplier 1	Supplier 2	Supplier 3	Supplier 4	Supplier 5	Supplier 6	Supplier 7	Supplier 8	Supplier 9	CONSTRUCT POLES
CONSTRUCTS (SUPPLIER ATTRIBUTES)										
1 Active relationship maintenance	*1*	*5*	*5*	3	1	3	5	1	3	No relationship maintenance
2 Committed	1	5	5	*2*	*1*	*2*	3	1	3	Uncommitted
3 Additional services	1	5	5	3	*1*	3	*5*	*1*	*3*	No additional services
4 Rated as A-customer	*3*	*5*	5	3	1	2	2	1	*4*	Rated as C-customer
5 High volume of turnover	1	5	*5*	*2*	1	2	1	*1*	1	Low volume of turnover
6 New product development capability	3	5	5	3	*1*	*2*	*5*	1	3	No new product development capability
7 Price level—lower	*1*	3	*1*	1	*3*	1	3	1	3	Price level—higher
8 Small family enterprise	5	*5*	5	*3*	1	*5*	1	1	3	Large enterprise
9 Special (unique) products	5	5	*5*	5	*5*	5	*5*	1	3	No special products
10 Personal relationship	3	5	5	*1*	1	*3*	3	*1*	3	Pure business relationship
11 Serious and reliable	1	*5*	*3*	3	*1*	2	2	1	3	Questionable
12 Dependent on supplier	4	2	1	*3*	*4*	1	*3*	5	5	Independent of supplier

Figure 6.4 A Repertory Grid on a Purchasing Manager's Perceptions of Automotive Suppliers (Respondent 5/9_5)

Note: The asterisks in the grid indicate which three cards were in each triad.

Table 6.4   Descriptive Statistics for a Purchasing Manager's Elements

Elements	Element's Best Score	Element's Mean Score	Element's Worst Score	Spread of Ratings
	Minimum	Mean	Maximum	Standard Dev.
1) Supplier 1	1	2.42	5	1.62
2) Supplier 2	2	4.58	5	0.99
3) Supplier 3	1	4.16	5	1.59
4) Supplier 4	1	2.66	5	1.07
5) Supplier 5	1	1.75	5	1.42
6) Supplier 6	1	2.58	5	1.31
7) Supplier 7	1	3.17	5	1.53
8) Supplier 8	1	1.33	5	1.15
9) Supplier 9	1	3.08	5	0.90

Table 6.5   Descriptive Statistics for the Constructs

Constructs	Best Rating	Mean Rating	Worst Rating	Spread of Ratings
	Min.	Mean	Max.	Variability (percent)
1) Active relationship maintenance	1	3.00	5	10.18
2) Committed	1	2.56	5	8.58
3) Additional services	1	3.00	5	10.18
4) Rated as A-customer	1	2.89	5	8.01
5) High volume of turnover	1	2.11	5	9.71
6) NPD capability	1	3.11	5	8.86
7) Price level	1	1.89	3	3.77
8) Small family enterprise	1	3.22	5	11.69
9) Special products	1	4.33	5	6.79
10) Personal relationship	1	2.78	5	8.29
11) Serious and reliable	1	2.33	5	5.94
12) Dependent on supplier	1	3.11	5	8.01

Statistics for the Constructs

Table 6.5 shows the descriptive statistics for the purchasing manager's constructs. It can be seen that on the construct "active relationship maintenance," the elements were rated from "1" to "5," with a mean of 3.00. The spread of the ratings against each construct varies and, for example, "price level" has a comparatively low spread. An important concept is the *variability* of each construct in a grid. The variability figure is the percentage of the total spread of ratings in a grid that is due to one construct. Variability is one indicator of a respondent's most important constructs, as it indicates the ones that differentiate most strongly between the elements.[26] Construct

Table 6.6 The Relationships between Constructs

Constructs	Construct Numbers											
	1	2	3	4	5	6	7	8	9	10	11	12
1) Active relationship maint.	1.00											
2) Committed	**0.91**	1.00										
3) Additional services	**1.00**	0.91	1.00									
4) Rated as A-customer	0.66	0.85	0.66	1.00								
5) High volume of turnover	0.68	0.86	0.68	0.77	1.00							
6) NPD capability	0.85	0.85	**0.89**	076	0.64	1.00						
7) Price level	0.27	0.27	0.27	0.07	-.06	0.23	1.00					
8) Small family enterprise	0.31	0.46	0.31	0.71	0.63	0.41	-.37	1.00				
9) Special products	0.41	0.30	0.41	0.31	0.35	0.47	0.11	0.44	1.00			
10) Personal relationship	0.74	0.86	0.74	0.82	0.77	0.80	0.13	0.71	0.38	1.00		
11) Serious and reliable	0.76	0.85	0.76	0.82	0.76	0.68	0.30	0.48	0.27	0.64	1.00	
12) Dependent on supplier	-.66	-.59	-.66	-.4	-.73	-.51	0.24	-.62	-.65	-.61	-.45	1.00

8 accounted for most of the variability, across all constructs, with a value of 11.69 percent.

A low variability with a high average rating indicates a construct on which all products are highly rated. Such a construct is not the most significant. An example is Construct 7 ("price"), with 3.77 percent variability and a mean rating of 1.89.

Particularly important are constructs with both a low variability and a low average rating—these can identify hidden or emergent issues. For instance, "special products" are important to the interviewee but few companies provide an adequate service (the mean rating is 4.33; the variability is 6.79 percent; and only Suppliers 8 and 9 offer better performance, with ratings of "1" and "3" respectively).

In addition to the statistics for the individual constructs, software packages calculate the correlations between the different constructs and therefore indicate which are potentially related. It can be seen from Table 6.6 that Construct 1 ("active relationship maintenance") and Construct 3 ("additional services") are perfectly correlated (1.00 shown in bold and underlined in the table). The other highly correlated constructs are 1 and 2 (0.91 correlation); 1 and 6 (a correlation of 0.89); 2 and 3 (correlated at 0.91); and 3 and 6 (0.89). Obviously

---

Box Case 6.5

Italian Wine—Designing the Packaging[27]

Wine producers know that in making their purchase decisions, consumers often perceive the bottle and packaging as an indication of the quality of the wine. To understand this phenomenon better, a leading Italian winery decided to have research conducted on its behalf by the University of Florence. A total of 30 interviews were conducted, with an equal sample of men and women, a range of ages, and different degrees of interest in wine. The interviews included a repertory grid elicitation and semistructured discussion. The repertory grid elements were different wines, which were actually shown to the interviewees in triads of three bottles (provided elements).

The results were analyzed to identify the key factors in the different grids; this task was easier as the respondents were all presented with the same (provided) elements. It was found that consumers' perceptions are based around two main dimensions: the color and shape of the bottle; and the "dress" (the label and the "capsule" [the cover over the top of the bottle]). Interestingly, in making their judgments of wine quality, consumers "applied" these two dimensions in different ways to white and rosé wines. A deeper understanding of the perception of bottles emerged, with interviewees using terms such as "traditional, bordolaise" bottles in "light-colored glass," versus "innovative bottle" and "dark colored glass." They also talked about "traditional" versus "small and gaudy" labels, and capsules with an embossed company symbol were perceived to indicate higher quality wine.

With a product like wine, a consumer without expert knowledge may be forced to take their cue on the quality from the packaging. Therefore, wineries that have a deeper understanding of perceptions gained through repertory grid are in a much better position to design their products, particularly if they want to project the right balance of innovation and quality in marketing a new wine.

a correlation does not prove causation but the correlations can enable market researchers to spot important links in the data.

The Cognitive Map

This is a two-dimensional representation of how an interviewee perceives the relationships between their elements and constructs. As long as researchers are aware of its limitations, it is a useful way of summarizing data, based on *Principle Components Analysis* (PCA). PCA uncovers the strongest relationships in the data and extracts two dimensions: *Component 1* and *Component 2*. Both components are mathematical combinations of the constructs, selected in a way as to explain in two dimensions as much as possible of the variation in the data. Taking a grid with many constructs and "forcing" this into two dimensions is a compromise.

Figure 6.5 shows the cognitive map for the purchasing manager and summarizes the data from the grid (Figure 6.4). The circle defines *component space*—the interviewee's frame of perception. It can be seen that the constructs are labeled around the circle and several of them are closely related to Component 1. For example, "questionable" [the pole of "committed"]; "c-customer"; and "pure business relationship" are all closely related to Component 1. In contrast, the only construct that is closely aligned to Component 2 is "higher price"). The brackets after the components on the diagram show that 63.208 percent of the variability in the grid can be explained by Component 1 and 14.42 percent by Component 2. Therefore,

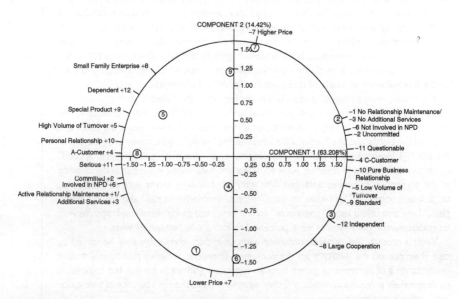

Figure 6.5   The Cognitive Map for the Purchasing Manager (Reference 5/9_5)

Components 1 and 2 explain in total 77.62 percent of the variability in the grid data. If the variation explained by the two components is not above 70 percent, then the map is too great a compromise, because the data cannot be adequately represented in two dimensions, therefore researchers should always check this before interpreting the cognitive map.

The elements are positioned in the component space, according to their ratings. For example, Suppliers 1 and 6 are positioned as being relatively low price but mid-performance on many of the constructs (that is, they are in the middle of the Component 1 scale). Suppliers 8 and 5 are perceived positively, as they provide active relationship maintenance, are serious (and reliable), offer special products, are dependable, and so on. It can be seen that the cognitive map provides a detailed insight into one interviewee's view of suppliers and summarizes how the elements (in this case suppliers) stack-up against the constructs. In key account management, where the market researcher is interested in a single organization's perception, then the cognitive map from the purchasing manager can bring unique insights and ideas for how to manage the relationship more effectively.

Analyzing a Series of Grids

From the 39 interviews with purchasing managers, a total of 411 personal constructs were elicited. Many of these were common, that is constructs that were mentioned by several respondents. The analysis of a series of grids therefore consists of:

- Collating the constructs into suitable categories.
- Identifying the most important constructs (see Box Case 6.5).

Collating the Constructs

To demonstrate how the constructs were collated, Table 6.7 gives two constructs with example quotes from respondents and the assigned labels. The words underlined in each quote indicate how the construct labels were derived. It can be seen that the construct "flexibility" was elicited from 23 of the interviewees (59 percent of the total). From the quotes, it can be seen that the respondents themselves used the word "flexible." An analysis of the transcripts showed that all 23 respondents actually used the words "flexible" or "flexibility" and so the latter was chosen as a label. The allocation of construct labels is not always as clear as in the case of flexibility. Respondents may use different terms in referring to the same issue and therefore the researcher must group these constructs under a suitable label. From Table 6.7 it can be seen that "joint problem solving" was the label assigned to a construct mentioned by six respondents. From the example quotes it can be seen that one respondent referred to solving problems "jointly" whereas another referred to solving problems "together."

Table 6.7 How Constructs Were Collated and Labels Assigned

Construct Label	Poles	Example Respondents' Explanations	Frequency
Flexibility	Flexible (1) Inflexible (5)	• "A flexible supplier is prepared to work on weekends to fulfill urgent orders for us. The supplier is able to quickly produce and deliver the parts. Other suppliers, inflexible ones, are unable to fulfill these wishes" (A managing director—electronics company). • "If we order something under a very short notice—let's say on a Friday—the supplier is so flexible that he even would work on Saturdays and Sundays to deliver the parts on the next business day; so on Monday. The same applies when ordering a small batch of parts. A flexible supplier can deliver various volume sizes and not only the large ones. An inflexible supplier cannot deliver parts at any other time or in any other volume than what has been agreed in the contract long ago" (A purchasing manager—engineering company).	23
Joint Problem Solving	Jointly (1) Alone (5)	• "I can call a supplier if I have a problem and I can ask him directly whether he can help me. Some help me to jointly solve a problem, others don't help us at all" (A managing director—electronics company). • "Some suppliers help us solving our problems. I really get full support in finding an answer to our problem. I can ring them at any time and I would be certain that we will find a way to overcome the problem together. I would also ring another supplier, but others have obvious difficulties to see our problems from our perspective and, therefore, are unable to solve it together with us. I even have to explain to them that I need help in solving the problem; they simply don't seem to understand what I mean by it. We always try to explain our position to them, but—for reasons I am not aware of—they seem to be unable to see the problem and the urgency to solve it. They don't do it" (A purchasing manager—electronics company).	6

To ensure that the collation of constructs is reliable, various approaches can be taken, sometimes in combination. Transcripts can be analyzed manually to give tables of similar constructs,[28] or they may be entered into a text analysis software program, such as *NVivo*[29] which is a very efficient tool for coding qualitative data. Different researchers can analyze the data in parallel and then an inter-coding reliability can be estimated.

Identifying Key Constructs

Once the constructs have been collated, a table of all of the distinct constructs can be produced, including their frequency. Table 6.8 shows the 20 most frequently mentioned constructs across the 39 interviews. Typically, constructs mentioned by at least 25 percent of respondents carry more importance. The constructs that fulfill this requirement are indicated by their frequencies being highlighted in the third column of Table 6.8 and there are 14 such constructs (numbers 1–14). In contrast, the bottom 6 constructs in the table, which were mentioned less than 10 times, are unlikely to be important ones.

Frequency is one indication of importance. Nevertheless, a high frequency of mention can also indicate that a construct was obvious and therefore readily mentioned. Variability is another indication of importance. A construct with

Table 6.8   Analysis of the Attributes of Partnership

No.	Constructs	Frequency (percent of respondents)	Average Normalized Variability (percent)	Key Construct?
1)	Flexibility	23 (59)	8.21	No
2)	Delivery Performance	20 (51)	6.83	No
3)	Personal Relationship	18 (46)	11.15	Yes
4)	Special Product Capability	17 (44)	12.76	Yes
5)	Quality	16 (41)	6.76	No
6)	Dependency	15 (38)	10.55	Yes
7)	Size of Organization	14 (36)	11.42	Yes
8)	Relationship Maintenance	13 (33)	10.08	Yes
9)	Volume of Turnover	13 (33)	12.45	Yes
10)	Price Level	11 (28)	4.93	No
11)	Feedback	11 (28)	10.21	Yes
12)	New Product Development	10 (26)	11.50	Yes
13)	Complaint Handling	10 (26)	9.58	Yes
14)	Location	10 (26)	9.48	No
15)	Customer Oriented	8 (21)	7.64	No
16)	Importance of Supplier (to Mfr)	8 (21)	10.24	No
17)	Openness	7 (18)	6.38	No
18)	Price Changes	7 (18)	6.35	No
19)	Commitment	6 (15)	11.00	No
20)	Reliability	6 (15)	7.81	No

a wide spread of ratings differentiates strongly between the elements and this spread (relative to the other constructs) is the variability that we mentioned in the previous section on the analysis of a single grid.

The variability measure is dependent on the number of constructs in an individual grid. For instance, if 5 constructs were elicited from a respondent, the average variability would be 20 percent (i.e., 100/5), whereas if 10 constructs were elicited, the average variability would be 10 percent. Therefore, the variability figures for constructs from grids with different numbers of constructs need to be normalized. This can be done by multiplying the variability of each construct by the number of constructs in that individual grid divided by the average number of constructs across all of the respondents—10.54. The normalized variability figures for a construct were then averaged across the grids.

As there were on average 10.54 constructs elicited per interview, the average variability per construct was 9.49 (that is 100/10.54). A construct with an *average normalized variability* (ANV) greater than 9.49 means that the construct differentiates more strongly between the suppliers. A construct with an ANV less than 9.49 indicates that the construct differentiates less strongly between suppliers. The 11 constructs (Numbers 3, 4, 6, 7, 8, 9, 11, 12, 13, 16, and 19) that have higher than average variability are highlighted in the fourth column of Table 6.8.

The construct "flexibility" has a frequency of 23 but an ANV of 8.21. This shows that "flexibility" was frequently mentioned by interviewees but that the performance of most suppliers was perceived as similar. The construct "special product capability" has both a high frequency (17) and a high ANV (12.76) and so can be designated a key attribute. Using the combination of frequency and variability, nine key constructs were identified, as indicated by shading in the right-hand column in Table 6.8 (Construct numbers 3, 4, 6, 7, 8, 9, 11, 12, and 13). These are the attributes that most clearly differentiate between suppliers.

Several of the attributes in Table 6.8 raise interesting points: "flexibility," "delivery performance," "quality," and "price level" are mentioned often but do not have high ANV (8.21; 6.83; 6.76; and 4.93 respectively). This finding shows that although these factors were mentioned by a large number of respondents, they do not differentiate strongly between the performance of each of the different suppliers. Another way of looking at this is that it indicates that the factors flexibility, delivery performance, quality, and price are what are termed "hygiene factors" (by marketing professionals) and "order qualifiers" (by manufacturing people), that is, manufacturers expect them but look for excellent performance in other areas when choosing suppliers. The key message to suppliers from the result summarized in Table 6.8 is that they need to strive to achieve top performance in not only the market attributes that are well-known in the industry but also offer excellent performance in building "personal relationships," "special product capability," and so on.

The Value of Grids

Overall, the repertory grids provide market researchers with:

- A deep understanding of how individual customers perceive products or services (or whatever else we have chosen as elements). This includes an appreciation of what an individual thinks are good and bad about the different products or elements chosen as elements.
- Clear insights into what are the most important constructs in a particular market segment. This includes ideas on the constructs that are related to hidden or emerging customer needs.
- Customers' constructs, which are invaluable in the preparation of surveys, focus groups, and so on.

LIMITATIONS TO CONSIDER

At this point, the many advantages of repertory grid technique will be clear. In order to be able to use grids effectively, however, it is important that market researchers recognize the following potential limitations:[30]

1. If the number of personal elements that can be identified is very low, there may not be enough possible triads.
2. Due to the number of variations in design, market researchers need to carefully select the most valid approach for their research.
3. The somewhat artificial nature of a repertory grid interview may influence an interviewee's constructs.[31]
4. The technique is time-consuming; typically 45–60 minutes per interview.
5. The interviewees' ratings of the elements are susceptible to the "halo" effect; ratings are not objective and their values tell us something about the interviewee as well as what is being rated.
6. The apparent simplicity of data tables and cognitive maps may seduce market researchers into making invalid interpretations of the data.

SUMMARY

Repertory grid technique has many advantages in market research and identifying customers' hidden needs. This chapter has shown the following:

- The technique is highly flexible and there are many different ways in which to apply it, for example, to understand product features, brand perception, feelings during the sales process, and so on.
- Single repertory grids provide deep insights into individuals' thinking and the cognitive map provides a useful way of summarizing the findings. For key account management, for example, it is very useful to understand the exact thinking of a client's purchasing manager.

- Series of grids allow market researchers to better understand the needs of market segments and identify opportunities for innovative products and service offerings.
- Repertory grid technique can be combined effectively with other techniques.
- Although superficially it appears to be a very simple technique, designing and conducting effective interviews to meet the goals of a specific market research project is complex and requires experience.

MANAGEMENT RECOMMENDATIONS

- Identify where repertory grid technique can generate ideas for innovation, in products, services, the sales process, and so on.
- Determine an appropriate sample for the research and design the interviews to ensure they generate sufficient numbers of reliable constructs.
- Combine repertory grid research with other techniques, in order to triangulate the results, or generate constructs that can be used in surveys or other approaches.
- Use the technique to generate ideas for products or services that can effectively differentiated from your competitors' offerings.

RECOMMENDED READING

1. Fransella, F. and Bannister, D., *A Manual for Repertory Grid Technique.* 2nd edition. Chicherster: Wiley, 2004. [Key handbook which covers the main issues in grid design, reliability, and validity.]
2. Pope, M. L. and Keen, T. R., *Personal Construct Psychology and Education.* London: Academic Press, 1981. [Also a useful handbook on the technique.]
3. Jankowitz, D., *The Easy Guide to Repertory Grids.* Chichester: Wiley, 2004. [This book has useful sections on analyzing multiple grids.]

7 INVOLVING THE USER

> Existing methods don't go nearly far enough in helping [marketers] move to a closer understanding of their customer.[1]

INTRODUCTION

Traditional market research keeps customers at arm's length in that they are asked *what* type of products and services they would like but then they have no further involvement in new product development. In short interactions with market researchers, it is difficult for customers to articulate the type of features they would like, particularly if they are unaware of the technological possibilities. However, some customers do have the expertise to know what is technologically possible, and others may have already modified their existing equipment to cope with its limitations. Some consumers are interested to have their views heard by their favorite companies, and yet others are even willing to assist with product development. *Involving the user* is the term we shall use for a range of techniques that companies can apply to collect customers' ideas and tap into their expertise in the development of innovative products and services.

The Internet has significantly increased the opportunities for companies to forge close links to large numbers of their customers or consumers. There are various ways to link users into product development and this chapter presents the most relevant ones covering:

- The history of involving the user in new product development.
- The importance of user involvement.
- Lead user technique.
- Virtual communities.
- Crowdsourcing.
- Experimentation and Prototyping.
- The advantages and limitations of the techniques.

HISTORY OF INVOLVING THE USER

The concept that the user can contribute to product development is not a new one. In 1776 Adam Smith recognized that many of the machines developed in the industrial revolution were the inventions of "common workmen."[2] Later, during the boom in manufactured products, users drove some of the development of products. The Model T Ford was designed as a saloon car, but in the 1920s farmers modified it for threshing corn and sawing wood. These modifications were the harbingers of the agricultural machinery industry. Later still, mountain bikes were invented by enthusiasts who cycled on mountain tracks and when their bikes failed mechanically, they began building more durable ones and adding components such as motorcycle brakes to match the rough terrains they were encountering. Even after the basic mountain bike concept emerged, enthusiasts have continued to modify and refine bikes, adding, for example, improved suspension and accessories.[3]

It was largely the work of Professor Eric von Hippel at MIT that showed the importance of user communities in driving innovation. In 1986, von Hippel introduced a process which is nowadays called the *lead user approach*. In his arguments for this approach, he criticized traditional market research methods,[4] stressing the value of involving users who have a deep expertise in the use (and abuse) of products.

Involving the user or consumer applies not only to manufacturing businesses but also service ones. In the 1960s, consumers were confronted with a new wave of self-service businesses, supermarkets, and fast-food restaurants. At the time, these were considered "real innovations" and supermarkets even produced advertisements explaining how to shop. The idea of self-service was new but it was very successful and it is being taken further today with leading stores such as IKEA encouraging their customers to use self-service checkouts.

The most important driver of user involvement in product development has been the Internet. At the end of the 1970s, academic researchers founded mailing lists and newsgroups in order to exchange their thoughts on specific topics. These were also the birthplace for user communities, as we know them today. Having started in the 1990s, the Internet has increased the opportunities for users to become involved with product development and has also made it much cheaper and easier for market researchers to manage such involvement (see, for example, Box Case 7.1). What is called *Web 1.0* (the first phase of the Internet) brought people together in chat rooms, enabled them to share personal information and ideas via personal homepages, which were the precursors to blogging and social networking. Part of the information that people began to share was their experiences (and frustrations) with products. The explosion of the Internet in the mid-1990s fostered a growth in these *virtual communities*, for example, independent groups of users of particular products and services. There are now countless virtual communities and those that focus on products and services are increasingly important to companies.

Web 2.0 emerged around 1994 and is characterized by a dynamic and not a static programming language. It is about interaction and collaboration and helps users to create personal content. The Web 2.0 wave of online communities caught the public imagination in the early 2000s, with social networks such as Flickr, Facebook, and Xing. A similar trend is starting to emerge within businesses where communities such as LinkedIn are becoming highly influential. Users can actively participate through blogging, uploading photos and videos, and so on. The possibilities offered by Web 2.0 are increasingly being used commercially. The most extreme form is known as *crowdsourcing*, where specific tasks are submitted to an unknown crowd on the Internet.

Box Case 7.1

Procter & Gamble—User Generated Content and Emotion[5]

The Fragrances Business Unit of P&G has its headquarters in Geneva, Switzerland. In addition to supplying fragrances to a string of household names such as Boss and Lacoste, P&G also have their own brands such as SK-II. In the industry, the luxury fragrances that are used in perfume, aftershave, and the like are referred to as "juice" and designing such a product is a mile away from the development of an engineered product such as a car. In fragrances, product development is something of an artistic process, in which emotion plays a key role.

Ryan Jones, an American with an MBA, has worked in Geneva as Brand Manager for the HUGO BOSS fragrance for four years. "In luxury products we have a bit of a different set of rules. We do conduct market research but we are also very much in contact with fashion houses, trend agencies and consumers to spot market opportunities. All of this information is gathered and essentially is the 'input' to our team of designers who are tasked with creating a juice that evokes the right emotions. In the end, the consumer is always the boss at P&G and so our product must work for them before we bring it to market." In working on ways to generate emotion, loyalty, and interest in the brand, the HUGO team introduced user-generated content, with a competition to design the packaging for a limited edition of the HUGO Man fragrance. A website, www.hugocreate.com, was created where Internet users could submit their designs and "the enthusiasm that was created and the quality of the submissions was superb, especially if you consider that we did no advertising for the first year ..." says Jones, "the message just spread via social networking."

The power of involving users and the way the Internet has changed much of the way marketing is done led Jones to be appointed as Head of e-commerce for P&G's Prestige Products Division in 2009. His background as an IT manager has "become hugely helpful in my work in managing innovation. It is amazing today the amount of market intelligence you can get listening to the web...you get instant on-line reviews of your products and I am increasingly working on closing the loop so that we can link this mass of information back into the R&D space to better develop products that delight our consumers."

The term *user-generated content* emerged in the late 1990s and refers to website information provided by customers and users of the Internet. Sometimes, user-generated content is only part of a website, for example, at amazon.com the majority of the content is prepared by the company but user reviews are also submitted by visitors. Other well-known examples of user-generated content are: wikipedia.com, tripadvisor.com, picasa.com, and myspace.com.

User-generated content can go much further than website pages and product development can be conducted by users, with *open source* software such as the Linux operating system being a prime example of user-driven product development. The way that users are willing to voluntarily develop open source software indicates that users of the Internet like to interact,[6] and user-driven innovation is therefore a social phenomenon. The original idea and the name "open source" came out of a strategy session held at Palo Alto[7] followed by the first "open source summit" in 1998. In the early 2000s, some companies began to publish parts of their source code, but one has to differentiate between the limited forms of open source software and fully open ones such as Linux (operating system), Apache (HTTP web server), Mozilla Firefox (web browser), and Mediawiki (wiki server software). The success of open source software is based on enthusiasm of the amateurs and the firms who benefit from using such products.[8]

For a number of years the users of video games have also been involved in product development to various degrees. Groups of players often share self-created tutorials about the games amongst themselves, make simple adjustments to games, and sometimes even develop complete games.[9] Leading companies in this area often provide tools to help users in their development work.

The importance of building close links with customers and users has never been greater and leading companies will, no doubt, be creative in developing new ways to harness the energy and enthusiasm of these customers. Much of this user involvement will be via the Internet and so it is likely to benefit from the work of ethnographers, who are currently developing ways to understand customers via *webnography*—studies of consumers conducted via the web but using ethnographic principles.[10]

IMPORTANCE OF USER INVOLVEMENT

Overview

Both companies and politicians have recognized the importance of user communities and involvement. Obama's successful presidential campaign is an often-quoted example of the power of social networks. The Danish government has targeted user-led innovation with an investment of 100 million Danish Krone (approximately 13.5M euro) between 2007 and 2010.[11] The aim of this program is to investigate the role of users in the innovation process, to identify best practices, and to boost the innovativeness of Danish companies through user involvement in R&D.

Studies have shown that 10 to 40 percent of users are engaged in the further development, modification, or improvement of existing consumer products.[12] Companies can quickly learn about their customers' perceptions of new technologies and the potential for new markets. This is especially important at a time when the majority of customers are unaware of emerging technology,[13] which makes it difficult for them to imagine future products.

Companies need to shorten the time between idea creation and market launch (*time- to-market*)[14] but they also need to ensure that products do not fail. Contact with potential customers via the Internet can be used in testing market acceptance[15] and can therefore reduce market failure. Similarly, user involvement can create a bond between brands and the consumer, as virtual communities create social interaction between a brand and a high volume of consumers.

Types of User Involvement

There are many ways how to involve users in market research and new product development, as illustrated by Figure 7.1. The term *user communities* is often used synonymously with *virtual* or *online communities*, but user communities that are recruited via the web can also meet face-to-face (see Box Case 7.4). Virtual communities only meet online but Web 2.0 technology has revolutionized the degree of interaction possible in market research and product development. For certain products, the lead user approach can be partly or fully managed via Web 2.0 instead of workshops (as indicated by the dotted line in Figure 7.1).

Box Case 7.2

United Airlines—Fashionable and Functional Uniforms[16]

United Airlines cabin crew uniforms had not been changed for over a decade when the company decided to bring in top fashion designer Cynthia Rowley in 2010. Rather than having her work from her studio, she was allowed to fly thousands of kilometers on United Airlines, to watch crew members at work and to directly collect ideas on how uniforms should look. Rowley knew she faced a real challenge in designing ten new types of uniforms (for males and females, for cabin crew, pilots, customer service and maintenance people), and she had to meet the needs of employees who told her that they wanted to look "professional" but at the same time their clothing had to be functional. For example, cabin crew need to be able to reach up and bend down easily, and be able to work in the restricted galley area. Instead of just implementing her own ideas, Rowley discussed possible solutions with staff, such as using elasticated waists and zips to increase crew members' ability to stretch easily.

United Airlines was clear that the investment in new uniforms is crucial and Tim Simons, MD of Marketing said, "new uniforms help folks [cabin crew] look and feel better, they're set-up for success which leads to better customer service, which leads to more customer loyalty."

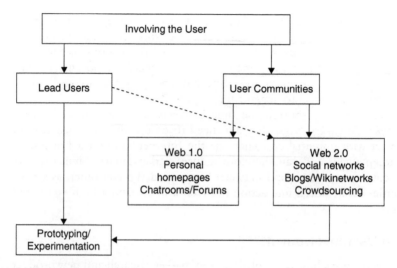

Figure 7.1   User Involvement

Timing of User Involvement

Due to the Internet, companies no longer have to rely on their R&D departments and internal know-how alone. User-led innovation and customer involvement can occur at different stages in the NPD process:[17]

- Ideation. Here, consumers and customers generate ideas for new products and/or services. Customer and user involvement is aimed at discovering needs and requirements.[18]
- Design and development. Here the customer co-develops new products in close cooperation with the company and/or other users. This is *user-led innovation* (see Box Case 7.2).
- Modification and novel use. Here, customers use existing products in new ways and/or modify them to add functionality.
- Market launch. Here the customer is involved in the test of the marketing mix before a product is finally launched (see Box Case 7.3).

Box Case 7.3

Sample U—Putting the Marketing Mix on Trial[19]

For a number of years, leading manufacturers have provided their key customers with prototypes or trial products, in order to capture their opinions and reactions. *Sample* U, a "Tryvertising research center" in San Diego, California, U.S. has optimized this technique. Michael Senger, President of *Sample* U, points out that "giving people

▸▸

---

the opportunity to try products is a great way to better understand what they are thinking." Consumers—or "Trysumers™" as Senger calls them—are asked to answer demographic and psychographic questionnaires, so that *Sample U* has a deep understanding of the psychological makeup of each of its respondents. Respondents then participate in product trials in an "Out of Home" controlled environment and researchers collect information about their reactions to specific product attributes, the overall performance, and user experience. In addition, respondents are encouraged to take the product home to see how it performs in their own environment. Companies that work with *Sample U* get actionable results in as little as 48 hours.

Involving the user is a powerful way to capture opinions "on virtually anything" Senger highlights, "be it the product, packaging, price, messaging, promotion or advertisement—actually, we learn everything about the entire marketing mix before the product is even launched which ensures our customer's success."

Several studies have shown that involving users in the early phases of new product development ensures that customer needs are met and market acceptance is faster. However, when "typical" users are involved in the early stages of complex product development, companies should not expect radical new product ideas to emerge directly. In such cases, early involvement of users will bring a greater understanding of users' current needs (which may, in turn, indicate that the business strategy needs reevaluating).[20]

Overall, the role of the customer in new product development is changing from that of a passive contributor to market research, to that of an active co-designer and sometimes even to an independent innovator.[21]

LEAD USER TECHNIQUE

Overview

Lead user technique is used by many leading companies around the world and it has been linked to a number of notable market successes. For example, Hilti a global leader in products for the construction and building maintenance industry based in Liechtenstein recruits lead users from universities and technical institutes and brings them in contact with in-house experts.[22] Other lead users are selected via a customer survey, which checks for those customers that are interested in being directly involved in product development. Once lead users have been recruited, the next step is a workshop to develop product concepts, the best of which are later developed into prototypes and tested with selected customers.

It is important to stress that there are distinct differences between lead users and normal ones. Lead users are customers that have very demanding needs and are experts at using a particular product or service. The requirements that lead users already face today will only be needed by the broader market in the future: "A true lead user should be a window into the future and not an anchor in the past."[23] In marketing language, lead users are *innovators* and therefore ahead of even the *early adopters*. Innovators are the first customers to buy and early adopters are fast to adopt. (For an explanation of the way early innovators and adopters influence markets see the work of Professor E.M. Rogers[24].)

Lead users have a strong interest in solving their specific problems and benefit significantly when they obtain a solution.[25] Consequently, lead users are often willing to contribute their ideas for a product and to participate in product testing. Sometimes lead users have greater knowledge about a particular product or service than the manufacturer (see Box Case 7.4). In contrast to traditional market research, which looks for customers that are representative, lead user technique focuses on a unique and often elite group of customers.

Box Case 7.4

Lego—Mindstorming Better Product Ideas[26]

Since its introduction in 1998, the Lego Mindstorms robot kit has been a huge success, selling upwards of 40,000 units a year. The kit includes a large robot brick that can be used in combination with a range of motors, lights, bricks, and sensors to build highly intelligent devices—for example, a robot that can manipulate and solve Rubik's Cube. Writing the control programs for such devices is a complex and challenging task, which is conducted on a laptop. The market for Mindstorms has developed into two distinct segments: parents buying the $200 kit for teenagers hooked on engineering, and adult enthusiasts ("geeks") who love programming in their spare time. Geeks love to exhibit their creations at the annual Lego "Brickfest" conference.

   When Lego decided to improve the Mindstorms product, they turned their attention to the geeks and chose to involve some of them in the new product development from a very early stage. After signing a nondisclosure agreement, four geeks were invited to exchange their ideas about the existing product in a secure chat room, hosted by Seren Lund, the director of Mindstorms. Over the next years, the four lead users were in regular contact with Lego, giving a wealth of ideas about how to make significant improvements to Mindstorms. Involving the four enthusiasts at such an early stage led Lego to develop a very different product, based on their suggestions. The new product, which was introduced in August 2006, looks very different and is not backwards compatible. The new robot brick has more computing power, uses an improved programming language, and comes with a vastly improved array of motors, sensors, and (new style) bricks. Interestingly, although the four dedicated enthusiasts were fundamental to the project and had a very strong influence over the final design, they were not paid by Lego—the prototype kits they were given, the peer recognition they received, and the opportunity to influence the new product were enough motivation for them.

   In the original Mindstorms development, Lego had learned the difficulties in managing a project including electronics and software (both of which are a mile away from plastic bricks). Therefore, making radical improvements to the Mindstorms software was outsourced. The shock came when within weeks of the product being introduced, a Stanford graduate had reverse-engineered the robot brick and posted all his findings about its control and software on the Internet. Lego considered legal action but decided that this would be counter to the spirit of Mindstorms. Now the software license that comes with every kit includes a clause allowing hacking. Consequently, the worldwide community of Mindstorms enthusiasts has grown fast. Lego's philosophy of deeply involving customers in NPD is here to stay.

Applying Lead User Technique

The lead user technique aims to increase the success rate of new products and new services by analyzing the future needs of customers. It is usually based on four main steps:[27]

- Identifying relevant trends.
- Recruiting lead users.
- Conducting a workshop with lead users.
- Developing product concepts.

Identifying Key Relevant Trends

This first stage involves identifying key relevant trends in customer and user requirements, industry, society, technology, and so on. Trend analysis is often part of a company's annual strategic planning process. In practice, looking for trends is often a combination of looking at factual data and forecasts for the future. (Note that forecasting, whether sales or technological performance, is notoriously difficult.) If the internal know-how of a company is limited, *trend workshops* with experts can be conducted, or telephone interviews with acknowledged experts in the field can be used.

Recruiting Lead Users

The best way to identify lead users is to find customers who have extreme needs (*extreme users*),[28] although this can be difficult.[29] Manufacturers of hiking boots typically approach professional hikers and climbers who are dependent on high-quality hiking boots. After a small number of extreme users have been identified, further extreme users can be found through recommendations (a snowball sample). In FMCG, lead users are often identified through surveys and/or telephone interviews. For industrial goods the number of extreme users can be small if the customer base is limited. One indication of extreme users of industrial goods is that their equipment may fail more often, as they use it in more demanding environments. In such cases, referring to customer service records and talking to service engineers can be useful.

Extreme users are "extreme" in terms of the demands they place on products and services and the in-depth knowledge they have on how to adapt products to their specific personal and/or professional needs.[30] They are not necessarily current customers but are generally opinion leaders in a particular field.

Another type of lead users is *analogous users,* who come from a different sector but face issues similar to those faced by extreme users. For example, the packaging of high-quality decorative glass requires a similar level of attention to detail to the packaging of fragile electronic sensors. Since analogous users stem from completely different sectors there are no competitive issues at stake and there is a willingness to share and discuss their experiences with users from other industries.

It is essential to recruit lead users with the relevant know-how and also good networks. Establishing a relationship with lead users requires a lot of management time and effort, therefore it is important to identify the users with the strongest networks, which are invaluable when a product or service is launched. The greater the benefit a given lead user can obtain from an improved product or service, the more likely they are to directly assist in developing that product or service.[31]

Conducting Workshops with Lead Users

Once the lead users have been selected, a workshop with them will be arranged, normally at a company's site (see Box Case 7.5 for a typical example). It is important to tell everyone involved up front that the company may have a commercial interest in the ideas being discussed and to clarify the issue of intellectual property. Some companies offer monetary compensation to lead users, but this is unnecessary as most of them feel honored to be asked to share their know-how. It is common practice, however, to cover at least the expenses for attending the workshop.

Lead user workshops usually have six distinct steps:

1. A preliminary session with team-building exercises to introduce the lead users to each other.
2. The trends identified by the company are reviewed by the lead users.
3. Each of the main trends is assigned to a subgroup, which discusses the issues further and thinks of possible solutions.
4. Each subgroup presents their ideas and solutions to the entire group.
5. The group judges the originality, feasibility, and completeness of each idea.
6. The most promising ideas are selected and merged into one or more concepts.

During the workshop, facilitators need to identify all of the new product ideas, especially the more radical ones.

Development of Product Concepts

Once the most promising concepts have been selected, they need to be tested with a wider set of customers to check if the idea is relevant to the mainstream. This check is necessary, because innovators and early adopters differ from the bulk of users.[32] Concept testing can use experimentation (covered later in this chapter). "It is rare for a manufacturer to simply adopt a lead user innovation 'as is'. Instead, a new product concept that suits a manufacturer's needs and market is most often based on information gained from a number of lead users and in-house developers."[33] Although the original lead user technique concentrated on structured face-to-face workshops, some lead user groups are being run via the Internet and virtual communities (to be discussed next).

Box Case 7.5

Nubert Speaker Factory—Users as Sources of Innovation[34]

How would you describe the sound of a perfect loudspeaker? Traditionally, loud-speaker manufacturers developed their products in sound-proof laboratories, and isolated the user from the development process. But Günther Nubert, founder of Nubert Electronic GmbH, knows that sound is experienced subjectively—and there is no scientifically defined, objectively "perfect" sound. This is why he and his company place such emphasis on involving the user in product development.

In 2007, Roland Spiegler, responsible for Marketing and Sales at Nubert, launched "nuDays." These are 1–2 day events, where about 80 customers are invited to meet at the company's headquarters in Schwäbisch Gmünd in Germany, in order to get a real insight into the company and also to discuss the product features. "During the last nuDays in June 2009," says Roland Spiegler, "we had a special review of the new 'nuVero' series, and we also had some test sessions. For example, we tested and compared the new nuVeros with models from the older 'nuLine' series." Depending on the room and the surroundings, some customers felt the new sound was "brighter," whilst others felt it was "darker." In fact, rooms have a great impact on a loudspeaker's sound reproduction because some rooms dampen sound whereas others do not. The direct customer contact during nuDays is extraordinarily impor-tant for the development team. Spiegler says, "we now offer the nuVero with three different switches, which enables customers to customize the output in order to match the acoustics of their rooms, allowing fine tuning within +/−2 to 3 dB."

Spiegler continues, "we have always asked our customers for feedback, which is why there is a special feedback-card attached to every loudspeaker. It is combined with a prize draw, in order to increase the response rate. Tips and comments from customers submitted by e-mail and letters are directly forwarded to the respective department and we always contact the customer; a small thing but important in building relationships with our customers."

As the Nubert team like to say, you need four things: the perfect loudspeaker, technical knowledge, a high level of creativity, and a pair of well-trained ears—to listen to the voice of the customer. The next nuDay event is already scheduled for Autumn 2010.

VIRTUAL COMMUNITIES

Virtual communities are now an established part of our society, and a multitude of websites can help with issues as diverse as looking for a partner, coping with an illness, concentrating on various hobbies, and selecting and using a product. So companies need to use the Internet for market research and innovation.

Overview

Virtual communities, also known as *e-communities* or *online communities*, are groups of people with a common interest who interact via online newsletters, email, online networks, social networking sites, and chat rooms, rather than meeting face-to-face. The purpose of the communication can be for social, professional, educational, or any other purpose. Virtual communications (such as the ubiquitous Facebook) also supplement direct meetings between people who know each other. Virtual communities' members like having fast and easy contact with each other. Sharing tips, recommendations, and experiences of products and services is also vital for community members. Sometimes they even develop into so-called *brand communities,* where members share certain values and beliefs, have similar rituals and traditions, and also feel a certain level of responsibility regarding a brand.[35] Examples are users of iPhone, drivers of the Mini, or Harley Davidson bikers. They share a common passion for a specific product or service. For example, the UK transport company Eddie Stobart has an online fan club.

Applying Virtual Communities

The Internet can facilitate contact with customers in several ways[36] and offers companies the opportunity to involve creative people from outside their organization in product development[37]. Instead of short interactions with customers during market research, companies are now able to establish a continuous and ongoing dialog with groups of customers, who share interests, know-how, and values. Table 7.1 illustrates the main differences between user innovation in real and virtual environments and shows, for example, the critical difference regarding the role of the customer (from passive to active) and the intensity of the contact (one-way question versus two-way dialog).

Table 7.1   Differences between User Innovation in Real and Virtual Environments

	Traditional Perspective Real Environments	Co-Creation Perspective Virtual Environments
Innovation Perspective	Firm-centric	Customer-centric
Role of the Customer	Passive—customer voice as an input to create and test products	Active—customer as a partner in the innovation process
Direction of Interaction	One way—firm to customers	Two way—dialog with customers
Intensity of Interaction	Spot—on contingent basis	Continuous—back-and-forth dialog
Richness of Interaction	Focus on individual knowledge	Focus on social and experiential knowledge
Size and Scope of Audience	Direct interaction with current customers	Internat as well as direct interactions with prospects and potential customers

Source: Reproduced with permission of Elsevier from Sawhney, M., Verona, G. and Prandelli, E. "Collaborating to Create: The Internet as a Platform for Customer Engagement in Product Innovation," *Journal of Interactive Marketing*, Vol. 19, No. 4, 2005, pp. 1–15.

Within such customer groups, there is often a pool of expertise which was previously difficult to tap. Therefore, social media sites, blogs, and the like are important sources of data. Market research via the Internet can help companies answer key questions such as: "What are the latest trends in our customer base?"[38] For example, a manufacturer of aircraft seats could participate in a "frequent flyer" blog, where the comfort with different airlines and the latest trends in business travel are discussed. The question "What suggestions do you have for new flavors?" has been posted on the Internet by the German company Alfred Ritter GmbH & Co. This company, which manufactures the well-known Ritter Sport brand with its snap-open pack, use the suggestions collected for their "limited summer edition" square chocolate bars.

Choosing Communities and Recruiting Members

Virtual community members typically exhibit different levels of interest. Participation ranges from adding comments and blogs to a message board, to posting suggestions for product improvements, to even making significant suggestions on product design. Similar to traditional user clubs, virtual communities often split into cliques, or even separate to form new communities.

The members of communities normally have "intrinsic" motivation. They are not necessarily looking for rewards and contribute for the fun of it. They are not reluctant to share their ideas and issues like intellectual property are typically not on their agenda. Many members of virtual communities are entrepreneurial, well educated, and highly skilled. Research has shown how new members become more active and, as they become more committed, may also act as community leaders.[39] Some leading members may leave as other commitments increase or their interest wanes.

Companies need to decide which customers should be involved in new product development. Then it is important to identify the communities where such customers are active. Many companies have user groups, so the first step is to evaluate the customers who are particularly active on this platform. Marketing departments need to monitor online communities even though some have only a very short life. Once a number of communities have been identified, it is important to evaluate the quality of interaction and the amount of traffic on the site. Contact with virtual communities should be organized via the webmaster, because members often react negatively to unsolicited questions from outsiders. Contact through the webmaster also ensures that legal issues and potential payments are dealt with in a professional way.

Practicalities

When working with virtual communities, it is important to use the language of the members. Staff from marketing and research departments need to adapt to the communities and not the other way round.[40] Members of virtual communities normally have no monetary or other expectations. Nevertheless, it is essential to confirm this, so that members do not suddenly claim intellectual property rights, based on their contributions to product development. Then instead of financial rewards, early access to new product information, samples, and the possibility to participate in the market launch can all be used to motivate members' participation.[41]

Before starting discussions with user communities, it is important to allocate the resources for analyzing the expected inputs. Most participants expect direct feedback on their ideas and also want to be informed of the progress of product development. Ignoring this can jeopardize the relationship with a community.

Table 7.2 Examples of Virtual Communities Used in Product Development

Company	Products or Services	Usage of Virtual Communities
Frosta[a]	German manufacturer of high-quality frozen foods	Uses the Web 2.0 and weblogs to communicate with customers. Management, product developers, and other Frosta employees take active part in web discussions. Consumers are encouraged to comment on products and this has helped Frosta to increase their market share significantly.[b]
Kraft General Food[c]	Leading international producer of food products	Invites consumers to participate in choosing new types of Philadelphia cream cheese via the company website. The initiative has different names in different countries. In Germany, it is called "Käsemeister Phil sucht Ihre Philadelphia Wunschsorte" ("Master cheese maker Phil is looking for your wish"). Kraft also wants to link the brand more strongly to consumers.
IBM[d]	Supplier of PC hardware	Used a worldwide "innovation jam," in which 330,000 employees and many customers contributed their ideas and comments on topics such as energy, mobility, healthcare, and so on. The IBM platform was based on various Web 2.0 tools, and about 150,000 users from 104 countries submitted 46,000 ideas. These were then clustered, discussed in various groups, and 31 selected ideas are being implemented.
Linux[e]	Software supplier	The Linux system has been developed by a network of software specialists—connected via the Internet—and is constantly being improved.
Threadless[f]	U.S.-based online clothes company	Invites Internet community to develop T-shirts and to vote each week about the favorite one which is then produced and sold via the website.

Notes: [a] Handelsblatt (2007). Erfolgreiches Innovationsmanagement, Handelsblatt Consulting, 24.9.2007, B1–B8; [b] www.frostablog.de (accessed on 06.05.2009); [c] www.horizon.net. Philadelphia sucht den Dialog (accessed on 09.21.2009); [d] Hartmann, M. (2007). Das Internet als Marktplatz der Ideen. Handelsblatt Consulting, 24.9.2007, B2; [e] Lee, G.K., Cole, R.E. (2003). From a Firm-Based to a Community-Based Model of Knowledge Creation: The Case of the Linux Kernel Development. *Organization Science*, 4(6), 633–649; [f] Weingarten, M. (2007). Project Runway for the t-shirt crows. Business 2.0 Magazine, 18.06.2007.

If the community was created for a limited time period or for a specific product, it is important to ask the participants if they are willing to participate again, and to get their permission to store their personal data. Ideally, a long-term relationship with users can result. Table 7.2 gives examples of companies that successfully work with online communities.

The examples in Table 7.2 are all large companies, but smaller firms are also now using virtual communities for market research and product development purposes.

CROWDSOURCING

Overview

The term *crowdsourcing* (from crowd and outsourcing) stems from an article in the *Wired* magazine in 2006.[42] It has been defined as "the act of a company or institution taking a function once performed by employees and outsourcing it to an undefined (and generally large) network of people in the form of an open call."[43] It has become popular with businesses to describe the trend of leveraging the mass collaboration by Web 2.0 technologies to achieve specific business goals.[44] However, crowdsourcing is fundamentally different to wikonomics, because it does not rely on market signals or open calls. It is also clearly different from regular outsourcing, because a task is given to an *undefined* public crowd, not to specific people or a specific company selected beforehand.

Crowdsourcing represents a significant change in the relationship between firms and their customers. Customers are now seen as "co-workers" who contribute to creating value in the company. Examples are Dell's "ideastorm" and the "innocentive" platform run by Procter & Gamble. People contribute to these sites "not because they want a reward, but because they are passionate" about the brand.[45]

Application

Many of the tasks posted on crowdsourcing websites replicate traditional market research activities.[46] However, real crowdsourcing is different.[47] For example, highly complex technological problems are often posted to a "crowd," rather than assigning them to a specialist supplier, whose core competence was in the technology in question. Today, problems are often solved by outsiders who respond to the posted problems and give their time free because of the "personal challenge," and to beat the others working on the same problem in being the first with a solution. Crowdsourcing is also used to find solutions to current customer problems. This can be part of a strategy to outsource mainly internal tasks to save money; or in the cases where a company cannot solve a problem internally.

Crowdsourcing is applied as eight steps, as illustrated by Figure 7.2.

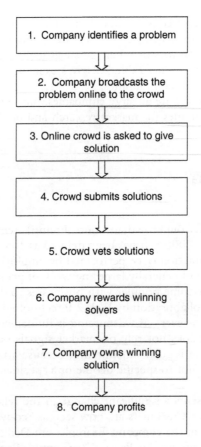

Figure 7.2   The Crowdsourcing Flowchart
Source: Brabham, D. http://darenbrabham.com, crowdsourcing researcher. Used with permission.

Although the concept of crowdsourcing is relatively new, it is being used extensively and some start-up companies are solely based on the idea (that is, they post problems to the crowd and then sell the solutions to interested companies for a higher price). Tools using collective intelligence have performed better than theorists can explain.[48] However, it is not yet clear which types of crowdsourcing will survive in the long-run.

EXPERIMENTATION AND PROTOTYPING

Overview

Whenever new products or services are being developed, it is essential to test ideas with customers from the start and often time and time again. The most common way for doing this with manufactured products is *rapid prototyping*, where new technologies mean that it is now easy and cost effective to produce physical models and trial software. Service products can also be tested using rapid prototyping; for example, Bank of America has test branches where new services are tested with customers and experiments are conducted to see how different service attributes impact customer satisfaction (for example, how waiting time influences customers' perceptions). Many companies check customers' reactions to prototypes. *Experimentation* goes further in that different aspects of products or services are varied and the resulting changes to customers' reactions are studied. Tests and experiments can be conducted as soon as product features have been identified and prototypes have been made and so it is now possible to make such test in the early stages of NPD. "Central to experimentation is the use of models, prototypes, controlled environments, and computer simulations that allow innovators to reflect, improvise, and evaluate the many ideas that are generated in organizations."[49]

Another reason for using experiments and prototypes is that users often do not have much technical knowledge and so cannot imagine possible solutions unless they are presented with mock-ups (see Box Case 7.6). Service products are intangible and so prototypes (within the sort of environment in which the full service will be delivered) help customers to generate more ideas. Working with prototypes allows innovators (from inside the company) and customers (from outside the company) to interact in a more productive way.[50] During this interaction, physical prototypes that can be touched, tried, and tested generate more insights than surveys of users' perceived needs.

Sometimes, experimentation and prototyping is used as an extension of the lead user approach, where observations are conducted to see how customers react to tangible product ideas in a realistic scenario. This may sometimes require expensive prototyping equipment, but most of the time experimentation is a quick and easy way to pilot things and to gain detailed insights into what works and what does not. The California-based consultancy Ideo is well-known for its ability to quickly prototype products and services.

Application

There are several points to consider when conducting experiments and using prototypes.[51] A *test protocol*, a list of the different product or service features that need to be tested with customers, is essential. Experiments isolate the variable that needs to be tested, because results get confusing if more than one variable is varied at one time[52] (for example, if you change the color and shape of a product at the same time instead of only the color or the shape). It is important to make sure that no outside influences can jeopardize the experiment (and therefore so-called *controlled environments* are needed) and that employees responsible for the development do not bias the findings by subjectively supporting the prototype of their personal choice. On the other hand, in controlled environments customers may behave differently to how they would in their natural environment.

There is a well-known story about when Sony conducted workshops where young people were shown the Walkman product for the first time. In discussions, the teenagers were asked which colors they preferred for the product and groups expressed a preference for bright colors. At the end of the session, attendees were told they would be given a Walkman as a reward for their participation and they could choose which one they wanted. From the different colors on offer, Sony engineers observed that black was the most popular and not the bright colors.[53] Also companies need to check that the results of testing apply to the real world and not just to the customers who took part in the prototyping session.

Box Case 7.6

Volvo Cars—American Women and the XC90[54]

For its first sports utility vehicle (SUV), managers at the Volvo Car group recognized that there was a lack of information on female drivers' perceptions of SUVs and decided it would be useful to involve a group of female drivers in product development. Some of the personnel involved in the project were skeptical, as they regarded the involvement of customers as "unscientific" but, nevertheless, a group of 24 women from California were recruited through a former Volvo employee who, with her technical and project management experience, was selected to moderate the group's meetings.

The group met with Volvo personnel every few months throughout the three-year project and informally discussed their views on SUVs. The presence of Volvo managers at each of the meetings was perceived positively by the women, as it indicated that the company was taking their views seriously. It quickly emerged that a relatively large engine was important but so was fuel efficiency, and it was perceived that the design of the car should not be "intimidating." To ensure that the discussions on exterior and interior design would be as effective as possible, early in the project Volvo showed the group a full-size plastic prototype and received feedback such as "not intimidating, yet still looks safe." At the group's final meeting, each member had the opportunity to test drive the final version of the XC90.

It is interesting to note that although the women were paid only $50 expenses for attending each two-hour meeting, attendance was good and 16 women remained involved from the start to the finish. In the final XC90, Volvo implemented a number of the group's ideas, including the "split-tail" boot, some of the points about the exterior design, the choice of interior textiles, and the fuel efficiency.

ADVANTAGES AND LIMITATIONS

Involving the user, whether via the lead user technique or any of the other approaches we have discussed, offers a variety of advantages and so this is the reason for their increased use in market research and new product development departments in recent years. As the different ways to involve are in many ways similar (and they are often combined—for example, virtual communities are often given software prototypes to trial), we will consider together the advantages and limitations for all of the methods for involving the user.

Advantages

Cost and Time Reductions

Contact with users is often cheaper and faster than conventional market research. The results can also be significant. For example, the companies that apply lead user technique have found that time to generate innovative ideas is shorter because of the clear steps in the method.[55] Thus, users can help speed up the development process, as a large number of ideas can be generated within a short time frame.

Virtual communities have an additional advantage, because these offer very low-cost access to users with the possibility to get in touch 24 hours a day, 7 days a week. Payments for ideas are not always required even in crowdsourcing projects where a particular problem needs to be solved. Prototyping also saves costs, in that the risk of poor market acceptance can be mitigated.

Increased Creativity

The involvement of users generally stimulates the creative processes within a company. For example, lead user workshops bring together very different users, stimulate intense discussions, and are normally hugely motivational for the company employees that are able to take part. When virtual communities are used, companies can profit from a wider range of know-how and talents compared with their own organization, because a huge amount of "resources" outside of the firm can be tapped. User communities enable direct communication and collaboration with large numbers of customers from which rich information can be gleaned.

High Customer Acceptance

The concepts derived from working intensively with users are often innovative and practical solutions to complex problems. Community members and lead user participants "declare" their approval to a new concept, business structure, or product[56] which is an ideal base for the product launch. This means that market failures are less likely (see Box Case 7.7). There is already clear evidence that lead user workshops generate products which have higher sales.[57] Market research via user communities also helps increase customers' identification with the brand and/or product. Allowing customers and users to test products at an early stage means that it is still possible to make changes to the final product or service. This increases customer acceptance still further.

> **Box Case 7.7**
>
> ### Unconventional Films—Taking the Pulse of the Movie Market[58]
>
> In 2003, Vernon Mortensen, Kelly Parks, and Neil Trusso founded *Unconventional Films, LLC* in Los Angeles. It is a full-service production company specializing in genre movies, TV, and new media films. The company takes an unconventional approach to the movie business. For instance, they produced different web series on the Internet. Vernon explains, "we are committed to being a pioneer in the Internet distribution World. If you don't provide what the market wants, you are out of business. Some ideas may come from people interested in watching a particular movie. We take note of such ideas." How?
>
> Vernon and his team have regular meetings with distributors to find out what they are looking for. Distributors are the direct customers and Vernon says, "distributors need a bankable movie star, they need to have a certain amount of production value and so forth. If we wouldn't offer it to them, they simply wouldn't accept it."
>
> Currently, distributors are asking for sports movies and the South American market is starting to pick up. "Without the input from distributors," says Verson, "we wouldn't have decided to make a boxing movie in the middle of Mexico City." The latest movie is called "Chamaco" and features the boxing champion Marco Antonio Barrera along with the film stars Martin Sheen, Michael Madsen, Alex Perea, and others. Eighty percent of actors are Latin Americans and in July 2010, it will be released to AMC Theatres across the U.S.

Improved Internal Processes

Involving users in the innovation process has several advantages for the internal NPD processes as well. Overall, user communities require a fundamental change to the innovation process, because it involves customers in a totally new way compared with traditional focus groups, interviews, or surveys (the customer's role changes from being passive to active). At the same time, customers contribute to better NPD performance,[59] due to the reduction in resources needed and the quality of results (as described in the sections above). Furthermore, the potential for conflict between R&D and marketing departments is reduced because everyone is involved in the dialog with users and can see how the product requirements are based on true customer insights. In a nutshell, user communities can be turned into a strategic asset by companies for their new product development.

Limitations

Although user communities are becoming more popular and are increasingly used in new product development, there are five main disadvantages which need to be kept in mind. The limitations can then be addressed (often by comparing the results of involving the user with the techniques discussed in other chapters of this book).

Time, Effort, and Experience Required

As explained earlier, identifying and recruiting lead users is difficult and time-consuming. Prototyping and experiments may also be costly. (On the other hand, the results can save money being invested in the wrong product or service.)

NPD teams are often poorly skilled to conduct lead user workshops. Involving users requires experience and always carries the risk of becoming too dependent on outsiders. If, for example, the lead user process itself is facilitated by external consultants, this can be dangerous, because "understanding the customer is one function that should not be outsourced."[60]

Nonrepresentative Users

Lead users and members of virtual communities are not always comparable to the main customer base. Thus, companies must not rely too much on the strong opinion of a minority and neglect the needs of other customers. This has been an issue for medical manufacturers that have based their new product development on the recommendations of leading surgeons.[61] It can also be difficult if customer needs are so sophisticated that a company is no longer able or willing to fulfill them.[62] The answers gained from crowdsourcing, where companies deal with an unknown online group, may also not correspond to the needs of the general public. Therefore, user involvement needs to be followed up with more market research to test the acceptance with "typical" customers, to estimate potential sales, pricing and so on. As the number of concepts generated through involving the user can be large, the costs of this type of evaluation can be high.

Techniques Do Not Apply

Involving the user sometimes does not work for highly complex developments such as chemical, pharmaceutical, biotech, or large mechanical products.

Not every question within a product development process can be solved on a "virtual" basis, because virtual contact cannot always replace a direct contact. This is especially true because perceptions and opinions are strongly supported by body language and tone of voice, but both of them cannot be captured in virtual environments. Based on this, user communities are often criticized for only developing incremental ideas and no radical innovations.

Incremental Ideas

A general problem when involving users in the innovation process is their tendency to focus on existing product solutions instead of suggesting creative new approaches. This can be an issue with virtual communities. The results are also criticized for being nonrepresentative, because lead user workshops take place outside of the normal working environment and because opinions in virtual communities cannot be double-checked and are in many applications from anonymous customers.

Competitive and IP Risks

It is also important to consider that user communities are likely to be observed by the competition, so such platforms carry a certain risk for "industry spies" and "malicious contributions." The absence of legal agreements or nondisclosure contracts is a risk in crowdsourcing projects. Legal claims for the exploitation of consumer ideas should therefore be managed in the very beginning to avoid any complications.

SUMMARY

Involving the user is still in its infancy but new opportunities will continue to arise. "The combination of social computing tools and an understanding of social networks will allow marketing researchers to build new types of research communities, in which respondents interact not only with the researchers but with the clients and most fertilely with each other."[63] This chapter has shown the following:

- There is a vast potential for learning about hidden needs within the existing and potential customer base of companies. Customer involvement can be achieved at various stages within the product development, from idea creation over co-development to testing prototypes.
- Lead users are a time-consuming but very efficient method to gather deep insights into the needs and requirements of "early adopters" and of those customers who might even know more about the product than the company that offers it.
- User communities based on virtual platforms on the Internet are an increasingly popular way to get easy access to a high number of customers and to tap on their needs and requirements. It is important to establish an ideal user profile and to select relevant communities. Ideally, a company-owned platform is established, especially for open calls and crowdsourcing processes.
- The advantages and limitations of user involvement have to be carefully considered, but evidence so far suggests that user involvement will become even more important in future.

MANAGEMENT RECOMMENDATIONS

- Determine the areas where involving the user can improve your new product development. (Remember: customers cannot solve every issue in new product development.)
- Select the customers and lead users carefully, because not every customer has the potential to positively contribute to the development process.
- Evaluate the effort of applying virtual communities with the benefits regarding the outcome, because the resources needed to handle the users are very often underestimated in the beginning.
- Develop ways of linking user involvement to market research and other aspects of new product development.

RECOMMENDED READING

1. Davis, R. E., "From Experience: The Role of Market Research in the Development of New Consumer Products," *Journal of Product Innovation Management*, Vol. 10, No. 2, 1993, pp. 309–317. [A frequently cited academic publication which provides a good introduction to user involvement.]
2. Surowiecki, J., *The Wisdom of Crowds: Why the Many Are Smarter than the Few and How Collective Wisdom Shapes Business, Economies, Societies and Nations.* Garden City: Doubleday, 2004. [This book explains the value of the collective wisdom of crowds.]
3. Von Hippel, E., *The Sources of Innovation.* New York: Oxford University Press, 1988. [A standard innovation text which is frequently quoted and gives useful insights.]

8 CONJOINT ANALYSIS

> In marketing, conjoint experiments have frequently been carried out to measure consumer preferences for the attributes of various products or services.[1]

INTRODUCTION

Before making a purchase decision, a customer will often compare several products, each of which is likely to have a different price and a different set of features. A more expensive product is likely to have higher performance but it may be visually less appealing. Another product will offer a combination of features with less performance but a more attractive design and reasonable price. For example, we might like the biggest LCD television, with the built-in DVD recorder but we may only be able to afford the mid-range products, which have some good features but not everything we would like. Before making their final decision, customers make subconscious assessment of the range of products on offer. *Conjoint analysis* (CA) is the method that allows us to understand this subconscious assessment—the way customers compare and assess different services or products.

This chapter on conjoint analysis covers the following topics:

- The history of conjoint analysis.
- An overview of the technique.
- How the technique is applied and analyzed.
- The limitations of CA.

HISTORY OF CONJOINT ANALYSIS

In the early 1960s, scholars from psychology started to explore the subtle nature of how decisions are made by individuals. In particular, they were interested in the *trade-offs* that need to be made when an optimum choice is not available. In deciding between different possibilities we are often forced to make a trade-off (a compromise), in choosing, for example, a product that we can afford but does not have every feature we would like. When we are faced with complex decisions, we weigh up the possibilities, either consciously or subconsciously, and reach our decision. To understand decision-making, psychologists started to apply mathematical modeling techniques. In 1964, Professors R. Duncan Luce (University of Pennsylvania) and John W. Tukey (Princeton University) published the results of their research on the psychology of decision-making[2] and the value of this work was quickly recognized by market researchers.

The first use of Luce and Tukey's work for market research was in 1971.[3] By the end of the 1970s, this technique had become highly sophisticated and widely known as conjoint analysis.[4] The term conjoint is based on *to join* or *become joined together* and symbolizes how people weigh up several factors at the same time—typically product features and price. Between 1986 and 1991, about 1,000 commercial projects are reported to have used conjoint analyses in Europe alone.[5] Today, the technique has found new applications, such as in assessing the quality of customer relationships.[6]

OVERVIEW OF THE TECHNIQUE

Every customer considering the purchase of a product or service will assess it and the rest of the market offering based on features, performance, and price. For example, a table in a furniture showroom will trigger customers to consider material, size, shape, the possibilities to extend the table, the brand, and, of course, the price. The important questions for market researchers (and product developers) are *which* factors trigger most interest and *which combinations* are preferred by the customers. The factors that customers consider are termed the *product attributes* (for example, size, brand, and price) and the *attribute levels* are the different values in the market offering (for example, the different sizes of table and the different prices on offer). If the ideal combination of attributes was always available at the price we could afford, all purchasing decisions would be easy but of course they are not (as anyone who has made a major purchase such as a new car, or a house will know). The central idea behind conjoint analysis is that interviewees are offered a range of realistic alternatives, each with different attributes and attribute levels. In choosing between the alternatives, respondents provide data from which the key characteristics of their purchasing decisions can be identified using mathematical modeling.

The first step is for market researchers to identify all of the attributes relevant to purchasing decisions. This necessitates a competitive analysis, to identify the full range of attributes and attribute levels available on the market. Too often, marketing departments have only a superficial knowledge of customer needs and hidden needs are often overlooked. Considering the attributes abstractly, each can be described as a dimension (for example, the "finish" of a table) with a specific range of possibilities (attribute levels—in this case the range of surface finishes available). Conjoint analysis considers a "product"

	Birch	Pine	Oak	*MEDIAN*
Plain Wood	5	6	4	*5*
French-polished	2	3	1	*2*
MEDIAN	*3.5*	*4.5*	*2.5*	

(Finish)

Figure 8.1   Trade-Off Method Matrix for a Table (Ranking)

to be a combination of different attributes and levels. Obviously, there could be hundreds of combinations of attributes and attribute levels for a table (and even more for a more complex product or service), and so it is also important to identify the most usual and meaningful combinations from a customer's perspective.

The next step in conjoint analysis is to present the potential customer with a number of combinations (so-called *stimuli*) and to have them to choose their preferences. To keep things simple, not every attribute level will be offered and respondents will compare and evaluate a limited number of combinations. There are various ways to do this and Figure 8.1 illustrates the *two-factor method* (or *trade-off method*). We will assume that customers are asked to evaluate a table based on only two attributes: the type of wood (birch, pine, or oak) and the finish (French-polished or simple plain wood). Given the two levels of finish and the three types of wood, the respondent has six different tables to choose from (shown in the gray area in the matrix). In the trade-off method, respondents rank their preferences from 1 (most attractive combination) to 6 (most unattractive combination).

The matrix shows that a French-polished oak table is the respondent's most favored combination (ranked "1"), a French-polished table made of birch is ranked "2," and a French-polished pine table is ranked "3." Since these first three preferences are all French-polished, it is evident that the interviewee puts more emphasis on "finish" than on "type of wood." The median value[7] on the right-hand side of the matrix also shows that the French-polished tables have a median ranking of "2" versus "5" for plain wood. Concerning the type of wood, we see that the interviewee prefers oak (median "2.5") to birch ("3.5") and is least attracted to pine ("4.5"). Trade-off matrices allow us to interpret a customer's preferences. When a number of respondents have given their preferences, it is possible to look at the purchasing tendencies across a group.

As ranking is an ordinal measure (see Chapter 2) it cannot be assumed that the distances between the ranks are equal. For example, the distance between ranks "1" and "2" may be different from the distance between the ranks "5" and "6." When collecting ranking data, companies explore additional aspects in order to better understand why and how preferences differ (see Box Case 8.1).

Box Case 8.1

Bentley Motors Limited—Identifying Customer Preferences[8]

The British automotive manufacturer *Bentley Motors Limited* is renowned for its crafts-manship of cars. "Bentley Mulliner" is the specialist personal commissioning department for Bentley and is known for handcrafted excellence by turning customers' desires and dreams into reality (for example, delivering a refrigerated bottle cooler, an extended wheelbase, or a fully functional mobile office).

Kiran Parmar is responsible for Bentley's global research and concept planning and overlooks the Mulliner unit from a market research perspective. Given the high level of customization offered, customers are faced with many options and so Kiran needed to understand the decision-making process from the customer's point of view. For instance, what does the customer value when selecting carpets for the car? And what is the importance of each product attribute when making the final decision?

For this project, Bentley first used a survey to identify the key attributes for carpets, such as quality, practicality, durability, luxury, and style. Based on this, Bentley selected different types of carpet and the marketing team presented five samples customers. The options included synthetic carpets, deep pile carpets, Wilton, lambswool, and woven silk. Based on the first research phase, Bentley knew the key attributes of each alternative. Now, by asking customers to rank the five samples from 1 (attractive) to 5 (unattractive), the marketing department developed an understanding of the impact of each attribute in the buying decision. Given the limitations of analyzing ranking data, Kiran also asked open-ended questions in the interview to shed light on the rankings. "I asked 'how important is practicality?' or 'is style just a by-product of having a luxury feel to you?' By exploring the similarities and differences of carpet types, I could understand the crucial factors and how they are perceived by customers," says Kiran.

Today, the marketing department is able to clearly distinguish between their customer groups, based on the preferences identified. The manufacturer is amazed by the results of this research: the well-established "traditional market segment" has an exclusive preference for lambswool, Wilton, as well as silk. In the future, Bentley will only present these options to this type of customer and will thus reduce the number of alternatives for carpets customers must choose between when individualizing their new Bentley.

Although it is simple to collect, ranking data are not recommended because of their limitations.[9] Most conjoint studies collect data on interval scales, which give more insights. Continuing our previous example of the type of wood and finish for a table, we would ask the respondent to rate each of the six tables on a scale of 1–100 in terms of "attractiveness" (1 being "unattractive" and 100 representing "very attractive"). For each wood-finish combination, ratings would be collected, with French-polished oak being rated "85" and plain birch "30," as shown in Figure 8.2.

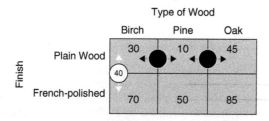

Figure 8.2   Trade-Off Method Matrix for a Table (Rating)

The numbers in the matrix are the *utility values*—ranging from 10 to 85 and the unit of measurement is referred to as a *utile*. Similar to Figure 8.1, the respondent has the same order of preferences but based on the utility values, we are now in the position to compute the differences between attribute levels (shown in white and black circles). The difference between the oak/plain wood (45 utiles) and pine/plain wood (10 utiles) is 35 utiles. Only the type of wood can explain the difference, as the finish is the same in both options. So, the respondent prefers oak to pine. The same can be said for birch, since it is 20 utiles more attractive than pine. We can also say that replacing pine with birch (+20 utiles) is perceived to be a greater difference than replacing birch with oak (+15 utiles). Comparing birch/plain with birch/French-polish it can be seen that the utility difference is 40. Finally, since changing the type of finish carries greater value (40 utiles) than changing the type of wood (35 utiles maximum), the attribute "finish" is deemed more important than the attribute "type of wood" by the respondent.

Products and services are typically compared using more than two attributes and this means that respondents have to state their preferences for "type of wood" versus "finish" (as in our example), as well as attributes such as "brand," "speed of delivery," "design," and so on. Therefore, the more attributes and attribute levels being considered, the more combinations for the respondent to evaluate. Calculating utility differences follows the same principle as discussed with Figure 8.2, but the increased number of combinations quickly turns our simplified example into a complex statistical exercise that goes beyond the scope of this book.[10]

Overall, conjoint analysis allows us to understand the trade-off decisions that customers make in purchasing and to identify the value (utility) they associate with different attributes. Importantly, it can also allow us to estimate the values placed on breakthrough features, based on analyzing hidden needs.

with N

APPLYING THE TECHNIQUE

Process

There are three main steps to effective conjoint analysis—preparation, application, and analysis—and (throughout the rest of this chapter) we will explain each step[11] using a real example.

Preparation

Identifying Customer Needs

In 2004, a leading manufacturer of washing machines, which for reasons of confidentiality, we call *WashMachineCo.*,[12] wanted to develop a new washing machine for its main customer segment. First a survey was conducted, but the results were disappointing, because it only verified what was already known: for example, that "quality" (clean washing and a long product working lifetime), "price," "ecology" (energy- or water consumption), and "brand" were all perceived as important. Next, focus groups elicited needs like "low noise" when washing and spin-drying, "identifying particularly dirty clothing," "avoiding shrinkage," and "faster cycle time" for the washing process. However, the marketing department at *WashMachineCo.* already knew these needs.

Finally, innovative repertory grid interviews and ethnographic market research were conducted with consumers. This uncovered several further needs. Repertory grid technique elicited the "sorting" of dirty clothes according to the temperature at which they should be washed, the "ease of ironing," the "folding" of clothes and not having to "reload" clothes from the washer into the tumble dryer. Ethnographic market research was used to look at "cleaning" in detail and put washing into the context of the activities conducted directly before and after washing. The following further needs were identified: "help" with the selection of the program, "storing" of washing materials (washing powder, fabric softener, decalcification), and also the "sorting" or "keeping clothes apart" (this relates to gender, since some religions strictly separate the clothes of men and women before washing). Through contextual interviews, it was found that if a colored piece of clothing was put into white washing by accident, a "warning signal" would be helpful.

In the professional segment, discussions with lead users were conducted. Investigations with rugby clubs, laundry companies, and big hotels showed that "productivity," "profitability," "reliability," "ease of service," ability to wash "large quantities" were additional needs.

By conducting qualitative research, *WashMachineCo.* identified several new criteria (attributes) which were understood from the customer standpoint, and also the potential levels of the new attributes were determined. It should be noted that, in contrast to *WashMachineCo.*'s approach, many marketing departments simply use the attributes they know—this limits the effectiveness of conjoint analysis.

Although several new attributes had been identified, their relative importance was unclear and conjoint analysis was used. As part of the preparation of conjoint analysis, an overview of product attributes (features) was prepared, with short explanations (from a customer perspective) of the attributes and their different levels (see Table 8.1).

Experience shows that the descriptions of product attributes must be carefully worded, otherwise respondents may misinterpret attributes and this will negatively influence the quality of conjoint analysis.

An attribute represents a *dimension* of a product or service on which customers base their purchasing decisions. In the case of *WashMachineCo.*, the attributes "price," "ecological performance," and "quality" are fairly generic and they could relate to a different product such as a car. Unfortunately many conjoint studies only analyze generic, somewhat superficial attributes. Therefore, it is essential to identify all possible attributes with approaches such as repertory grid.

Determining the Attribute Levels

Attributes of products and services are called "dimensions" because they have different levels which need to be determined. It is very important to ensure that the description of attributes and their levels are clear and unambiguous to respondents. Equally, the range of attribute levels that are selected should be appropriate for the attribute without overloading respondents with too many levels to consider.

Simplistic level descriptions such as "expensive" or "cheap" (attribute: price) as well as "high consumption" and "low consumption" (attribute: energy consumption) are poor, because they are subjective. Therefore, the descriptions of the levels should be specific and meaningful from a customer's standpoint. Unfortunately, many companies rush this stage and the attribute level descriptions they use are ambiguous (for example, "excellent customer service") and it is impossible to determine attribute levels after a conjoint study has been completed.

Single attributes can be bipolar, where only two realistic dimensions are imaginable (for example, a left or right-hand drive car). Other attributes such as "color," can theoretically have hundreds of tones which could be used as levels. Too many levels are impractical in conjoint studies and so not every level will be included. Often, it is possible to select a representative section of levels, for example, red, yellow, green, and blue might be sufficient for "color." Focus groups can be used to check that the most appropriate levels are selected and can also help ensure that the attribute descriptions are clear (because, by definition, hidden needs will lead to attributes that are not immediately obvious to customers).

Product experts should also advise on how many attribute levels are needed, as they can decide where more levels are needed to uncover nuances in the way customers evaluate services and products. Consumers will feel overwhelmed if they are confronted with too many different levels. The choice of the number of levels is about balancing the volume of information to be obtained against the time required by the respondent (and the complexity of the task they are given). The optimal balance should be determined through pilot studies. In practice, three levels for each attribute is a good compromise, because this covers the range of a dimension and offers a middle value.

Table 8.1 lists ten attributes and their levels from the washing machine research. The manufacturer decided to base the "energy consumption" levels on European Union regulations for electrical household goods as householders are becoming familiar with this. This is a scale of "A" to "G" but only "A," "C,"

Table 8.1 Attribute (Definitions and Levels) Table

Attribute	Definition	Levels
1) Noise	Level of noise while washing (excluding spin-drying)	A (quiet; below 50 db)
		C (average; between 50–60 db)
		E (loud; more than 60 db)
2) Storage	Storage and organization of washing materials (powder, stain remover, fabric softener, and calcification)	Integrated storage unit for washing powders in the washing machine
		Storage next to the washing machine
		No storage
3) Energy consumption	Ecological consideration of variable electricity costs	A (low good; below 0.19 kWh/kg clothes)
		C (average; 0.23 kWh–0.27 kWh/kg clothes)
		E (high; 0.31 kWh–0.35 kWh/kg clothes)
4) Capacity	The maximum weight of a washing load, measured in kilogram of dry clothes	Small (3–4 kg dry weight)
		Medium (5–6 kg dry weight)
		Large (7–8 kg dry weight)
5) Help instructions	Clear simple instructions on a display of the best program for a particular wash	Detailed, graphic instructions are provided on a display
		Short instructions are provided on a display
		No instructions are given
6) Expected product working lifetime	Length of the expected life (number of years in use)	25 years
		10 years
		5 years
7) Washing result	Quality of the washing process	Washing result A (very good)
		Washing result C (average)
		Washing result E (poor)
8) Washing speed	Time saving due to fast washing programs	All washing programs are faster
		Some programs are faster
		Washing speeds are standard
9) Water consumption	Ecological consideration or variable monthly water costs	A (low)
		C (average)
		E (high)
10) Brand	Name of Manufacturer	Internationally established brand
		Nationally established brand
		No-name

and "E" were selected. The attributes in Table 8.1 are a mix of known needs and less obvious ones. For example, the attribute "help instructions" emerged from observations and context interviews where researchers saw post-it notes on washing machines, marking the most frequently used washing programs. These notes were typically attached by women, so that their husbands are able to operate the machine in the event of them not being around. Similarly, relatives provided such notes for pensioners. Appending the attribute table with such examples in the form of notes or photographs can help in deciding which attributes should be included in the conjoint study.

Selecting Attribute-level Combinations

A set of the attributes, ten in our example, with specific combinations characterizes a complete product. Not all combinations are realistic and, for example, a washing machine would not have the performance on every attribute and the lowest price. Therefore, not every attribute-levels combination needs to be presented to the respondent—unrealistic combinations need to be excluded (see Box Case 8.2).

Box Case 8.2

IKEA—Excluding Unrealistic Combinations[13]

The importance of products that are manufactured in an environmentally friendly way has been clear for years. IKEA, the Swedish furniture manufacturer and retailer, focuses on environmentally friendly manufacturing and was interested in the influence of sustainable wood (with an eco-label) on the purchasing of a table (model SÖRGAARDEN). Interviews with 258 customers in Norway and the UK were conducted based on conjoint analysis.

The table considered had many attributes but, to match the focus of the study, only three were selected: "price" (three levels: "base price"/"plus 10 percent"/"plus 25 percent"), type of wood (two levels: "birch"/"pine"), and "eco-label" (two levels: "yes"/"no"). This gave 12 combinations, but two were found to be unrealistic: the combination of no-eco-label with a 25 percent higher price; similarly, an eco-label table and the base price were eliminated. Both combinations could theoretically be offered in birch as well as in pine, but this would give four unrealistic combinations. Excluding these from the study reduced the number of combinations to eight. This made the conjoint analysis realistic, easier, and faster for interviewees to respond.

Interestingly, the study showed that customers in England were willing to pay 16 percent more for a table with an eco-label, whereas customers in Norway were only willing to pay 2 percent more.

Application

Selection and Presentation of Stimuli

During a conjoint-based interview, stimuli in the form of attribute-level combinations can be presented to the respondent in different ways. The *trade-off* or *two-factor*

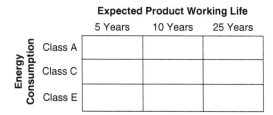

Figure 8.3   Trade-Off Method (Washing Machine)

method is illustrated in Figure 8.3. It is easy to understand and to answer, with respondents comparing two attributes at a time (for example, "Expected Product Working Lifetime" and "Energy Consumption"). In the figure, each of the two attributes has three levels and the respondent needs to assign rankings from "1" to "9" in the matrix. In real purchasing decisions, customers consider all attributes and so comparing only two at a time can appear artificial. Also, although trade-off matrices are easy for the respondent to fill out, a large number of them are needed (since each attribute has to be compared with every other attribute[14]). There is a risk that respondents will become bored and simply write the same rankings into successive matrices, with, for example, starting with the most preferred rank in the top right corner and ending with the least preferred option in the bottom left.

In contrast, in the *full profile method* respondents consider a full set of attributes, rather than just two at a time. Figure 8.4 shows the profile of a washing machine with six attributes (selected from Table 8.1). More than six attributes should not be presented to the interviewee in the full profile method because psychologists have found that individuals cannot comprehend more than six pieces of information at one time.[15] When interviewees are overloaded with information, they subconsciously adopt coping strategies and consider only 2–3 attributes in their decision.

The *pair-wise comparison* approach makes it easier for interviewees to decide on their preferences. Two profiles are presented at once and the respondents first give their preferences and then give a rating on the scale. With real products, customers have to consider every attribute simultaneously at once[16] and so the six that are listed in the profiles on the cards need to be rotated through the full list of attributes to be realistic. Changing the order of the attributes also helps prevent respondents from being biased by the position of an attribute on the profile cards. Depending on the number of profiles, it is advisable for the interviewee to first sort the profiles roughly into an order of preference. Afterwards, a specific rating for each profile is made, for example, using the scale "2" ("very good") to "–2" ("very poor") shown in Figure 8.5.

For a typical conjoint study with three attributes with three levels each resulting in 3x3x3=3^3 = 27 profiles, it is possible to present every profile to the interviewee for evaluation. In this case, we would talk of a *full factorial design*.

- Quiet when in use (Class A, below 50 db)
- Energy consumption: average (Class C, 0.23 kWh—0.27 kWh/kg clothes)
- High water consumption (Class E)
- Expected product working life: 10 years
- Storage possibility of washing material next to the washing machine
- No support instructions are given

Figure 8.4   Full Profile Method for a Washing Machine

• Quiet when in use (Class A, below 50 db) • Energy consumption: average (Class C, 0.23 kWh—0.27 kWh/kg clothes) • High water consumption (Class E) • Expected product working life: 10 years • Storage possibility of washing material next to the washing machine • No support instructions are given	• Loud when in use (Class E, more than 60 db) • Energy consumption: very good (Class A, below 0.19 kWh/kg clothes) • Low water consumption (Class A) • Expected product working life: 5 years • No storage possibility of washing materials • Support instructions are provided when choosing the program on the display

–2	–1	0	1	2

Figure 8.5   Full Profile—Pair-wise Comparison for Washing Machines

However, when more complex products are being considered, the number of profiles is too many for every one to be rated by the respondent.

For a product with six attributes, each with three levels there are $3^6 = 729$ possible profiles and the full factorial design method is impractical. The alternative is the *fractional factorial design*, where only a "fraction" of all theoretically possible profiles are presented to the interviewees. In our examples, it is easy to recognize that some of the profiles would be very similar. Imagine we would first present the profile pair of Figure 8.5 to the respondent. Next, we would replace the profile on the left with a profile which is identical except the "expected product working lifetime" is "5 years" (instead of "10"). As the profile on the right stays the same, the overall stimulus is too similar to the previous one. Therefore, *orthogonal* profiles need to be selected, that is, the ones that are as diverse as possible.[17] In addition, every attribute level needs to be included in at least one profile, to provide balanced stimuli. Selection of orthogonal attribute-level combinations is a complex process[18] that is conducted with a software package (for example, PASW [formerly SPSS][19]).

WashMachineCo. wanted to investigate ten attributes with three levels and this would result in over 50,000 combinations! Table 8.2 illustrates the 27 representative profiles selected using software. In the first row the ten attributes are

Table 8.2 Orthogonal Design for Washing Machine Research

Washing machine profiles	1 Noise	2 Storage	3 Energy consumption	4 Capacity	5 Instructions	6 Working lifetime	7 Washing result	8 Washing speed	9 Water consumption	10 Brand
#1	Quiet	Next to	Low	Large	Short	10	Very good	All	Average	No-name
#2	Loud	Next to	Average	Large	None	25	Average	All	High	Internat.
#3	Average	None	Average	Large	Detailed	25	Very good	Some	Average	National
#4	Average	Integrated	Average	Medium	Short	10	Very good	Some	High	Internat.
#5	Loud	Integrated	Low	Medium	Detailed	5	Poor	Some	Average	No-name
#6	Average	None	High	Medium	Short	25	Poor	All	Average	Internat.
#7	Quiet	Integrated	High	Medium	None	25	Average	Some	Low	National
#8	Average	Next to	Low	Medium	Short	5	Average	Standard	Low	Internat.
#9	Loud	None	Average	Medium	Detailed	10	Average	All	Low	No-name
#10	Loud	Integrated	High	Large	None	5	Very good	Standard	Average	Internat.
#11	Average	None	Low	Small	None	25	Average	Standard	Average	No-name
#12	Quiet	None	Average	Small	Detailed	5	Poor	Standard	High	Internat.
#13	Quiet	Next to	High	Small	Detailed	10	Average	Some	Average	Internat.
#14	Loud	None	High	Small	Short	10	Very good	Standard	Low	National
#15	Quiet	None	Low	Medium	None	5	Very good	All	High	National

Washing Machine Attributes

Continued

Table 8.2 Continued

Washing Machine Attributes

	1	2	3	4	5	6	7	8	9	10
Washing machine profiles	Noise	Storage	Energy consumption	Capacity	Instructions	Working lifetime	Washing result	Washing speed	Water consumption	Brand
#16	Average	Integrated	Low	Large	Detailed	10	Average	Standard	High	National
#17	Quiet	Integrated	Average	Large	Short	25	Poor	Standard	Low	No-name
#18	Quiet	Integrated	Low	Small	Detailed	25	Very good	All	Low	Internat.
#19	Loud	Next to	Low	Small	Short	25	Poor	Some	High	National
#20	Quiet	None	High	Large	Short	5	Average	Some	High	No-name
#21	Loud	Integrated	Average	Small	Short	5	Average	All	Average	National
#22	Average	Integrated	High	Small	None	10	Poor	All	High	No-name
#23	Quiet	Next to	Average	Medium	None	10	Poor	Standard	Average	National
#24	Loud	Next to	High	Medium	Detailed	25	Very good	Standard	High	No-name
#25	Average	Next to	High	Large	Detailed	5	Poor	All	Low	National
#26	Loud	None	Low	Large	None	10	Poor	Some	Low	Internat.
#27	Average	Next to	Average	Small	None	5	Very good	Some	Low	No-name

shown, with levels matching Table 8.1. As soon as manufacturers understand which hypothetical profile customers prefer, they will be in a good position to define their own offers (see Box Case 8.3).

Box Case 8.3

Bayernwerk AG—Defining an Offer with Conjoint Analysis[20]

When the German energy market was deregulated, new suppliers such as "Yello" and "Privatstrom" entered what was to become a very competitive market. Electricity became a commodity, the market price quickly fell by 20 percent, Bayernwerk AG was losing customers, and Lars Weber, head of market research, needed to find a suitable response. He was interested in whether electricity is simply a commodity, or whether customers differentiate between suppliers? To obtain an objective answer, he conducted a competitive analysis and produced an overview of the market offerings, including the price per kWh, the energy source (for example, nuclear or coal-fired, local and "remote" suppliers, and the type of customer service (helpline and Internet)). The next step was to investigate the value customers placed on each of the various attributes using a conjoint study.

Weber found that there was a market segment that would pay more for electricity generated in a sustainable way and also more for electricity from a local supplier. As Bayernwerk is located close to the Bavarian Alps it had the possibility to generate all of its electricity from hydroelectric generation. As the conjoint study had clearly demonstrated the higher perceived value of hydro power, a new product was defined and named "AquaPower"—to clearly differentiate it from the competition. This was unique at the time that it was introduced and it has been very successful for Bayernwerk.

ANALYZING THE RESULTS

Calculating the Part-worths

In conjoint studies, interviewees have to evaluate either a pair of attributes (the trade-off method) or full profiles. Every product has a certain "value" for each customer and, in conjoint terminology, this is called the *utility* and the total utility of a product is the sum of each of the attribute level utilities (so-called *part-worths*). Utilities are calculated by conjoint software packages (for example, ACA[21]) based on the customer preferences (refer to Figure 8.2 where we explained the utility differences of attribute levels). The utility values can be computed for individual respondents or as average values across all respondents.[22]

For the washing machine, the part-worths for the three levels of the attribute "capacity" are shown in Table 8.3. The part-worths range from –70 to +45 utiles. The range is dependent on the preferences of customers and we will explain this aspect later. It is worth noting that negative values do not necessarily mean that this is unattractive to the respondents, but it simply means that it is less preferred compared with the other levels. Overall, part-worths add up

Table 8.3 Part-worth Value per Level for the
Attribute "Capacity"

Levels	Part-worth (utiles)
Low 3–4 kg dry weight	–70
Medium 5–6 kg dry weight	+25
Large 7–8 kg dry weight	+45

Table 8.4 Influence of Attributes to the Total Value

Attribute	Level	Range of part-worths	Total range*	Attribute Importance (percent)
Capacity	Large (7–8 kg) to Small (3–4 kg)	+45 to –70	115	46.00
Brand	International to No-name	+60 to –30	90	36.00
Price	€300–€6,000	+15 to –30	45	18.00
		Total	250	100

Note: *The units are typically called "utiles" from the English term "utility values."

to zero and so are interdependent. The example shows that—on average—the respondents prefer a large capacity. A product is made up of several attributes and the impact of each attribute on the total utility varies. For example, a customer might put more emphasis on capacity than on the price when buying a washing machine. The impact of a particular attribute depends on how large its range of part-worths is compared to the total utility of the product. The ranges are converted to percentages in order to obtain a set of attribute importance values that add up to 100.

Table 8.4 compares three attributes ("capacity," "brand," and "price"). ACA software shows the utility of the washing machine to be 250 utiles. The "capacity" range is 115, whereas the ranges for "brand" and "price" are "90" and "45" utiles respectively. It can be seen that, as a percentage of the total range of "250," "capacity" has the greatest impact on the purchasing decision—46 percent. This is another way of saying that "capacity" is more important than "price" in the purchasing decision for this particular group of customers.

In most studies, the average values for attributes are calculated but if the respondents are not homogenous, then customer segments should be analyzed separately (see Box Case 8.4). For example, in the case of the washing machine, the household and professional cleaners would be analyzed as separate segments.

Box Case 8.4

Motorola—Talking Two-ways[23]

The Motorola company was established in 1928 and is a world leader in communications and electronics. For example, the company spearheaded car radios in the 1930s, invented the world's first commercial portable cellular phone in 1983, and good value for money compact "TalkAbout" two-way radios in the late 1990s.

At the end of the 1990s, it was not obvious which two-way radio features customers valued most and whether they would be willing to pay for new features. The "TalkAbout" product is well suited for outdoor activities, such as hiking, camping, mountaineering, sailing, and biking. Marketing manager Maria Townsend-Metz's challenge was to capture customers' perceptions of a large number of possible features, including visual design, technical specifications, battery life, range, and so forth. "We couldn't put all the different options we were thinking about on the radio, so we needed to know which ones were going to be of most value to the consumer, and help sell the most radios," Townsend-Metz explains.

Motorola brought in market research company POPULUS to help run a conjoint study and focused on six markets across the U.S. In the study, the team analyzed 18 different attributes, including price. On the basis of the study, the company developed a deep understanding of the outdoor customer's needs and today, Motorola offers 18 highly different versions of its TalkAbout model, in order to meet the specific needs of the growing outdoor customer segment.

Calculating the Utility Indices

Once the part-worths of each level of all attributes have been calculated (Table 8.3) and their impact on the purchasing decision is understood (Table 8.4), the *utility index* (UI) of each product profile can be calculated. This is done using following equation:

$$UI = (\text{Attribute}_1 \text{ PW} \times \text{Attribute}_1 \text{ AI}) + (\text{Attribute}_2 \text{ PW} \times \text{Attribute}_2 \text{ AI}) + (\text{Attribute}_n \text{ PW} \times \text{Attribute}_n \text{ AI})$$

UI	=	utility index
PW	=	part-worth
AI	=	attribute importance

The utility indices provide the basis for comparing product profiles. For example, the UI for a "professional" washing machine with a capacity of 7–8 kg dry weight and an international brand name for 6,000 euro would be calculated in the following way (see Table 8.4):

$$UI = (+45 \times 0.46) + (+60 \times 0.36) + (-30 \times 0.18) = 36.90 \text{ utiles}$$

In comparison to this, a low-cost washing machine with a capacity of 3–4 kg dry weight, from a no-name manufacturer and sold at 300 euros would have the following utility index:

$$UI = (-70 \times 0.46) + (-30 \times 0.36) + (+15 \times 0.18) = -40.30 \text{ utiles}$$

This shows that the first washing machine is preferred over the second one, because it has a higher utility index ("36.9" versus "–40.3" utiles). A conjoint analysis is in many ways similar to an experiment. The utility index is the dependent variable and the attributes represent the independent variables. As the attribute levels change, the customer's perception of the product will also change.

Selection of the Analysis Model

There are three main models for analyzing the data:[24]

- First Choice model.
- Share of Preference model.
- Purchase Likelihood model.

The *first choice model* assumes that a customer will always choose the product or service with the highest overall utility (the *maximum utility rule*). It focuses only on the customer's "first choice" and, for example, if 3,000 interviewees' responses are collected, it is possible to calculate the hypothetical market share of the two different washing machines (profiles). For example, if 900 out of the 3,000 respondents prefer the "professional" washing machine, then this machine is expected to capture 30 percent market share. The limitation of the first choice model is that it calculates extreme preferences and, thus, unrealistic market shares may result.

The *share of preference* model considers that not all customers make rational decisions and the product with the highest utility is not always chosen. It compares alternative products and forecasts the probability of the selection of each product. Since all products are considered in the model, each one also gets a share of preference. The market is then split between all products on offer.

The *purchase likelihood* model looks at the probability of the selection of each product independently of the others. Thus, the result is particularly important for breakthrough (first-to-market) products and services that do not face any direct competition. However, as soon as other companies introduce their competitive offers, we recommend basing the forecast on the share of preference model (if the purchase is less rational, for example, a spontaneous purchase), or on the first choice model (if the product is perceived more as an investment). In some commercial and academic studies, the data are analyzed with all three models and the different results stimulate further insights.

Overall, WashMachineCo. identified the ideal combination of attribute levels in their new washing machine based on customer preferences. This is why

Box Case 8.5

The UK Tractor Market—Brand Rules OK?[25]

The market in the UK for agricultural tractors is approximately 15,000 units a year and a number of well-known brands are present in the market: including Massey-Ferguson, Fendt, New Holland, and John Deere. In a university-led study, conjoint analysis was selected to determine the importance of brand compared with other factors in farmers' purchasing decisions. Five attributes with different levels were selected for the study: brand name (five levels with the leading brands), price (£30,000; £35,000; and £40,000), the proximity of the dealership (0–15; 16–30; over 30 miles), the dealer's quality of service ("average"; "good"; "very good"), and the buyer's experience of the dealer (two levels: "have never bought a tractor from the dealer before"; "bought one or more tractors from the dealer before"). Interestingly, although initially considered, the attribute "technical performance" for tractors was not included in the analysis. The attributes and levels were combined into 25 profiles which were presented to the respondents in a postal survey, in which they ranked their preferences. From a database of 15,000 farmers, a random sample of approximately 1,500 farmers was surveyed and the response rate was 28 percent.

Superficially, the absolute power of the brand was clear from the results: 39 percent of the purchasing decision could be explained by it. Price (26 percent) and service (15 percent) were the next most important attributes. However, the study chose to use attributes from an old (1979) study, supplemented by interviews with just two farmers and one contractor. A more effective approach would have been to use repertory grid interviews to establish today's key factors and to take these as the attributes in the conjoint study.

conjoint analysis can play a significant role in the early product development phases of any company.

LIMITATIONS

The limitations of conjoint analysis include the following:

1. If conjoint analysis is to be effective, every important attribute from the customer's perspective must be identified and included (see Box Case 8.5). Traditional approaches are not sufficient and so conjoint studies need to be linked to full hidden needs analysis.
2. The complexity of the analysis grows with the number of attributes and levels and interviewees can become overwhelmed.[26]
3. If price is included as an attribute, it has to be interpreted carefully. Often customers will pay more if they receive more for it and so price is made relative to what is on offer and so cannot be regarded as an independent attribute. It can require a more complex analysis.[27]
4. Customers' opinions change over time, and so conjoint studies only provide a "snapshot" of a given point in time.

5. The descriptions of attributes and levels presented to respondents are relatively short and do not necessarily convey the same meaning to all interviewees, or may be hard for some interviewees to understand. For this reason, the descriptions should use the "language of the customer."
6. Purchasing decisions are sometimes made by a group (a *decision-making unit* [DMU]). For example, a family may make the choice about a new plasma television. Conjoint studies look at individual preferences and the group dynamics are not captured.

SUMMARY

Although conjoint analysis does not uncover customer needs, it is an important technique for establishing the perceived value of product attributes, including known and hidden needs, across large samples. Therefore, it is an essential tool for checking how a service or product which addresses hidden needs will be perceived. This chapter has shown the following:

- The first step is to determine all of the important product attributes and their levels.
- From the many possible combinations (profiles), a manageable set of diverse (orthogonal) ones are selected.
- For each of the selected profiles, cards are prepared with a maximum of six attributes and these are best presented to the respondent in pairs.
- Respondents indicate their preferences by rating the different profiles, always presented in a pair-wise fashion.
- The ratings from each individual respondent are then averaged using the software package ACA, and this also calculates the utility indices of the various profiles.
- This analysis of a number of profiles enables the optimum set of product features to be identified, uncovers customer segments, and shows the price that customers will pay.

MANAGEMENT RECOMMENDATIONS

- Use conjoint studies to ensure that your products and services have the ideal feature set, an appropriate pricing, and are competitive. Such studies can also determine the perceived value of features that address hidden needs.
- Make sure that all of the attributes are included in analysis.
- Use dedicated conjoint software to make the analysis faster and simpler.

RECOMMENDED READING

1. Curry, J., "Understanding Conjoint Analysis in 15 Minutes," Sawtooth Software Research Paper Series, Sequim, USA: Sawtooth Software, 1996. [This report provides a very quick overview of conjoint analysis and takes the reader through the basic CA principles with a practical example.]
2. Gustaffson, A., Herrmann, A. and Huber, F. (eds.) *Conjoint Measurement: Methods and Applications.* Berlin: Springer-Verlag, 2001. [Gives an overview of current developments in conjoint analysis and explains the different methods with examples.]
3. Louviere, J. J., Hensher D. A. and Swait, J. D., *Stated Choice Methods: Analysis and Application.* Cambridge: Cambridge University Press, 2000. [Discusses the theory behind choice modeling methods and stated preference methods; it explains how data can be combined from both ways, and illustrates the implementation in case studies and explains the validation of results.]

Part 3
Designing Breakthrough Products

9 COMBINING THE TECHNIQUES: DESIGNING BREAKTHROUGH PRODUCTS AND SERVICES

[C]ompanies say they want breakthrough products, but most are far more adept at making incremental improvements to existing lines. Eric von Hippel *et al.*, MIT[1]

INTRODUCTION

We opened this book by commenting on the large number of new products and services that fail and we have stressed throughout that understanding customers' hidden needs is essential to the successful development of breakthrough products. To identify hidden needs, innovative techniques for market research need to be combined with more traditional ones. Using a combination of techniques generates deeper insights and also allows the results to be *triangulated* (cross-checked). But recognizing hidden needs is only the first challenge; creative product and service concepts need to be developed that address the hidden needs. In this chapter we explain how to combine different market research techniques to gain deeper market insights and then we discuss how these insights can be used to design breakthrough products. The approach we will present is not theoretical; it is based on our experiences working with a number of leading organizations including Agilent Technologies and Bosch Packaging Technology in the manufacturing sector, and VirginMoney in the financial services sector.

The main sections in this chapter are as follows:

- Explain the critical phases in moving from hidden needs to breakthrough products and services.
- Discuss the market research phase, in which customers' issues are identified using a combination of techniques.
- Give details on how to manage the concept development stage by formulating problem statements and applying creativity techniques to design breakthrough products and services.

FROM HIDDEN NEEDS TO BREAKTHROUGHS

Key Phases

In Chapter 1 we defined hidden needs as: issues and problems that customers face but have not yet realized. When hidden needs are addressed by product design, customers are both surprised and delighted. As shown in Figure 9.1, there are two main phases to generating breakthrough products: the exploratory phase and the concept development phase. In the former (exploratory) phase, an appropriate combination of market research techniques must be selected to generate deep market insights—an understanding of the central problems and issues customers face. In previous chapters we have explained how ethnographic market research and other techniques allow us to probe into what customers are thinking (but may not be articulating), and identify hidden needs. Innovative techniques, such as repertory grid, will normally be combined with traditional surveys and focus groups.

In the second phase, the results of the market research are formulated into *customer problem statements* (which express the problems and issues customers face), and then creativity techniques are applied to find ways of solving these issues. It should be noted that understanding the customer (Phase 1) will focus on their language but the customer problem statement itself does not normally use customer language. This is because the problem statement focuses on hidden needs that have not been directly articulated. For example, the German vacuum

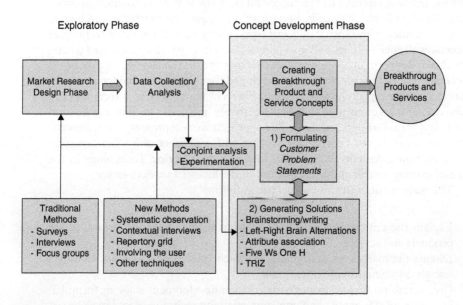

Figure 9.1   Hidden Needs Analysis in Product Development

cleaner manufacturer Miele recognized from contextual interviews that people whose children have dust allergies clean several times a week. Such parents were seen to vacuum their children's mattresses several times and, when asked why, answered, "Because then I know it is clean." This customer quote demonstrates the subtle nature of hidden needs—parents were so used to existing vacuum cleaners that they did not realize the problem they had (having to clean several times to feel convinced that a mattress was dust-free). Such an insight can be used to formulate a customer problem statement: *parents of children with allergies are forced to spend time cleaning several times because they have no way of knowing when the mattresses they are cleaning are completely dust-free*. The solution was a vacuum cleaner with a breakthrough feature to solve the issue—a dust-level indicator (see Box Case 9.1).

Figure 9.1 shows that creativity techniques are used to develop solutions to customer problem statements (that is, addressing hidden needs). The creativity techniques that can be used include *attribute association* (where each attribute of a product or service is considered and ideas for modifications generated); *brainstorming;* and what is known as *TRIZ*—a methodology for problem-solving based on databases of patents. In the concept development phase, the attributes of a new product or service can also be tested with potential customers through *experimentation* (for example, *rapid prototyping*). Similarly, customers' preferences and the trade-offs they are willing to make (for example, between features and price) can be better understood by *conjoint analysis* (see Chapter 8). It can be seen that experimentation and conjoint analysis typically span the two phases, as both of them are useful in gauging customers' reactions to new product and service concepts.

Box Case 9.1

Miele—Listen and Watch Teams[2]

Seizing an opportunity is what a German household products manufacturer has done in recognizing the influence on their markets of the growing number of people with allergies. The Miele company has introduced a vacuum cleaner that indicates when the floor being cleaned is dust-free. A hygiene sensor at the nozzle has a "traffic light" indicator, which turns from red, through amber, to green as cleaning progresses. This sensor is a breakthrough feature for the increasing number of people who have allergies: because it allows the user to know when a room really is clean, or that an allergic child's mattress is free of dust and house mites have been eliminated.

The market research behind this product was conducted in close cooperation with the *Deutscher Allergie- und Asthmabund* (German Allergy and Asthma Foundation—DAAB), an association for people with allergies. Through an innovative approach to its market research, Miele not only recognized the need for a hygiene sensor but also identified an important new segment. People with allergies also have to be careful with

▶▶

their washing. Consequently, Miele has introduced a new washing machine, which has a special program for washing pillows and a rinsing process to remove detergent residues. In addition, a tumble drier has been designed to minimize static electricity, as it exacerbates allergies.

Both these products were based on market research and ideas generated from working closely with the DAAB and customer groups. As Olaf Dietrich, Marketing and New Product Development Manager Vacuum Cleaners says: "We are in regular contact with users and have a 'listen and watch' philosophy at Miele. By this we mean that we realize that it is essential for not only marketing but also engineers to actually see the issues first-hand. Only if you are present do you really understand the issues." The links established with the DAAB and other similar organizations also mean that Miele has established a lead over its competitors and is making its innovations harder to copy.

Core to Miele's approach is regular and intensive customer contact and the use of both marketing and technical perspectives. "For us, market research is all about understanding the customer's real problems. Once we have identified these, we use cross-functional teams to determine suitable solutions," says Herr Dietrich.

Table 9.1 Characteristics of Breakthrough Products

	Category	Attributes	Implications
1)	Market/Customer	• New to customer. • Tied to emerging customer trends. • Often change market structures. • Require customers to learn and change their behavior. • Typically take longer to diffuse. • Create new categories.	Breakthrough products are usually "first-to-market" and so effective marketing/customer education is required to convince innovators, then early adopters, and then the early majority.[a]
2)	Product	• Offer unique benefits. • Evolution is less predictable. • Need to be hard to copy. • Need to incorporate design thinking[b] into both the product and the packaging (see Box Case 9.2).	Companies must ensure that their breakthrough products are hard to copy, to prevent competitors capitalizing on their pioneering work.
3)	Technology	• Incorporate new technologies. • May embody new processes that need new infrastructure.	Process technology can often make products and services hard to copy.

Notes: [a]Rogers, E. M., *Diffusion of Innovations*. New York: The Free Press, 1995; [b]Verganti, R., *Design-Driven Innovation—Changing the Rules of Competition by Radically Innovating What Things Mean*. Boston, MA: Harvard Business Press, 2009.

Characteristics of Breakthrough Products and Services

Applying the different creativity tools and techniques to develop product or service concepts is normally an iterative process. During the iterations it is useful to keep the NPD team focused on the outcome: breakthrough products and services (or breakthrough product/service combinations). The key characteristics of breakthrough products that should be kept in mind and their implications are given in Table 9.1.[3] From this it can be seen that the challenge is to create products and services with unique value; to educate and develop markets; and to ensure that competitors cannot easily copy the innovation. As we have stressed throughout this book, "traditional market research and development approaches [have] proved to be particularly ill-suited to breakthrough products."[4]

Box Case 9.2

BlandfordConsulting—Packaging the Brand[5]

Kate Blandford has over 20 years' experience of design and brand management in the retail sector. Having started her career in a design agency, Blandford worked for ten years for the UK supermarket Sainsbury's and was responsible for the packaging design for all of this retailer's own brands. Now she heads her own consultancy focused on relaunching brands.

Studies show that in the food sector the success rate for new products is, on average, only 10 percent. With thousands of new food products being introduced each year worldwide, companies need to think carefully about every aspect of the product and that, according to Blandford, must include the packaging. "I have seen so many products that are presented in an inappropriate way. I fundamentally believe that effective design is the cornerstone of brand management. Truly great packaging is aesthetically pleasing, ergonomic, environmentally friendly, commercially viable, and so on. But it is also the face of your brand when the consumer makes their purchase decision. A brand can thrive or fail because of the packaging and so it's essential to get it right!"

Blandford works with both food manufacturers and retailers, linking them to design agencies. "One of my challenges is that design agencies are often sceptical about involving customers. They are worried that their packaging designs will be judged by customers—like 'a beauty parade'. But I need to involve customers to understand their perceptions of packaging, particularly their unarticulated, emotional responses. You have to understand these responses, if you are going to come up with a design that personifies your brand values," explains Blandford. Her approach involves a blend of techniques: both talking to and observing customers (generating insight from their actions rather than taking their words at face value); and using intelligent stimulus material in traditional focus groups but also in-home observation.

An example of Blandford's work and the impact of packaging is her redesign of Sainsbury's SO organic range, where she did not simply take one or two products

▶▶

but worked on refreshing and repositioning the whole category. The packaging had, until that time, largely been in beige colors, which were found through market research to imply to customers that the product would be tasteless. A change to deeper colors and the use of photographs on key products changed the customer's perception of both value and taste and sales of the whole category went up.

In the future, Blandford thinks that "there will be a greater understanding of the value of design, packaging and the brand in the boardroom—after all, without it, the customer may never get to find out how good the product is!"

MANAGING THE EXPLORATORY PHASE

One of the critical elements of adopting a philosophy of hidden needs is the recognition that newer market research techniques need to be used in combination with traditional ones. This enables deeper insights and triangulation—the comparison of results from different techniques to generate more reliable conclusions. The importance of using multiple methods cannot be overstressed because: "One method of hidden needs insights doesn't work, it must be a combination of methods."[6]

Choosing an Appropriate Combination of Techniques

The most appropriate combination of techniques needs to be chosen for each market research project. To help this decision, Table 9.2 gives the advantages and limitations of the techniques discussed in this book. In general, innovative techniques such as ethnographic market research, repertory grid, and lead user technique are used at the beginning of the exploratory phase, where a broad understanding of the market is needed. Observing customers and conducting contextual interviews provide such information but an expert on market research has said: "Observation of behaviour is rarely sufficient by itself."[7] So we need to decide which other technique will provide a different perspective because, "All consumers have relevant conscious thoughts that they need special help in articulating. In addition, all consumers have relevant *hidden thoughts*: ideas that they are not aware of possessing but are willing to share once discovered."[8] Repertory grid and projection unveil factors that would not be elicited by direct questioning and it also allows researchers to differentiate between the factors that customers mention most frequently (for example, because they are obvious) and those factors that are most important. It should be stressed that "frequency of mention does not appear a good surrogate for importance."[9]

In the exploratory phase the aim is to identify hidden needs through intensive techniques used with smaller numbers of customers and then to test whether the insights apply to wider numbers of customers. To achieve this second point, interviews, surveys, and focus groups are typically used with the questions used being based on earlier insights.

Table 9.2 Different Approaches to Identifying Customer Problems and Requirements

	Approach	Overview	Applications/Advantages	Limitations
1)	Surveys, Interviews and More (Chapter 2)	• Use of direct questions to determine customers' views on what they think are their requirements. • Open-ended questions allowing respondents some freedom to give creative ideas. • Can be applied as a postal survey, telephone, Internet, or direct interviews. • Projection: uses indirect questions to probe the views that respondents would not share directly. • ZMET: concentrates on respondents' usage of metaphors…	• Widely used method of collecting customer inputs. • Ideal to collect a higher number of customer inputs compared to other approaches (sample size is usually bigger). • Respondents are asked, for example, for their view on somebody else's actions. • Encourages respondents to engage with the subject through the use of visual and other stimuli.	• Questionnaires are often thought to be easy to design. In fact, it is the opposite and many surveys are poorly designed and consequently produce equivocal results. • Response rates are often low, which raises the question of whether the results are representative of the market. • High response rates (for example, via the Internet) may not be representative. • Respondents may find it difficult to articulate their answers to open questions. • Very difficult to analyze the results. • Different researchers may come to very different conclusions. • Needs specialist training to be applied effectively.

Continued

Table 9.2 Continued

Approach	Overview	Applications/Advantages	Limitations
2) Focus Groups and Variations (Chapter 3)	• Small groups of selected users or nonusers, paid to discuss product needs. • Discussions are stimulated by an initial question and by having example products in the room. • A moderator guides discussions. • Market researchers often observe the discussions through a two-way mirror.	• Help to define customer problems and give background information, rather than identifying solutions. • Users are taken outside their normal environment. • Focus groups can be used to help interpret survey findings and statistical data. • Focus groups can be used to provide a more in-depth picture of the topic of interest after a survey has been conducted and analyzed	• The somewhat artificial nature of the situation can limit the effectiveness. • Particular individuals can dominate the discussions. Therefore good moderation is required. • Some companies try to save costs by using inexperienced moderators; this wastes the potential of focus groups discussion.
3) Ethnographic Market Research (Chapters 4 and 5)	• A range of approaches of which the main ones are systematic observation and contextual interviews. • Many anecdotal examples show that the approaches can lead to breakthrough products.	• Becoming more popular. • Gives an in-depth and cultural understanding of customers' and users' product use models. • Contextual interviews are *in vivo* and the environment gives valuable information.	• Systematic observation is not easy and using specialists may be the best approach (otherwise base studies on a suitable coding scheme developed from Table 5.3). • Vast amounts of qualitative data may be generated, which requires effective analysis strategies.
4) Repertory Grid Technique (Chapter 6)	• Users or customers undergo a structured interview discussing *elements* (typically products or services). • Interviewees are stimulated to identify *constructs*—product attributes—by being asked to compare triads of different products and/or services.	• Repertory grid technique is powerful at enabling users and customers to articulate their issues. • Very useful to identify key and emerging attributes that might appeal to customers. • Often an ideal way to prepare for a survey. • The technique taps tacit knowledge of hidden needs	• The technique is not well-known. • Interviewees need to have experience with 5–6 different products and services to make the technique work. • Interviewer needs specific training in the technique, although it is easy to apply. • Time-consuming interviews.

	Technique	Advantages	Disadvantages
5)	Involving the User (Chapter 7)	• Lead users: identification of users with extreme needs and analogous users in related sectors. It is usual to run a workshop with extreme and analogous users, to develop product concepts.	• Workshop brings together very different users and stimulates creative discussions. • Can be combined with experimentation, to test the concepts identified in the workshop.	• Difficulties in identifying lead users. • Workshops are time-consuming and lead users may need to be motivated to give their time. • Workshop is outside the normal working environment (although it can be combined with a visit to a lead user environment).
		• Virtual communities: the countless number of groups that share a common interest and take the time to regularly communicate on the web.	• Allows companies to contact large numbers of enthusiastic customers. • Gives the opportunity to discuss specific issues with wider groups of customers	• Time consuming to set-up and maintain the links to these groups. • Not necessarily representative groups.
		• Crowdsourcing: posting specific problems or ideas on the internet to gain voluntary but potentially large volumes of feedback.	• Enables companies to tap outside potential and not always to focus on internally-generated ideas and solutions.	• Relatively new approach for which both the advantages and the limitations are still emerging.
6)	Conjoint Analysis (Chapter 8)	• Identifies the trade-offs customers make in deciding between different products. • Customers are presented with descriptions of products (or services) with different *attribute levels* and must choose their preferences.	• Identification of the product attributes that customers perceive as their key priorities. • Development of pricing models, in which the implicit trade-offs customers make between features and price are understood.	• If the wrong attributes are fed into the analysis, then the prioritization will not be useful (it will encourage a continuing focus on incremental products). • The somewhat artificial nature of the decisions can limit the accuracy of the findings. • Relatively complex method that usually needs expert support.

Source: Based on but significantly extended from Table 5.5: Goffin, K. and Mitchell, R., *Innovation Management: Strategy and Implementation Using the Pentathlon Framework.* Basingstoke: Palgrave Macmillan, 2010, pp. 173–174.

Evidence for the Utility of Techniques

In Chapter 1, Table 1.2 (page 17) we gave many examples where different techniques for identifying hidden needs had led to successful new products and services. Unfortunately, such evidence is engaging but anecdotal and there have been (too) few studies on the value of the newer techniques for market research. Overall, there is an urgent need for good research to identify the advantages and limitations of each method for market research (this is an area where we in Cranfield School of Management are currently active[10]).

One survey of 160 U.S. companies investigated managers' perceptions of the different methods (see Figure 1.4; page 19). The researchers commented that ethnographic market research was "not so popular among practitioners...[Although] the method provides perhaps the greatest insights and depth of knowledge into users' unmet and unarticulated needs."[11] The main limitations of this study were that it used managers' perceptions as a "measure" of the effectiveness of methods and did not investigate how methods could be used in combination. Overall, the study concluded: "there is a lack of substantial research to reveal the most effective sources [of ideas for new products]."[12]

Figure 9.2 shows the results of an important study by Professors Abbie Griffin (now at the University of Utah) and John Hauser (MIT)—one that compared the effectiveness of focus groups and interviews.[13] It showed that quite a number

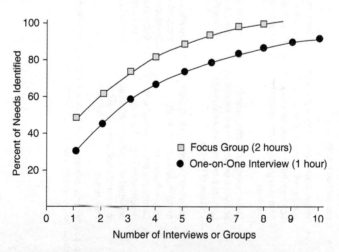

Figure 9.2   Comparison of Interviews and Focus Groups

Source: Reprinted by permission, Griffin, A. and Hauser, J. R., "The Voice of the Customer," *Marketing Science*, Vol. 12, No. 1, Winter 1993, pp. 1–27. Copyright (1993), the Institute for Operations Research and the Management Sciences (INFORMS), 7240 Parkway Drive, Suite 300, Hanover, MD 21076 USA.

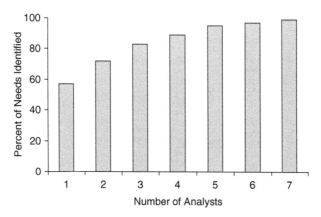

Figure 9.3 Number of Analysts Required

Source: By permission (redrawn), Griffin, A. and Hauser, J. R., "The Voice of the Customer," *Marketing Science*, Vol. 12, No. 1, Winter 1993, pp. 1–27. Copyright (1993), the Institute for Operations Research and the Management Sciences (INFORMS), 7240 Parkway Drive, Suite 300, Hanover, MD 21076 USA.

of interviews or focus groups are required to identify a comprehensive list of market needs. For example, 5 one-to-one interviews or 3 focus groups were needed to identify approximately 70 percent of market needs; 10 interviews or 6 focus groups were needed to identify approximately 90 percent of needs. Figure 9.2 gives an idea of the number of interviews or focus groups required but it is important to always use a Pareto analysis to check for theoretical saturation (see Figure 6.3, page 131).

Another important finding of this work is that, ideally, three or more researchers ("analysts") should check the data. Figure 9.3 shows that over 80 percent of customer needs from focus groups or interviews are identified when three researchers analyze the data in parallel.

Unfortunately, the Griffin and Hauser study only compared focus groups and interviews and did not attempt to differentiate between known, unmet, and hidden needs. As the scientific evidence for the best combinations of techniques is not yet available, we will describe a typical approach (based on one of the many projects we have conducted for companies).

Combining Techniques

Every market research project which aims to discover hidden needs must use the most appropriate combination of techniques—"mixing and matching" market research. Figure 9.4 shows a very typical combination from a confidential project to understand personal computer users' needs. Repertory grid technique was used to understand customers' perceptions of existing products including: the

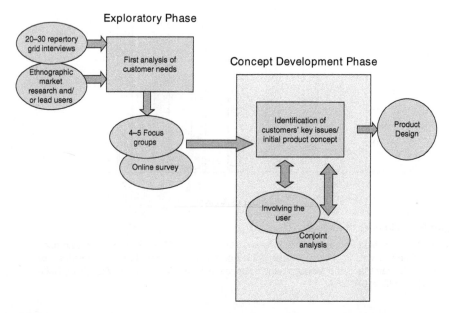

Figure 9.4 A Typical Combination of Methods (for a Personal Computer Market Study)

attributes that they found most important; attributes that existing products did not fulfill; and the language customers used in discussing products. Parallel to the repertory grid interviews, ethnographic market research (and lead user technique) was used: to systematically observe customers using products; to identify the central issues they faced; and to draw out the culture of key customer segments. The data from these two sources were checked for theoretical saturation and then triangulated to identify hidden needs. This first analysis gave a strong indication of the issues that the customers face, which were then verified with a wider sample in focus groups and an online survey. In this way, the unmet and hidden needs of the smaller group of customers were confirmed as being important to a broad spectrum of customers.

Once the key issues were identified, a customer problem statement was formulated, which was discussed with users who were involved in commenting on the product concept, and later the prototype. In parallel, conjoint analysis was used to estimate the ideal combination of product attributes (including the price). Note that the attributes used in the conjoint analysis were based on those which emerged from the repertory grid interviews and the focus groups, rather than being the product manager's view of what she thought the market valued most. (For another example of how different techniques can be used in combination, see Box Case 10.1 on Bosch Packaging Technology in Chapter 10.)

MANAGING THE CONCEPT DEVELOPMENT PHASE

During the concept development phase we need to:

- Apply creativity theory to the way we challenge individuals and teams to develop breakthrough product concepts.
- Write problem statements that capture the essence of the issues that our products and services should address.
- Use creativity techniques with our new product development teams.

Pointers from Creativity Theory

There are three types of business creativity: *serendipitous, exploratory,* and *normative creativity.* Serendipitous creativity is accidental and the most famous example is 3M's "Post-It," where an adhesive that was being developed for gluing things together failed but for which a very successful alternative use was found. Serendipitous creativity, by definition, cannot easily be managed although looking for ideas from different sectors or bringing in experts from other fields can help because "the best innovators aren't lone geniuses, they're people who can take an idea that is obvious in one context and apply it in not-so-obvious ways to a different context."[14]

Exploratory creativity matches most people's understanding of creativity, where the goal is to identify new ("outside the box") opportunities. It is "unconventional thinking, which modifies or rejects previous ideas, clarifies vague or ill-defined problems in developing new views, or solutions."[15] Identifying problems which create real business opportunities is what hidden needs identification is all about. But it is important for managers to clearly specify the markets and segments that they want their employees to focus on. For example, Bosch Packaging Technology (see Box Case 10.1) specified a new market that it wanted to enter and assigned marketing to explore the needs and opportunities in this market.

In normative creativity, original thinking is used to solve known problems and this is central to hidden needs. Research has shown innovation to be a series of problems that need to be solved, including solving customer issues and solving the many technical problems that arise in, for example, the design of a car.[16] Clearly specifying problems and issues is a key step in maximizing creativity and so that is the reason we recommend that the results of exploratory market research need to be formulated into customer problem statements.

The vast majority of innovation projects involve teams of people. Therefore, managers need to stimulate team creativity. Professor Teresa Amabile of Harvard has conducted a number of studies and found that managers need to focus on six issues:[17]

1. Providing the right group of individuals with the right challenge—matching the people to the project.

2. Giving teams the autonomy to choose the means by which they solve clearly defined problems.
3. Making suitable resources available (including time and money). A certain amount of time pressure can be positive but realistic schedules are essential.
4. Creating diverse teams and motivating them to be excited about the project.
5. Ensuring timely and appropriate support. For example, if management takes too long to make decisions this impacts team motivation negatively.
6. Protecting teams from organizational politics.

So creativity theory shows us the importance of formulating clear problem statements and using diverse groups (for example, cross-functional internal teams supplemented by external experts). For example, designers with their focus on materials, aesthetics, and creating iconic services or products can bring

---

Box Case 9.3

Boxer—Bacon Butties, Brazilian Beer, and Branding Birmingham[18]

What is the real value of design? Is it just a way of making products look good? Or a way of bringing creativity into business? How valuable is design to most companies? The team at Boxer Design Consultants, based in Birmingham, England and Chicago are faced with these questions on a day-to-day basis and see their challenge as balancing the creative and the rational aspects of business. Their business has 45 staff and a turnover of £5 million.

When most people think of design they tend to think of the aerodynamic lines of a sports car, or a visually stunning kitchen utensil from Alessi. However, design is more than pure aesthetics and Boxer has conducted a number of challenging projects ranging from rebranding of a Brazilian beer, to fast-food packaging, to working on the image of a city. The challenge with the beer was to help Brazil's best-selling beer position itself in the UK as a premium brand for the style-conscious segment and an innovative approach was needed. Boxer came up with the idea of a competition for budding artists to design wrapping for the beer bottles and packaging. Over two million bottle and pack wraps were printed with the winning designs, specially painted buses toured cities to visit clubs and promote the beer, and the campaign was nominated as one of the best in the industry.

From Brazilian beer to Birmingham's brand: Boxer was tasked with creating a campaign that not only challenged outdated perceptions of England's second city, but also presented Birmingham as a city reborn, bursting with energy and enriched by cultural diversity. Boxer strategically defined The City of Birmingham's brand identity and built the campaign upon the proposition, "Many worlds, one great city." The campaign was rolled out across a variety of media including advertising, print, and online and given the extensive range of organizations and companies who would use the brand, Boxer also created brand guidelines.

▶▶

In order to constantly come up with such creative ideas, part of Boxer's culture is the "Soak-It-Up" Friday team gathering. The whole of the studio and client services teams chat over Brummie bacon butties (Birmingham bacon sandwiches), discussing examples of design practice the teams have collected over the previous week. The purpose is two fold; seeking ideas from the wider world and to stimulate debate around other people's designs to inform decisions in current projects.

Angelique Green, Chief Operating Officer for Boxer, not only has responsibility for managing the company but she also plays a major role in creative projects such as those with McDonald's in the U.S. "My role is to guide and inspire the overall direction of the business, so the Soak-It-Up initiatives are very important. Clients look for inspirational creative solutions that lead to real business benefits. We therefore have to partner both at a practical level with our designers and on strategic level leading the business direction." The key to producing leading-edge solutions for business is to understand the challenges and balance the creative and the rational, so she is assisted by other directors such as Julian Glyn-Owen. With a design degree, international business experience, and an MBA, Julian can focus on rational business benefits for clients whilst designers create breakthrough design. Julian's interests lie in developing the skills required to translate and transition client needs into breakthrough design. "Often we see global brand owners carrying out leading-edge positioning and analysis. But what they don't do, for understandable cultural, organisational and professional reasons, is to make the leap from their valuable analysis to an emotional, meaningful experience for the consumer. Our clients need help in *translating* the literal into the *emotional*—this is what we do everyday in creating attractive, powerful, even magnetic context for the targeted consumer."

a very valuable different perspective (see Box Case 9.3). Above all, managers need to "instill [in teams] a sense of wonder and adventure into the product development process."[19]

Writing Customer Problem Statements

Correctly applied market research will identify customers' and users' needs, priorities, and also their hidden needs. The next step is to formulate market insights into problem statements with cultural insights. Table 9.3 shows three examples. Some readers may wonder whether the effort of writing a formal problem statement is worthwhile. In answer, we stress that research on creativity that we discussed above shows the value of a clear statement (and similarly, in the field of quality management the value of problem statements is well-known). Clear problem statements arise from intensive customer contact (see Box Case 9.4). In addition, readers should remember the

Table 9.3   Example Customer-focused Problem Statements

	Company	Central Problem/Cultural Issues	Resulting Breakthrough Product
1)	Miele (see Box Case 9.1)	• The parents of children with allergies have to clean rooms more often and several times to ensure they are dust-free. • Cultural element is that parents only have "peace of mind" if they have cleaned mattresses, for example, several times ("Because then I *know* it is clean").	• Vacuum cleaner with a dust level indicator. • Co-branding with an association for people with allergies. • Whole new product line focused on families with members who have allergies.
2)	Bosch Packaging Technology (Case 10.1)	• When pharmaceutical companies buy high-speed production line equipment, the installation, approval, and "ramp-up" (to high volumes of high quality) takes too long (and is costly). • Pharmaceutical packaging equipment reliability and flexibility is not as good as customers require. • The integration of pharmaceutical packaging equipment to other parts of the production process causes problems (such as access and space requirements).	• The Bosch FXS5100 system has - Solved many of the reliability issues compared with existing systems. - Requires less space and gives easy (one-side) access - Has related services for installation and training.
3)	WarehouseEquipCo. (see Chapter 5)	• Mixed pallet preparation in warehouses is time-consuming, costly, and such pallets are prone to damage and late requests for changes. • Cultural aspect is that warehouse employees enjoy the challenge of preparing mixed pallets, if they have the time.	• Confidential—still in development

---

Box Case 9.4

Fiat Iveco—Testing Products to the Extreme[20]

Iveco is the arm of Fiat responsible for manufacturing and marketing commercial and industrial vehicles, buses, and diesel engines. The company is 30 years old and is organized around business units: light commercial vehicles, trucks,

Company. In a typical year Fiat Iveco produces 160,000 trucks across the four business units and 400,000 diesel engines are sold worldwide. The company's headquarters are in Torino and it has a number of engineering and manufacturing facilities in Europe.

Truck drivers live in their vehicles on long journeys and so part of developing a vehicle is designing a living space. Massimo Fumarola, the Platform Development Manager for trucks says, "you just cannot understand truckers' needs from the results of a survey or focus group. These guys are demanding because their work is extremely demanding." To really understand truck drivers' needs, Fumarola moved his whole marketing team for two weeks to a motorway truck stop just south of the Alps. His people had extensive contact with drivers all hours of the day. "We lived with the truckers for two weeks, literally not going home at night. We accompanied drivers on journeys, ate with them, slept in trucks and collected a mountain of ideas...now our challenge is to find ways of incorporating these ideas into the next product."

Trucks are used relentlessly and so the design must be robust. One of Iveco's heavy trucks was recently serviced and had an incredible 250,000 km "on the clock" after only one year (compared with the industry average of 120,000 km per year). This vehicle is used for nonstop international runs across Western Europe with different drivers working shifts. Iveco uses such vehicles as a test bed for ideas. Such demanding usage leads to a vast array of design requirements.

Many manufacturers design the next generation product by focusing on what the users' needs will be at the time of the product introduction. "We have learnt to look further into the future, as our product life cycles are long. So we design products with features that will still be relevant in the market towards the end of the product life cycle, not just at the time of introduction—that can mean thinking 20 years ahead," says Fumarola. He has recently moved from trucks and is working at Iveco's Engine Business Unit but finds many of the issues similar, "in both business units effective new product development is crucial—but the real challenge is being innovative in everything we do, throughout our business, and in every process."

saying that "you do not think clearly unless you are writing"—the process of formulating a statement is a good discipline to develop clear thinking.

Creativity Techniques for Innovation

A wide range of creativity techniques is relevant to innovation projects. Professor Daniel Couger from the University of Colorado describes 22 creativity techniques, with recommendations on when to use them with individuals or teams, and whether they can be used for exploratory or normative creativity.[21] We will discuss five alternatives that we have found to be most effective. Companies can choose the most suitable techniques to match the issues at hand and so avoid the overuse of *brainstorming*, which causes employees to lose interest.

Brainstorming and Brainwriting

The most widely known creativity technique is brainstorming, which was developed in the 1950s. A group of people are asked to describe any ideas that come to mind as solutions to a problem (normative creativity), or as opportunities for new products, services of businesses (exploratory creativity). The ideas are written on a flip chart where everyone can read them and one idea leads to another. An experienced moderator typically records the ideas and reflects these back to the group to stimulate further discussion. The evaluation of the feasibility of each idea is suspended during the idea collection phase, so that potentially good ideas are not prematurely rejected and the group develops momentum and many ideas.

Brainstorming assumes people are naturally creative and deferring judgment on the quality of ideas until a sufficient quantity has been generated ensures that from the range of ideas available some really good ones can be selected. A limitation of brainstorming is that certain individuals may dominate the discussion and so in the variation *brainwriting*, ideas are written down by individuals before they are shared with the group.

Left-Right Brain Alternations

This technique helps a "whole-brain approach" to identifying an opportunity or solving a problem. Typical left-brain functions include speaking, writing, calculating, logic and deliberating, and so on. In contrast, our right brains control our abilities for intuition, spatial perception, art, and visualization. The creativity task at hand can be formulated to require thinking driven from both our left and right brains and two columns on a flip chart are used to summarize the contrasting ideas. Properly developed services and products should evoke customers' emotions and the right brain thinking of designers brings a valuable counterpole to logical engineering thinking.[22]

For example, the technique can be used to improve a service product by analyzing the service from a left (analytical) perspective, asking such questions as: What is the core product? How quickly is it delivered? What are the key performance indicators? In contrast, the right brain approach would lead us to ask questions such as: How does the customer perceive our service? How do they feel about the service? The contrast between the insights gained from the left and right brain focused questions help to generate new ideas.

Attribute Association

Attribute association can be used to solve a known problem with a product, process, or service (normative creativity), or identify new opportunities. The starting point is to create a list of the attributes (that is, the features) of an existing service or product. This can be based on looking at the existing products, or it can be based on results of repertory grid interviews. For a vacuum cleaner the list of attributes would include the ability to clean

Table 9.4   Example Approaches to Attribute Association

	Approach	Explanation	Service and Manufacturing Examples
1)	Modifying the nature of attributes	Also called *product morphology analysis*, this approach takes the main product attributes and sees how these can be modified.	• Home insurance normally covers the costs of repairs. The German Allianz Group has gone further and offers a home "breakdown" service, with fast call-out of qualified tradesmen guaranteed for any household problem. • Originally domestic coffee machines had a simple glass pot to hold the freshly brewed coffee. However, companies such as Braun have changed this attribute to a vacuum flask, which keeps the coffee warm until needed.
2)	Subtraction or simplification of attributes	Removing certain attributes may simplify a product and make it more attractive to certain segments. This is an attempt to prevent what some writers have called *feature* or *specification creep*—the tendency for development teams to always add more features to products.	• Some mobile telephone companies have successfully marketed a "receive calls only" contract, which is popular with parents that want to be able to contact their children but do not want them making outgoing calls. • Not every subtraction attempt will be successful or positively perceived by customers. For example, the colorless Crystal Pepsi failed when it was introduced to the market in 1993.
3)	Multiplication of attributes	An existing product attribute is copied and offered, with a modification of the function of the repeated attribute, multiple times in the product. The multiplication leads to a specific benefit.	• A classic example is the Mach 3 razor from Gillette. The three blades all cut but the first two, which are set at different angles, drag across the skin to raise the beard for cutting by the second or third blade. • A service example is Europcar's multiple rental agreement. Busy executives can purchase rental agreements of, for example, five days a month but these can be multiple rentals, such as one-day at five different airports.

Source: Based on Goldenberg, J., Horowitz, R., Levav, A. and Mazursky, D., "Finding Your Innovation Sweet Spot," *Harvard Business Review*, Vol. 81, No. 3, March 2003, pp. 3–11 supplemented by examples collected by the authors.

carpets, smooth surfaces, stairs, corners, and so on, plus other factors such as the maneuverability, design, and so on. Each of the product, service, or process attributes is then reviewed using one or more of the approaches summarized in Table 9.4.[23]

The process of reviewing and modifying the attributes requires practice and there are no hard and fast rules for which of the approaches given in Table 9.4 (for example, subtraction or multiplication) is the most appropriate for a particular service or manufactured product. Complex products will most benefit from subtraction or task unification. Of course the review of product attributes does not simply have to be conducted internally; it is more effective when conducted with customers or users.

Five Ws, One H Technique

This is a versatile technique that can be used at all stages of innovation. It helps enhance our understanding of a problem or an opportunity by asking five "W" questions ("who," "what," "where," "when," and "why"?) and one "H" ("how"?). Specific W and H questions are developed for the topic and the answers to the Ws tell us more about the issues. The answer to the H question provides ways to implement the ideas generated by the Ws. The technique is very useful for investigating reports of product problems and using these to generate new product concepts.

TRIZ

No discussion about the use of innovation and creativity tools and techniques would be complete without stressing the value of TRIZ, a creative form of problem-solving developed by the Russian Genrich Altshuller.[24] The acronym TRIZ is based on the four Russian words for the *Theory of Inventive Problem Solving*. Altshuller, who worked in the Moscow patents office, based his ideas on his study of patents. His work started in the 1940s and since that time over 2.8 million international patents have been analyzed.

Patents document how certain problems are solved and looking at large numbers of patents allows particular patterns to be identified. First, patents can be grouped by the generic problem they are solving—for example, an automotive patent might be specifically concerned with engine temperature control but at a generic level it is concerned with cooling. Altshuller grouped patterns by generic problems and found that, based on the underlying physical properties of materials, there are typically a limited number of ways to solve a particular problem. So the first advantage of a TRIZ database is that engineers involved with finding a specific problem can look up all the generic ways to approach the issue. In this way, rather than relying on brainstorming (which is dependent on the knowledge around the table), problem-solving based on a TRIZ database ensures that no possible solution is forgotten and provides example ways that problems have been solved. A TRIZ database provides access to the knowledge of previous generations of scientists and engineers.

The second advantage of TRIZ is that design trends can be identified and so opportunities for improvement can be spotted. For example, design tends to start with straight lines and forms and, over time, more complex lines emerge. Comparing the type of products in a particular industry against these trends can bring useful ideas. The Mars group uses TRIZ regularly and a good example is the packaging of the ubiquitous Mars Bar. The wrapper used to have straight lines and was sealed like a parcel. Consequently, it was awkward to open. Nowadays, the ends of the wrapper have a serrated edge, which means that they can be torn open easily.

The third way that TRIZ helps is by providing insights into how *design trade-offs* can be managed. Say, for example, a particular component needed to be strengthened to withstand wear but could not be heavier. TRIZ matrices allow designers to look at the ways in which this particular trade-off and many others have been solved previously. Once again, the theory of creative problem solving provides access to a body of knowledge summarizing millions of inventions. Somewhere, sometime, the technical problems facing a product development team have been solved previously and so learning from this can be quicker and more effective that starting from scratch.

The Cold War led to TRIZ being largely unknown in the West until relatively recently. Now, it is being widely applied as a way of finding quicker solutions to product design problems. Slowly TRIZ is also being adopted into the service domain,[25] although currently there are no comprehensive databases of ideas available as there are for patents.

Answers to the Customer Problem Statement

The range of creativity techniques we have described should, when used with cross-functional teams, quickly provide answers and solutions to the issues described in

---

Box Case 9.5

Grundfos—Pumping 24/7 and Understanding the "Customer"[26]

Grundfos is a Danish company and a manufacturer at the forefront of technology for pumps and pumping systems. The company's pumps are used in central heating systems and so their installed base of millions of pumps is working 24/7 during the winter months. Founded in 1947 and with 8 manufacturing sites and over 14,000 employees worldwide, Grundfos generated revenues of over 91 M euros in 2007. Probably the major factors in the success of the company have been its understanding of its "customers" and its constant strive to build close links to them. Few companies have such a broad understanding of "customers" but then few companies have been so good at creating a differentiating factor.

Dr. Peter Elvekjær is Group Senior Vice President Global Research and Technology at Grundfos and he explains: "It is quite hard to really know our customers as it is a very long chain to the end-user and everyone involved has different views and needs." This is one of the reasons that Grundfos has used university-based anthropologists to

conduct ethnographic studies of the different players involved in the purchasing decision for heating pumps. This has involved looking at the needs of domestic end-users,
heating installation and service companies, the engineers who design domestic heating
systems, and so on. "By using an ethnographic approach we have been able to produce
a pamphlet summarizing the 'persona', that is the characteristics and needs of our different types of customers, and this has been very useful in raising internal awareness
of our market needs," says Elvekjær. Having run two projects with anthropologists he
advises, "Such studies can produce big results but it is important to stay focused and
make sure that ethnographic work produces results that are not just academically
interesting but add real commercial value."

Many companies compete on technology but at Grundfos they also focus on all their
different types of "customers," including political decision-makers. In the late 1980s the
company recognized that the power consumed by the 200 million heating pumps in
Europe is significant. Grundfos had the first-mover advantage when they introduced
their first generation of low-power consumption pumps but it went further in forging
links to the European Parliament, to understand how legislation for heating equipment
is drawn up. Over several years, Grundfos has played a leading role in the drive by
Europump (the European Pump Manufacturers' Association) to have legislation requiring pumps to be labeled with their power consumption. The success of this move,
coupled with the technological advantage of Grundfos pumps (which require less than
10 percent of the power that they did 20 years ago), has put the company in a unique
competitive position. For example, in Germany domestic users who replace their heating systems only receive a government grant of 1–2000 Euro if they also replace the
circulation pump with an ultra low-power one—such as the Grundfos Alpha2 product
(which meets the norm EnEV §14.3 and consumes only 90 kWh per year compared
with the 400 kWh of the typical pumps it replaces). "Gaining political and legislative
support was a long process but it has been key for us. Now legislation is also being
drawn up to require electric motors to be more efficient. That's another significant part
of our business and, naturally, we already have the right technology."

At Grundfos, R&D always takes a pragmatic approach: "overall our mission is:
'Research for Business'. Everything we do in R&D must be technologically sound,
based on real customer insights, and make a significant commercial contribution" says
Elvekjær.

the customer problem statement. Beware though, the process will be iterative and
it will take time and effort. However, it can be one of the most rewarding stages
of new product and service development. Creativity at this stage can also generate
ideas for how a commodity product can be differentiated (see Box Case 9.5).

SUMMARY

In this chapter we described how market insights are used to generate ideas for
breakthrough new products and services. Breakthrough products and services
include not only basic and performance features but they also offer customers

excitement features (Kano model—see Chapter 1). To create such breakthrough product and services we have shown the importance of:

- Generating deep market insights through the use of a suitable combination of research techniques, which are applied in parallel and with some iteration.
- Triangulating the results of different market research techniques.
- Taking market insights and formulating them into customer problem statements that capture the issues that customers face, their cultural background, and the key elements of the environment in which the product or service is used.
- Addressing customer problem statements using creativity techniques, and generating breakthrough product concepts.

In this chapter we have concentrated on the process by which market insights lead to breakthrough products and services. However, hidden needs analysis must become embedded in a company's culture if it is to become successful. This aspect is what we will cover in Chapter 10.

MANAGEMENT RECOMMENDATIONS

- Ensure that your organization conducts effective market research to identify all types of customer needs.
- Treat the problems and hidden needs that customers have as new product and service opportunities—create concepts that will both surprise and delight customers.
- Through an understanding of the theory of creativity, use diverse groups.
- Apply an appropriate mix of creativity techniques to generate solutions.

RECOMMENDED READING

1. Cooper, R. G. and Edgett, S. J., *Generating Breakthrough New Product Ideas: Feeding the Innovation Funnel.* Product Development Institute, 2007. [Useful overview of internal and external sources of ideas for new product development. Unfortunately gives very little detail on the techniques themselves.]
2. Evans, S., Burns, A. and Barrett, R., *Empathic Design Tutor.* Bedford: Cranfield University, 2002. [Short booklet with very useful ideas on different "empathic design tools."]
3. Deszca, G., Munro, H. and Noori, H., "Developing Breakthrough Products: Challenges and Options for Market Assessment," *Journal of Operations Management,* Vol. 17, No. 6, 1999, pp. 613–630. [Good paper on the challenges of finding the right ways to gain the insights necessary for developing breakthrough products.]
4. Verganti, R., *Design-Driven Innovation—Changing the Rules of Competition by Radically Innovating What Things Mean.* Boston, MA: Harvard Business Press, 2009. [Excellent discussion of the value that design can bring in creating products that evoke positive emotions.]

10 CREATING A CULTURE FOCUSED ON HIDDEN NEEDS

> Innovation cannot be prescribed from above...it does not consist in following existing routines.[1]

INTRODUCTION

For organizations that always strive to be at the leading edge, the decision to adopt new techniques for market research and to focus on hidden needs will be an easy one. However, in many organizations, there can be significant barriers to the adoption of a philosophy of hidden needs. Sometimes the senior management team is unaware of the powerful new techniques for understanding customers. Sometimes it is R&D departments, with little knowledge of the social sciences, that are skeptical. However, it is often marketing departments that present the greatest opposition. Some marketers feel they are the guardians of their company's knowledge on customers' needs and are reluctant to admit that they need to learn new approaches, as this admission might be perceived as a sign of weakness. In fact, recognizing that more insightful customer data need to be generated using enhanced techniques is a sign of strength but one that only top marketing departments exhibit. In addition to marketing opposition, there are a number of reasons why it can be challenging for organizations to focus on hidden needs and so this chapter:

- Starts with a detailed case study on a business unit of the German company Bosch, and how it made the decision to introduce new methods for market research.
- Comments on the Bosch case study, and the issues it raises.
- Identifies the barriers that companies face in moving toward a philosophy of hidden needs.
- Summarizes the key steps required to create a culture that is focused on hidden needs and which develops breakthrough products and services.

BOSCH PACKAGING TECHNOLOGY CASE STUDY

This case study tells the story of the development of a complex piece of manufacturing equipment for the pharmaceutical sector by Bosch Packaging Technology. It demonstrates that hidden needs techniques can be applied in the business-to-business (B2B) sector with just as must success as in consumer (B2C) markets. The Bosch case study is the story of a very successful product development. So readers should consider what it was that enabled the Packaging organization to quickly adopt a hidden needs approach.

Box Case 10.1

Bosch Packaging Technology—Making the FXS 5100 Stand-out[2]

The Bosch Group employs 280,000 people worldwide and its Packaging Technology Division serves the food, pharmaceutical, cosmetics, and chemicals industries. Part of this Division, the Bosch factory at Crailsheim (northeast of Stuttgart), designs and manufactures high-technology production line equipment for the pharmaceutical sector. Crailsheim produces a range of products for packaging pharmaceuticals, such as systems for filling vials with liquid pharmaceuticals. Packaging systems are significant investments for pharmaceutical companies. Such systems cost up to several million euros but are able to automatically fill hundreds of vials per minute and provide the highly accurate and sterile filling capabilities needed to meet the demanding FDA (Food and Drugs Administration) manufacturing regulations.

The emergence of biotech pharmaceutical products in the 1990s generated new packaging requirements. Biotech products are so expensive that filling accuracy is essential, high speed filling is needed, and sterile handling is a must. By 2000, liquid pharmaceuticals were increasingly being filled directly into presterilized single-use syringes rather than vials. There were two reasons for this. First, single-use syringes are easier for medical staff to use (they do not need to fill a syringe from a vial) and, second, with expensive biotech products there is less wastage (there is always residual waste when a syringe is filled from a vial).

And so an attractive market was developing for Bosch...but there were complications.

THE "4TH-TO-MARKET CHALLENGE"

In 2003 senior management at Crailsheim were considering whether to make major investments in developing a product to enter the presterilized syringe filling market—often known as the "sterile-clean-fill market" (derived from the SCF™ product name used by the original supplier of presterilized syringes, Becton & Dickinson). The problem facing Bosch was that several companies already offered packaging systems for filling presterilized syringes. In particular, three leading competitors—Inova, Groninger, and Bausch + Ströbel—offered products with a full set of features and had considerable market presence.

▶▶

An analysis of the competitors' products and visits to key customers had enabled Bosch marketing to identify the typical features required for the presterilized syringe filling market. In addition, the Crailsheim engineering team had conducted a preliminary analysis and believed it could develop a product with higher specifications than the incumbents'. However, Crailsheim management was seriously concerned that, being the fourth major entrant to the market, competition would be so intense that only a clearly differentiated product would be successful—one that would really stand out. As the R&D investment to develop a SCF system was high, management decided to delay the decision long enough to take another look at the market.

And so Marketing was given four months to identify whether there was an opportunity for Bosch to develop a product that could be differentiated from the competition.

MARKET RESEARCH—REVISITED

To gain the market insights required, the Crailsheim Marketing team decided it was time to apply a new approach. "We needed to understand the whole environment in which the SCF filling systems were being used and not just the features that were currently offered" says Klaus Schreiber, Head of Product Management Pharma Liquid. In the summer of 2003 he began the quest to identify market needs, together with Product Manager Klaus Ullherr.

In their previous research, the Crailsheim Marketing Department had conducted a feature-for-feature analysis of the competitors' products. In addition, they had interviewed customers who already had presterilized syringe filling lines. Although this provided a good overview of the market, "we had a feeling that what the customers were telling us was too strongly focused on the features offered by our competitors and the views being expressed were already out-of-date," says Schreiber. Therefore, Bosch Crailsheim took the decision to enlist the support of a business school in planning the second round of market research. Another important decision taken by the Crailsheim marketing department was to look at the need for a "service package" to support the product offering. As filling and packaging systems are complex, pharmaceutical companies need help with installation and equipment maintenance. "We knew we needed the right product-service combination," says Ullherr.

And so, it was decided to apply three market research techniques: contextual interviews; a survey; and repertory grid interviews.

CONTEXTUAL INTERVIEWS

In-depth contextual interviews with pharmaceutical production managers and line operators were arranged in factories in both Europe and the U.S. These interviews were designed to generate a deep understanding of the way presterilized syringe filling equipment is used, the features required, and the issues faced with operating filling systems on pharmaceutical production lines. Compared with the earlier customer visits, these interviews used open-ended questions and were conducted in "context"—in

▶▶

the factories where the presterilized syringe filling equipment was being used. This allowed questions to be asked based on what was seen in the physical environment. For example, graphs of the key manufacturing performance measures were often seen next to production lines and this led to questions such as: "How does your current filling system help or hinder you achieving these targets?" This stimulated interviewees to point out some of the problems with their current equipment.

Some points from the interviews, such as the number of syringes to be filled per minute (customers said they needed 300 per minute), had been obvious from the competitor analysis, whereas others were not. The interviews identified the typical problems with filling systems, such as broken syringes, poor stopper insertion (in the syringes), and bent insertion rods. Another piece of information from the interviews was about the need for flexibility: "*it was clear that a filling system must be highly flexible, that is able to quickly switch between batches, or syringe sizes, or drugs, and be physically compatible with the space and layout restrictions in a typical factory*," says Ullherr.

The contextual interviews also placed a strong emphasis on identifying service issues. Rather than just discussing installation and maintenance, the interviews looked to identify all of the post-sales service issues that pharmaceutical manufacturers face. It quickly emerged that there were a number of service issues that were perceived as key: fast installation; the training of production line employees; equipment "uptime"; and "validation." Uptime is the amount of time that a filling system is functioning 100 percent and is important because a faulty system can stop a whole production line. Validation is defined by the FDA as "establishing documented evidence, which provides a high degree of assurance that specific processes will consistently produce a product meeting its predetermined specifications and quality attributes." Although the competitors offered after-sales service, it became clear that Bosch had an opportunity to produce a much better service package, as pharmaceutical companies perceived the current validation process for new filling systems to be awkward and time-consuming.

As the data from the contextual interviews began to come in, "*we started to think that we were on to something. It appeared that there were customer needs that the competitors had missed…but we didn't know if we had enough to convince management to make the investment*," says Schreiber.

IDENTIFYING PRIORITIES—A SURVEY

The next part of the market research was a survey of pharmaceutical companies' priorities for product and service features. The questions were based on the product features and the types of service that had emerged from the contextual interviews. It was found that service aspects were perceived as just as important as the design of the filling system itself, because it was the combination of the product and service that determined how fast a new filling system could be validated. For example, overly complex equipment with computer monitoring was not always liked because, as one interviewee said, "we don't use the data monitoring feature [of our filling systems] as it extends the validation process by 3–6 months." "*Another important finding was that*

▶▶

customers had a long list of priorities," says Ullherr. The survey results showed that customers perceived 11 factors including flexibility, speed of validation, and a "fully automated system" as equally important. And several of these priorities were not addressed by the competitors' products.

And so, *"that made us wonder if our competitors, with their years of market experience, hadn't solved some of the big issues would we—as the new entrant—be able to do it,"* says Schreiber.

REPERTORY GRID INTERVIEWS

The third part of the market research consisted of repertory grid interviews with production managers. Obtaining the agreement of managers to spend a full hour discussing presterilized syringe filling equipment took some persuasion but these interviews were to provide some critical insights for Bosch.

The idea behind the repertory grid interviews was to probe for the limitations in the design of the current filling systems that managers had not articulated in the contextual interviews. To do this, the key stages of a filling system were used as the elements of the repertory grid technique. Bosch knew that a typical presterilized syringe filling system consisted of six stages:

- A conveyor belt that takes tubs of presterilized syringes and moves them to a sterile area.
- Mechanical scissors and other devices to open the tubs.
- Handling equipment to take the syringes out of the tub, typically in "nests" of one hundred.
- A filling station to accurately and quickly fill the nest of syringes with liquid drugs.
- A machine to apply the stoppers to the syringes.
- Final sterile packaging of the syringes.

Interestingly, the repertory grid interviewees identified intermediary stages that they perceived to be critical—for example, subcomponents that they often experienced issues with. Once the elements were elicited, the interviewees were presented with random groups of three elements (triads) with the question: "How are two of these stages similar and different from the third?" The interviews elicited over 30 constructs—such as "automatic cleaning" and "critical for the process." In explaining their constructs, the interviewees provided valuable details of the problems that production managers and employees faced in operating existing presterilized syringe filling systems. Critically, many of the details of these problems had not been identified from the contextual interviews.

The three types of market research produced, *"a mass of data and the analysis was over 100 pages long. We needed to condense that down into a presentation for the management team,"* says Ullherr. *"The investment required to develop a new filling system is significant and so we were all on edge, to see what management would decide,"* says Schreiber.

▶▶

THE DECISION IS MADE

At the October 2003 meeting, senior management concentrated on whether a really differentiated product could be developed, so that the Bosch offering would stand out from the competition. The volume of data collected by the Marketing Department was to prove its worth. Each of the recommendations on the possible product and service features were shown by Marketing to be based on customer-derived data. The deep understanding of the customer's view of the problems associated with each of the stages of the filling process was also perceived positively by the management. In the event, the decision to invest in developing a presterilized syringe filling system was made by the senior management team, more quickly than maybe Marketing had expected. In addition to giving the go-ahead, management suggested that a phased introduction of products was appropriate, with a presterilized syringe filling station first, and then a fully automated system.

DESIGNING THE FXS 5100 PRODUCT

Filling hundreds of presterilized syringes per minute requires a complex mix of mechanical and electrical engineering, industrial design, and mechatronics. The moment the investment decision had been taken by senior management, the R&D laboratory at Crailsheim assigned a full new product development (NPD) team. The market research provided them with a deep understanding of the key areas in which they could design a better product than the competitors'. Werner Mayer, Director Engineering/Development and Documentation, manages over 70 mechanical designers and says that, "*marketing gave us a lot of technical challenges but I'm pleased to say that my guys found creative ways to solve the issues that customers had found problematic with competitors' products.*" For example, the R&D team designed the FXS 5100 so that it could be operated, cleaned, and serviced from one side, which means that the system can be installed against a wall, saving space in a factory.

During the two year development project, the engineering team was also presented with somewhat of a moving target. Initially the goal for the filling speed was 300 syringes per minute but during the project this increased first to 400 per minute, and then to 500 per minute. The presterilized syringe filling market was changing and so, "*Getting the concept right and keeping up with the market was essential and it took long, hard but ultimately positive discussions*" says Mayer. Part way through the project Crailsheim had some luck—two engineers with SCF filling experience from other companies applied for positions at Bosch and their knowledge came in very useful in addressing the evolving market requirements.

The FXS 5100 filling station is several meters long, 2 meters high, and the Bosch engineers are proud that the glass enclosed, stainless steel equipment not only works efficiently but also looks like a technological work of art. As part of the phased introduction strategy, the FXS 5100 was shown for the first time at the *Interphex USA* trade fair in New York in March 2006. Although the FXS 5100 did not have the fully automated features (such as tub opening) at that time, showing it "*was an important signal to the market, it generated interest and got us into further interesting conversations with customers,*" says Schreiber.

▸▸

INSIGHTS FROM APPLICATIONS ENGINEERING

The work of Marketing and R&D and the evolving design of the FXS 5100 were also influenced by the Applications Engineering Department at Crailsheim. This is managed by Herr Markus Kurz, Head of Project Management Bosch Crailsheim. Application Engineering's role is to manage modifications that customers request when ordering equipment. Most pharmaceutical companies have specific requirements and so application engineers are installation experts who know the "ins and outs" of production equipment—in particular the "upstream" (bag and tub opening) and "downstream" (repackaging of filling syringes) requirements of fully automated packaging systems. Based on their constant interaction with customers at a technical level, a deep understanding of fully automated presterilized syringe filling systems emerged. *"Our constant dialogue with customers was very important. It allowed us to report on trends and give detailed information on technical designs for upstream and downstream,"* says Kurz. For example, his engineers were able to provide key insights on the functioning of ABO equipment (automatic bag opening machines). *"We also were able to help recommend how the product-service package could be configured,"* says Kurz.

MARKET SUCCESS

Even considering the high investment costs, the FXS 5100 has been a resounding success and the worries about being a late entrant are a thing of the past. The first full "reference site"—a fully automated filling system, including upstream and downstream components—was installed at a major pharmaceutical company in May 2007. Prospective customers visit regularly and sales of the FXS 5100 have exceeded Crailsheim's expectations. Similarly, related products such as the ATO (automatic tub opening) and the FXS 2050 (specially designed for the Asian market) have sold well.

From an organizational perspective, the FXS 5100 project has also been important for Crailsheim. *"Bosch wouldn't have made the decision to enter the market without the depth of findings from the second market study,"* says Schreiber, *"it has changed the way we look at market research."* Overall, the FXS 5100 team from Marketing, R&D, and Applications Engineering conducted a very successful development project and maybe this is the reason that Bosch Crailsheim has been chosen by the Packaging Technology Division to be specifically responsible for finding ways to enhance the NPD process used by the Division.

Lessons from the Bosch Case Study

There are a number of key lessons from the case:

- At Bosch Packaging there was a pressing need to try another approach to market research because management recognized the danger of being fourth-to-market with a me-too product.
- The marketing department at Crailsheim realized that a new approach was necessary, as their previous attempt to identify the best way to compete with

the incumbents had focused on current market features. Similarly, marketing had no reservations in working with a business school to help them design an enhanced market study.

- Management was initially skeptical of the ability of new techniques to identify customers' hidden needs but was open enough to provide funding for the project.
- The research project blended several techniques and enough time was allocated to conducting a thorough analysis—there was no unrealistic pressure to get results too soon.
- The market research techniques were applied in an open-minded, systematic, and objective way. (Some companies misuse the techniques simply to gather data to justify an existing point of view.)
- Bosch Crailsheim already had a working environment and culture that allowed innovation to flourish. For example, the strategy and approach to innovation were well aligned; senior management provided support; there was a willingness to try new techniques even though there was a risk they might fail; and there was strong encouragement for collaboration between R&D, Marketing, and Applications Engineering.
- The FXS 5100 project has not been a "one-off"; rather the use of multiple methods for market research is one of a number of innovative approaches that has led Crailsheim to be given responsibility for optimizing the NPD process within the Packaging Technology Division.

It would be good if we could say that the Bosch case is typical but, unfortunately, it is not—normally there are barriers within companies to the adoption of a hidden needs approach.

THE BARRIERS TO THE HIDDEN NEEDS VISION

Our own research with numerous organizations has shown that circumstances often block companies from adopting a hidden needs approach to innovation. In addition, an interesting exploratory study by Dr. Ceri Batchelder and colleagues investigated 14 organizations.[3] It looked at the market research techniques used by the companies and the organizational issues they had faced in adopting such techniques. The study concluded: "competitive advantage is not attained by hidden insights methodologies and techniques alone but through multiple [cultural and process] factors."[4] So it is important to discuss how the cultural and organization barriers can be overcome.

The Two Barriers

There are two main barriers to be overcome before a philosophy of hidden needs can be embedded in an organization. Figure 10.1 shows that the first barrier hinders many organizations from developing the *intention to use* new

BARRIER ONE (INTENTION TO USE)
1) Relying on internally generated product ideas
2) Lack of awareness of hidden needs approaches
3) Company culture does not support use of hidden needs techniques
4) Company strategy/direction is not aligned with the use of hidden needs analysis for breakthrough innovation

BARRIER TWO *(EFFECTIVE USAGE)*
1) Lack of leadership/champions
2) Time and effort to learn the techniques
3) Lack of cross-functional team involvement
4) Gaps in communication processes

Figure 10.1 Organizational Barriers to the Adoption of Hidden Needs Techniques
Source: Diagram enhanced and used with permission from: Batchelder, C., Pinto, C., Bogg, D., Sharples, C. and Hill, A., "Capturing Best Practice in Establishing Customers' Hidden Needs for Smith and Nephew," Manchester Business School, International Business Project 2006, December 2006, p. 31.

techniques. Four factors typically contribute to this barrier: many organizations are used to (and satisfied with) relying on internally generated ideas for new products and services; *hidden needs* is an aspect of innovation management that is not *yet* well-known (other aspects of innovation management such as *open innovation*[5] are the current buzzwords); in many organizations company culture does not support trying something new; and often company strategy does not adequately focus on breakthrough products and services (see Box Case 10.2).

Even when a company intends to adopt new techniques for identifying customers' hidden needs, it does not guarantee success. A second barrier hinders the *effective usage* of the techniques. This barrier consist of four factors: there are not enough people who have the knowledge of hidden needs techniques and the leadership skills required to change a company's approach; time and effort is required to become efficient in the new techniques; to be totally effective, hidden needs analysis needs to be applied using cross-functional teams (but many organizations have functional silos); and finally a good communications process is essential.

In overcoming the barriers to the adoption of a philosophy of hidden needs, managers need to think where *change management* tools can be applied, such as the analysis of which stakeholders will be supportive and which will be against (see recommended reading at the end of this chapter). Similarly, it is important not to try and introduce hidden needs as part of a new process for product development. It is much more effective to choose a key project on which the new approaches can be applied. A successful project sends a strong signal throughout an organization, a much stronger signal than a (somewhat abstract) change to the new product development process.

Box Case 10.2

Black & Decker—Focusing on Breakthrough Products[6]

Black & Decker is famous for its power tools but it reserves a distinct brand—DeWalt—for its line of professional tools, such as drills and miter saws. The company is well aware of the challenges of the professional market, in which the decision-makers are looking for innovative, reliable, and efficient tools and are not loyal to a single brand. John Schiech, President of DeWalt has adopted a first-to-market strategy and has developed the core capabilities of his organization to match this. For instance, he explains that deep customer insights are obtained by "engineers and marketing product managers spending hours and hours on building sites talking to the guys who are trying to make their living with these tools." Observing professionals working with power tools allows DeWalt to identify the problems and issues they face and to develop products to solve these. Schiech wants his organization to focus on breakthroughs because, "It's only when you come with a breakthrough product that you can really change the game in terms of market share." To be successful at breakthrough innovation, the company not only focuses on customer insights but also rapid prototyping, in the 40–50 projects that are running at any one time. The first-to-market strategy has been very successful and is tracked using a key performance measure that DeWalt calls *product vitality*—the percentage of sales from products launched in the previous three years. This performance measure is typically around 30 percent and some years it has even exceeded 50 percent.

Overcoming the Barriers—*Intention to Use*

As shown in Table 10.1, actions must be taken to address the factors that stop companies even making the decision to adopt a philosophy of hidden needs. For example, the reliance on internally generated ideas can be overcome by analyzing whether customers perceive your company's current product offering to be exciting. Similarly, actions need to be taken to create awareness; create the right organizational culture (where the adoption of new ideas becomes the norm); and to ensure that company strategy is focused on breakthrough products. Audi has the right organizational culture in that market research is regarded as highly important and something that every senior manager must have experience of (see Box Case 10.3).

One reason that the value of hidden needs is not well-known is that the companies that develop breakthrough products and significant sales are reluctant to disclose either the amounts that they had to invest to develop internal capabilities in hidden needs or the return they generated through sales. (Academic research is needed to close this gap.)

Box Case 10.3

Audi—Vorsprung durch Technik...and Market Insights[7]

The Audi company is famous for its level of innovation and the slogan *Vorsprung durch Technik*. Less well-known is the strong emphasis Audi places on market understanding. Johann Gessler the Head of the Engine Development Test Center, a mechanical engineer by training, manages over 500 engineers, technicians, and craftsmen working on the development of car engines at two locations in Germany. In most automotive companies the development of car engines is the realm of technology and is far removed from the customer. But not at Audi. In 2006, as part of a management development program, Gessler spent two weeks conducting market research in China. Together with 20 other managers from a range of functional areas including finance, marketing and R&D, Gessler was trained in cross-cultural observation. Then he was immersed in the Chinese markets: together with a colleague and a translator he visited dealers, interviewed Chinese families in their homes, visited dealers and distributors, and traveled with business people on their way to and from work. By spending so much time with Chinese consumers, Gessler and the other managers were able to generate a deep understanding of the Chinese market—an important one for Audi and very useful in the development of the A8 product that was introduced on November 30, 2009. As Gessler says, "Visiting China to conduct the market research allowed me to understand one of our major markets much better but it also gave me first-hand experience of the value of market research generated through intense teamwork."

There are two particularly interesting aspects about Audi's approach: first, the time and effort that the company invested in understanding the Chinese market for their A8 model; second, it is striking that Audi has such a focus on the customer that senior managers from all functional areas are required to have firsthand experience of market research. Many other organizations talk about being market-driven but Audi has put market understanding high on the list of the skills that it regards as essential for senior managers.

Overcoming the Barriers—*to Effective Usage*

Once the intention to adopt a philosophy of hidden needs is there, a second barrier needs to be overcome. As indicated by Table 10.1, management sponsorship and *hidden needs champions* (managers who have expertise in the techniques and the ability to provide leadership in their adoption within a company) are needed; and time and effort must be invested in gaining knowledge of the new techniques (otherwise ethnographic and other studies will be rushed and will produce superficial results). Similarly, cross-functional teams should be involved to gain the most from the new methods; and the success of hidden needs approaches is dependent on clear and precise communication on why they are necessary and how they will be applied.

Table 10.1 Overcoming the Barriers to the Adoption of a Philosophy of Hidden Needs

Category	Factors	Typical Issues	Actions to Overcome the Barriers
BARRIER ONE (*Intention to use*)	Reliance on internally generated ideas for new products and services.	• Organizations that use only internal ideas may not recognize that they only develop incremental innovations. • Lack of understanding that creativity relies on different perspectives. • Market research is misused in being used to support marketing decisions that have already been made	• Analyze the main sources of ideas for the new products and services introduced in the past five years versus the success of these products. • Conduct a competitive analysis to identify how strongly your company's products are differentiated from the competition. • Conduct a Kano analysis (see Chapter 1) to determine how many of your current products have excitement features. Make sure that this analysis is based on customers' and not internal perspectives!
	Lack of awareness of hidden needs techniques.	• Ethnographic market research, repertory grid technique, and the like are not well-known (see Chapter 1). • The commercial returns from investments in hidden needs are not clear.	• Encourage employees to attend conferences on innovation best practice. • Organize visits for cross-functional teams to see how leading companies in other segments generate a deep understanding of customers.
	Organizational culture is not supportive.	• Current new product development processes can lead to a reliance on current approaches. • Marketing department often perceives hidden needs philosophy as a threat to their authority (on customers' needs). • All departments need to actively think how the company's capabilities can solve customer issues.[a]	• Encourage an organizational culture that is open to new ideas, where learning is the norm, and where market insights are highly valued (see Box Case 10.3 on Audi). • Ensure that your marketing department does not feel threatened by assigning marketing professionals some of the key responsibilities in the move to a philosophy of hidden needs. • Ensure that your engineers are not skeptical of social science approaches.[b]
	Company strategy does not align with hidden needs.	• Lack of urgency to try new techniques. • Company vision does not mention innovation. • No focus on breakthrough products.	• Focus on innovation (see Box Case 10.2 on Black & Decker). • Conduct a stakeholder analysis to identify which decision-makers/functional areas will be supportive and which will not. • Take your next major product (or service) innovation project and apply new approaches to generate market insights. Make this project such a success that your company strategy can take innovation as a key component.

Continued

Table 10.1 Continued

Category	Factors	Typical Issues	Actions to Overcome the Barriers
BARRIER TWO (*Effective usage*)	Lack of leadership/ champions.	• The adoption of hidden needs approaches is not easy. • The way that a philosophy of hidden needs can best be implemented depends on the specific history and situation of a company. Both top management sponsors and hidden needs champions are needed.	• Have cross-functional teams trained in the techniques. • Innovation champions need to be experts in the approaches and their application (see Box Case 10.4 on Whirlpool). • Senior management sponsors and a "champion" to take responsibility for the implementation are needed. The latter person needs to become an expert in the techniques and to pro-actively work on overcoming Barrier Two.
	Time and effort required to learn and apply new techniques.	• Almost no marketing courses or MBA programs cover the new techniques. • Market research agencies do not share their knowledge of techniques. • Management takes a long time to decide to adopt new techniques and then expects the results overnight.[c] • Techniques are not applied in a systematic and objective way.	• Providing sufficient resources is important. Ensure that sufficient time is allocated to the investigation phase of new product development. • Do not use agencies just to provide you with market insights, negotiate with them to involve your staff and provide training on techniques and how to apply them.
	Lack of cross-functional team involvement.	• If departments such as R&D are not involved in the market research they may be skeptical about the results.	• Always involve cross-functional teams in hidden needs projects (remember that creativity theory tells us that different perspectives lead to innovative ideas).
	Gaps in the communication process.	• Senior management often do not communicate the reasons for focusing on hidden needs and breakthrough innovation. • Without adequate explanation, hidden needs techniques can be perceived as unnecessary effort without clear returns.	• Clearly identify and communicate the costs and the risks of focusing on hidden needs and breakthrough products. • Identify and promote the need to make the (relatively low) investments required to develop internal competencies in hidden needs. • Measure and discuss the return on the investments in learning and applying hidden needs techniques.

Note: Based on the work of the authors with a number of organizations which are described in case studies in this book plus a number of confidential projects. Cranfield School of Management is now conducting formal research into these issues. [a]De Young, G., "'Listen, 'Then Design'," *Industry Week*, No. 246, February 17, p. 76; [b]Leinbach, C., "Managing for Breakthroughs: A View from Industrial Design." In Squires, S. and Byrne, B. (eds.) *Creating Breakthrough Ideas: The Collaboration of Anthropologists and Designers in the Product Development Industry*. Westport, CT: Bergin and Garvey, 2002, pp. 3–16; [c]At Cranfield School of Management we have recently worked with a software company that took over three months to decide to apply ethnographic market research and repertory grid technique and then, having decided, wanted the results within an unrealistic four weeks.

Box Case 10.4

Whirlpool—Innovation Champions[8]

Whirlpool Corporation is a world leading international manufacturer of home appliances and generates over $19 billion sales per year. Founded in 1911 and having produced washing machines under different names since that time, it was in 1949 that the name Whirlpool Corporation was adopted and the company became a leading supplier of innovative products. However, by the mid-1990s, the household appliance market had become a commodity one. There were too many manufacturers competing in the market; they were offering similar products and so price became the key purchase criterion and Whirpool, with its engineering and manufacturing culture, focused on cost-cutting. It took a new CEO to realize that market-driven innovation could produce products that would stand out. This entailed a fresh approach to new product development and the extensive use of systematic observation and other techniques. Whirlpool developed a vision called "Innovation from Everyone Everywhere" and, as the company has over 70,000 employees, creating a culture of innovation was complex. "Innovation champions" were trained in the key aspects of innovation management but, in addition, every employee received a short training on innovation. Today, the message of the Whirlpool website is: "Wrinkles, Confusing Settings, Lots of Laundry, Energy Bills, Tough Stains.... We Hear You."

SUMMARY

Companies that are successful at adopting a philosophy of hidden needs have an open attitude, take the time and effort to train their people in different techniques, and employ innovation champions to push the ideas through. This book has shown:

- A culture (or philosophy) of hidden needs has four key components. It recognizes that traditional methods of market research are inadequate; that new techniques should be applied in combination with traditional ones to give deep market insights (and more reliable results); it stresses that market insights should be formulated as customer problems for which solutions— breakthrough products and services—are needed; to develop breakthrough products and services, the right organizational culture is essential.
- The main methods that give deep market insights are ethnographic market research (systematic observation and contextual interviewing); repertory grid technique; and involving the user. These should be applied in combination with interviews, focus groups, and surveys.
- Companies need to be proactive in developing the intention to use hidden needs techniques. This means that the complacency of using internally generated ideas needs to be challenged, awareness of the new methods and their advantages needs to be generated; the right organizational culture must be created; and a strategy focused on breakthrough innovation is essential.

- Once a company intends to apply hidden needs analysis, it needs to focus on identifying management sponsors and hidden needs champions; training cross-functional teams in the techniques; taking the time and effort to conduct meaningful research; and communicating effectively.
- That choosing the right project on which to apply hidden needs techniques is essential, as when this project is successful this will send a positive message and will help to quickly embed the hidden needs approach throughout the organization.

The message of the final chapter is a simple one: adopt the culture of innovation, develop a deep understanding of your customers and their hidden needs, and turn these insights into breakthrough products and services features. Although the message is simple, achieving a culture of hidden needs is not always easy and so we wish you and your company every success in solving the challenges.

MANAGEMENT RECOMMENDATIONS

- Identify the factors which currently block the adoption of hidden needs techniques and develop plans to address them (use Table 10.1).
- Choose a key project on which to apply the new techniques.
- Have key staff trained in both the individual techniques and in how to apply techniques in parallel, to obtain more reliable results.
- Create a culture of innovation in which cross-functional teams, skilled in the relevant techniques, conduct market research and design breakthrough products.

RECOMMENDED READING

1. Tushman, M. L. and Anderson, P. (eds.) *Managing Strategic Innovation and Change*, Oxford: Oxford University Press, 1997. [Classic collection of readings on culture, leadership, and innovation. Not specifically focused on market insights but still very useful.]

2. Balogun, J., Hope Hailey, V. with Johnson, G. and Scholes, K., *Exploring Strategic Change*, London: Prentice Hall, 1999. [Useful text which explains the key tools and techniques for change management.]

Appendix 1: Form for Observers' Notes at Focus Groups

FOCUS GROUP DATA CAPTURE PRO-FORMA				
Study Title:				
Date:				
Moderator Name:				
Pro-forma Completed by:				
Group Detail:				
No. Participants:				
Start Time:				
End Time:				
Participant Demographics: *enter column headings as appropriate*				
Gender/Age	Job			

Participants' Positions:

Draw diagram of table and note participant seating positions.

Discussion Question 1	
Data/Quotes/Observations *(Note down relevant quotes and enter time in right hand column)*	Time

Discussion Question 2	
Data/Quote/Observations *(Note down relevant quotes and enter time in right hand column)*	Time

Discussion Question 3	
Data/Quotes/Observations *(Note down relevant quotes and enter time in right hand column)*	Time

Additional Comments and Reflections
Consider comments on strongest individual opinion and group dynamics.

Appendix 2: Field Notes Form for Ethnographic Market Research (See Chapter 4)

Field Notes made by................

Research Project:
Case: #
Location / Date:

Actors:

Field Observations:

-
-
-
-
-
-
-
-

Initial Reflections

-
-
-

Remember!

- Notes should cover: space; actor(s); activities; object(s) and physical traces; events; time sequences; goals; feelings; and explanatory variables.

Appendix 3: Repertory Grid for Six Elements (See Chapter 6)

Date:
Interviewer:

Purpose:
Start:

Interviewee:
Finish:

Tape:

Order of personal elements: 5; 1; 6; 4; 3; 2
Stars in grid indicate the triads

CONSTRUCTS	Elements 1	Elements 2	Elements 3	Elements 4	Elements 5	Elements 6	POLE
1	*	*	*				
2				*	*	*	
3	*		*		*		
4		*		*		*	
5	*	*		*			
6	*		*	*		*	
7		*	*		*		
8				*			
9	*				*	*	
10		*			*	*	
11			*		*	*	
12			*	*	*	*	

Appendix 4: Repertory Grid for Ten Elements (See Chapter 6)

Date:
Interviewer:

Purpose:
Start:

Interviewee:
Finish:

Order of personal elements: 5; 1; 8; 6; 9; 10; 4; 7; 3; 2
Stars indicate the triads

CONSTRUCTS	Element 1	Element 2	Element 3	Element 4	Element 5	Element 6	Element 7	Element 8	Element 9	Element 10	POLES
1	*	*	*								
2				*	*						
3				*		*		*			
4	*		*			*					
5											
6		*			*						
7				*		*	*				
8	*				*	*	*				
9					*		*		*		
10	*			*				*		*	
11										*	
12											

241

REFERENCES AND NOTES

1 INTRODUCTION TO CUSTOMERS' HIDDEN NEEDS

1. Gill, G. K., "Sony Corporation: Workstation Division," *Harvard Business School*, Case Study 9–690-031 (1989) (quote on p. 1).
2. Balachandra, R. and Friar, J. H., "Factors for Success in R&D Projects and New Product Innovation: A Contextual Framework," *IEEE Trans. on Engineering Management*, Vol. 44, No. 3, August 1997, pp. 276–287.
3. Cooper, R. G. and Kleinschmidt, E. J., "Major New Products: What Distinguishes the Winners in the Chemical Industry?" *Journal of Product Innovation Management*, Vol. 10, No. 2, March 1993, pp. 90–111.
4. Ohno, T., *Toyota Production System: Beyond Large-scale Production*. New York: Productivity Press, 1995.
5. Cooper, R. G., *Product Leadership: Creating and Launching Superior New Products*. Reading, MA: Perseus Books, 1998.
6. Kärkkainen, H., Piippo, P., Puumalainen, K. and Tuominen, M., "Assessment of Hidden and Future Customer Needs in Finnish Business-to-Business Companies," *R&D Management*, Vol. 31, No. 4, 2001, pp. 391–407.
7. Jordan, M. and Karp, J., "Whirlpool Launches Affordable Washer in Brazil and China," *The Wall Street Journal Europe*, Tuesday, December 9, 2003, p. A8.
8. Rust, R. T., Thompson, D. V. and Hamilton, R. W. "Defeating Feature Fatigue," *Harvard Business Review*, Vol. 84, No. 2, February 2006, pp. 98–107.
9. Green, P. E., Tull, D. S. and Albaum, G., *Research for Marketing Decisions*. London: Prentice-Hall International, 1988.
10. Ulwick, A. W., "Turn Customer Input into Innovation," *Harvard Business Review*, Vol. 80, No. 1, January 2002, pp. 91–97 (quote on p. 91).
11. Sorensen, J., "The Eye on the Shelf: Point-of-Purchase Research," *Marketing News*, Vol. 33, No. 1, January 4, 1999, p. 4.
12. *Ibid.*
13. Sandberg, K. D., "Focus on the Benefits," *Harvard Management Communication Newsletter*, Vol. 5, No. 4, 2002, pp. 3–4.
14. Magnusson, P. R., Matthing, J. and Kristensson, P., "Managing Service Involvement in Service Innovation: Experiments with Innovating End Users," *Journal of Service Research*, Vol. 6, No. 2, November 2003, pp. 111–124.
15. Deszca, G., Munro, H. and Noori, H., "Developing Breakthrough Products: Challenges and Options for Market Assessment," *Journal of Operations Management*, Vol. 17, No. 6, 1999, p. 613.
16. Ulrich, K. T. and Eppinger, S. D., *Product Design and Development*. 2nd edition. Boston, MA: McGraw-Hill, 2000.
17. Huston, L. and Sakkab, N., "Connect and Develop: Inside Proctor and Gamble's New Model for Innovation," *Harvard Business Review*, Vol. 84, No. 3, March 2006, p. 62.

18. Kano, N., Saraku, N., Takahashi, F. and Tsuji, S., "Attractive Quality and Must-be Quality." In Hromi, J. D. (ed.) *The Best on Quality*, Vol. 7, Ch. 10, Milwaukee: ASQC, 1996, pp. 165–186.

19. Matzler, K. and Hinterhuber, H., "How to Make Product Development Projects More Successful by Integrating Kano's Model of Customer Satisfaction into Quality Function Deployment," *Technovation* Vol. 18, No. 1, 1998, pp. 25–38.

20. Fellman, M. W., "Breaking Tradition," *Marketing Research*, Vol. 11, No. 3, Fall 1999, pp. 20–24.

21. Based on discussions with Chris Towns of Clarks and: Towns, C. and Humphries, D., "Breaking New Ground in Customer Behavioural Research: Experience from Clarks/PDD," *Product Development Management Association UK & Ireland Conference*, London, November, 2001.

22. Rosier, B., "From the Dreams of Children to the Future of Technology," *The Independent on Sunday* (UK), July 15, 2001, p. 8.

23. Macht, J. D., "The New Market Research," *Inc. Magazine*, Vol. 20, No. 10, July 1998, pp. 86–94.

24. Case based on company documentation, an interview, and personal correspondence with Cobra managers in May 2004 and January 2009.

25. Useful guidelines on market research ethics include—Market Research Society (see http://www.mrs.org.uk/standards/codeconduct)—American Marketing Association (see http://www.marketingpower.com/)—The British Psychological Society (see http://www.bps.org.uk/the-society/code-of-conduct/).

26. Squires, S. and Byrne, B. (eds.) *Creating Breakthrough Ideas: The Collaboration of Anthropologists and Designers in the Product Development Industry*. Westport, CT: Bergin and Garvey, 2002.

27. Meyer, C. and Ruggles, R., "Search Parties," *Harvard Business Review*, Vol. 80, No. 8, August 2002, pp. 14–15 (quote on p. 14).

28. Fellman, 1999, pp. 20–24.

29. Goffin, K. and Szwejczewski, M., "Keep a Close Eye on the Market," *Management Focus* (Cranfield School of Management), Autumn 2009, pp. 17–19.

30. For details of these approaches see Goffin, K. and Mitchell, R., *Innovation Management: Strategy and Implementation Using the Pentathlon Framework*. Basingstoke: Palgrave Macmillan Academic Publishers, 2nd edition. March 2010.

31. Venkatesh, A., "The Home of the Future: An Ethnographic Study of New Information Technologies in the Home," *Advances in Consumer Research*, Vol. XXVIII, 2001, pp. 88–96.

32. Christensen, C.M., Cook, S. and Hall, T. "Marketing Malpractice: The Cause and the Cure," *Harvard Business Review*, Vol. 83, No. 12, December 2005, pp. 74–83.

2   SURVEYS AND INTERVIEWS

1. Neuman, W. L., *Social Research Methods: Qualitative and Quantitative Approaches*. 3rd edition. London: Allyn and Bacon, 1997, p. 31.

2. The Holy Bible, *Holy Bible,* Giant Print Deluxe Edition: King James Version. USA, The National Publishing Company, 1997, pp. 1085–1086, St. Luke 2: 4–5.

3. Booth, C. (ed.) *Labour and Life of the People of London*, 17 volumes. London: Macmillan, 1889–1902.

4. For example, India is currently embarking on the world's biggest census, which aims to collect data, fingerprints and photographs from everyone in its 1.2 billion population: Burke, J., "India Begins Mega-census," *Guardian Weekly*, Vol. 182, No. 17, 2010, p. 10.

5. Squire, P., "Why the 1936 Literary Digest Poll Failed," *Public Opinion Quarterly*, Vol. 52, 1988, pp. 125–133.

6. *Chicago Daily Tribune*, "Dewey Defeats Truman," November 3, 1948, p. 1.

7. Moser, C. A. and Kalton, G., *Survey Methods in Social Investigation*. 2nd edition. London: Gower, 1971.

8. Robson, S., "Group Discussions." In Birn, R. J. (ed.) *The Handbook of International Market Research Techniques*. London: Kogan Page, 2000, pp. 297–316.

9. Lilienfeld, S. O., Wood, J. M. and Garb, H. N., "The Scientific Status of Projective Techniques," *Psychological Science in the Public Interest*, Vol. 1, No. 2, 2000, pp. 27–66.

10. Catterall, M. and Ibbotson, P., "Using Projective Techniques in Education Research," *British Education Research Journal*, Vol. 26, No. 2, 2000, pp. 245–256.

11. Fram, E. H. and Cibotti, E., "The Shopping List Studies and Projective Techniques: A 40 Year View," *Marketing Research*, Vol. 3, No. 4, 1991, pp. 14–22.

12. Haire, M., "Projective Techniques in Marketing Research," *Journal of Marketing*, Vol. 14, No. 5, 1950, pp. 15–33.

13. Will, V., Eadie, D. and MacAskill, S., "Projective and Enabling Techniques Explored," *Marketing Intelligence and Planning*, Vol. 14, No. 6, 1996, pp. 38–43.

14. Catchings-Castello, G., "The ZMET Alternative," *Marketing Research*, Vol. 12 No. 2, 2000, pp. 6–12.

15. Zaltman, G. "Metaphorically Speaking," *Marketing Research*, Summer 1996, Vol. 8, No. 2, pp. 13–20.

16. *Ibid.*, pp. 13–20.

17. U.S. Patent Number 54536830 registered in 1995.

18. Tom Brailsford quoted in: Eakin, Emily (2002) "Penetrating the Mind by Metaphor," *The New York Times*, February 23.

19. Kerlinger, F. N., *Foundations of Behavioral Research*. 3rd edition. London: Harcourt Brace College Publishers, 1992, p. 443.

20. Campbell, D. T., "The Informant in Quantitative Research," *The American Journal of Sociology*, Vol. 60, No. 4, 1955, pp. 339–342. John, G. and Reve, T., "The Reliability and Validity of Key Informant Data from Dyadic Relationships in Marketing Channels," *Journal of Marketing Research*, Vol. XIX, No. 4, 1982, pp. 517–524.

21. Janis, I. L., *Groupthink: Psychological Studies of Policy Decisions and Fiascoes*. 2nd edition. Boston: Houghton Mifflin, 1982.

22. Oppenheim, A. N., *Questionnaire Design, Interviewing and Attitude Measurement*. New edition. London: Printer Publishers, 1992, pp. 103–106.

23. Calvillo, J. P. and Lal, L., "Pilot Study of a Survey of US Residents Purchasing Medications in Mexico: Demographics, Reasons, and Types of Medications Purchased," *Clinical Therapeutics*, Vol. 25, No. 2, 2003, pp. 561–577.

24. Haddock, G. and Zanna, M. P., "On the Use of Open-ended Measures to Assess Attitudinal Components," *British Journal of Social Psychology*, Vol. 37, No. 2, 1998, pp. 129–149.

25. Dillman, D. A., Smyth, J. D. and Christian, L. M., *Internet, Mail, and Mixed-mode Surveys: The Tailored Design Method*. 3rd edition. New Jersey: John Wiley & Sons, 2009. Oppenheim, A. N., *Questionnaire Design, Interviewing and Attitude Measurement*. New edition. London: Printer Publishers, 1992.

26. Eagly, A. H. and Chaiken, S., *The Psychology of Attitudes*. London: Harcourt Brace Jovanovich College Publishers, 1993. Babbie, E., *The Practice of Social Research*. 11th edition. London: Wadsworth Publishing, 2006.

27. Case based on interview with Kiran Parmar conducted by F. Lemke on January 25, 2010 and several conversations in January and February 2010.

28. Based on Webb, J. R., *Understanding and Designing Marketing Research*. 2nd edition. London: Thomson Learning, 2002, pp. 105–106.

29. Thompson, M. E., *Theory of Sample Surveys*. London: Chapman & Hall, 1997. Bryman, A., *Social Research Methods*. 3rd edition. Oxford: Oxford University Press, 2008.

30. Grimmett, G. R. and Stirzaker, D. R., *Probability and Random Processes*. 2nd edition. Oxford: Clarendon Press, 1992. Howell, D. C., *Statistical Methods for Psychology*. International edition. London: Wadsworth, 2009. Coolican, H., *Research Methods and Statistics in Psychology*. 2nd edition. London: Hodder & Stoughton, 1997.

31. Case based on interviews conducted with Martina Lovcikova and Tomáš Hejkal by F. Lemke in January 2010 and multiple conversations between Martina Lovcikova, Tomáš Hejkal, and F. Lemke in February and March 2010.

32. Case based on interviews with Thomas Müller conducted by F. Lemke in January and February 2010.

33. For quantitative data analysis, refer to: Mason, R. D., Lind, D. A. and Marchal, W. G., *Statistics: An Introduction*. Belmont: Duxbury Press, 1994. Norman, G. R. and Streiner, D. L., *Biostatistics: The Bare Essentials*. 2nd edition. London: B.C. Decker, 2000. Gravetter, F. J. and Wallnau, L. B., *Statistics for the Behavioral Sciences*. 6th edition. London: Thomson Learning, 2003. For qualitative data analysis, refer to: Miles, M. B. and Huberman, A. M., *Qualitative Data Analysis: An Expanded Sourcebook*. 2nd edition. London: Sage, 1994. Banister, P., Burman, E., Parker, I., Taylor, M. and Tindall, C., *Qualitative Methods in Psychology: A Research Guide*. Buckingham: Open University Press,

1994. Creswell, J. W., *Qualitative Inquiry and Research Design: Choosing Among Five Traditions.* 2nd edition. London: Sage, 2007.

34. Johnson, P. and Harris, D., "Qualitative and Quantitative Issues in Research Design." In Partington, D. (ed.) *Essential Skills for Management Research,* London: Sage, 2002, p. 105.

35. Churchill, G. A., Brown, T. J. and Suter, T. A., *Basic Marketing Research.* 7th edition. Mason, OH: South-Western, 2010.

36. Norman, G. R. and Streiner, D. L., *Biostatistics: The Bare Essentials.* 2nd edition. London: B.C. Decker, 2000.

37. Oxford University Press Dictionary of Psychology, in: Colman, A. M. (2001) A Dictionary of Psychology, Projective Tests, www. Oxfordreference.com

38. Jacques, D. (2005) "Projective Techniques: Eliciting Deeper Thoughts," *Customer Input Journal,* www.customerinput.com (accessed 5.25.2009).

39. Easterby-Smith, M., Thorpe, R. and Lowe, A., *Management Research: An Introduction.* London: Sage Publication, 1991.

40. Pettigrew, S. and Charters, S., "Tasting as a Projective Technique," *Qualitative Market Research: An International Journal,* Vol. 11, No. 3, 2008, pp. 331–343.

41. Levy, S. J., "Interpreting Consumer Mythology: Structural Approach to Consumer Behavior Focuses on Story Telling," *Marketing Management,* Vol. 2, No. 4, 4–9.

42. Boddy, C. (2005). "Projective Techniques in Market Research: Valueless Subjectivity or Insightful Reality?" *International Journal of Market Research,* Vol. 47, No. 3, 1994, pp. 239–254.

43. Chandler, J. and Owen, M., *Developing Brand with Qualitative Market Research.* London: Sage, 2002.

44. Grant, I., "Creative Approaches to New Media Research," *Young Consumers,* Quarter 2 2006, pp. 51–56.

45. Boddy, C., 2005, pp. 239–254.

46. Yoell, W. A., "The Fallacy of Projective Techniques," *Journal of Advertising,* Vol. 3, No. 1, 1974, pp. 33–36.

47. Will, V., Eadie, D. and MacAskill, S., "Projective and Enabling Techniques Explored," *Marketing Intelligence and Planning,* Vol. 14, No. 6, 1996, pp. 38–43.

48. Catchings-Castello, 2000, pp. 6–12.

49. Zaltman, 1996, pp. 13–20.

50. *Ibid.*

51. Slater, S. G. and Narver, J. C., "Customer-led and Market-oriented: Let's Not Confuse the Two," *Strategic Management Journal,* Vol. 19, 1998, pp. 1001–1006.

52. Catchings-Castello, 2000, pp. 6–12.

53. Lee, M. S. Y., McGoldrick, P. J., Keeling, K. A. and Doherty, J., "Using ZMET to Explore Barriers to the Adoption of 3G Mobile Banking Services," *International Journal of Retail & Distribution Management,* Vol. 31, No. 6, 2003, pp. 340–348.

54. Hoffmann, J., www.olsonzaltman.com, Deep Dives, Vol. IV, Fall 2009, p. 4.

3   FOCUS GROUPS (AND VARIATIONS)

1. Sandberg, K. D., "Focus on Benefits," *Harvard Management Communication Newsletter,* Vol. 5, No. 4, 2002, pp. 3–4.

2. Powell, R. A. and Single, H. M., "Focus Groups," *International Journal for Quality in Health Care,* Vol. 8, 1996, pp. 499–504.

3. McDonagh-Philp, D. and Bruseberg, A., "Using Focus Groups to Support New Product Development," *Institution of Engineering Designers Journal,* Vol. 26, No. 4, 2000, pp. 9–11.

4. McDonagh-Philp, D. and Denton, H., "Using Focus Groups to Support the Designer in the Evaluation of Existing Products: A Case Study," *The Design Journal,* Vol. 2, No. 20, 1999, p. 131.

5. Eriksson, P. and Kovalainen, A., *Qualitative Methods in Business Research.* London: Sage, 2008.

6. Robert K. Merton is the father of well-known terms such as "self-fulfilling prophecy" and "role models". Both terms passed from his academic work into everyday language.

7. Denzin, N. and Lincoln, Y. (eds.) *Handbook of Qualitative Research*. Thousand Oaks, CA: Sage, 1994.

8. Emberger, W. and Kromer, R., *Treue Kunden wachsen nicht auf Bäumen—Strategien und Instrumente zur Kundenbindung*. Wien: WEKA Verlag, 2000.

9. Langford, J. and McDonnagh, D., "What Can Focus Groups Offer Us?" In McCabe, P. T. (ed.) *Contemporary Ergonomics*. London: Taylor & Francis, 2002.

10. Weatherchem corporation (2009) "The Spice of Life in India". Growth opportunity for spice manufacturers in India. http://www.weatherchem.com (accessed June 2009).

11. Krueger, R. A., *Developing Questions for Focus Groups*. London: Sage, 1998.

12. In 2010 we observed focus groups conducted by an American company in London. Here the company's culture (with a very strong work ethic) led them to run the groups for 2.25 hours—after 1.5 hours the participants were obviously very tired and the quality of the discussions dropped significantly.

13. Durgee, J., "New Product Ideas from Focus Groups," *The Journal of Consumer Marketing*, Vol. 4, No. 4, Fall 1987, pp. 57–65.

14. Koners, U., "Learning from Research & Development Projects: The Role of Post-project Reviews," PhD Thesis, Cranfield School of Management, 2006.

15. Kepper, G., *Qualitative Marktforschung: Methoden, Einsatzmöglichkeiten und Beurteilunskriterien*. 2nd edition. Wiesbaden: Deutscher Universitätsverlag, 1996.

16. Morgan, D., "Focus Groups," *Annual Review of Sociology*, Vol. 22, 1996, pp. 129–152.

17. Calder, A., "Focus Groups and the Nature of Qualitative Marketing Research," *Journal of Marketing Research*, Vol. 14, 1977, pp. 353–364.

18. In 2010 these cost £650 for three hours in the evening, see www.allglobalviewing.com.

19. Walker, R., *Applied Qualitative Research*, Aldershot: UK Gower Publishing Company, 1985, p. 5.

20. Easterby-Smith, M., Thorpe, R. and Lower, A., *Management Research: An Introduction*. London: Sage, 1991.

21. Krueger, R. A., *Moderating Focus Groups*. London: Sage, 1998.

22. Prince, M. and Davies, M., "Moderator Teams: An Extension to Focus Group Methodology," *Qualitative Market Research*, Vol. 4, No. 4, 2001, pp. 207–216.

23. Krueger, R. A., *Focus Groups: A Practical Guide for Applied Research*. London: Sage, 1988.

24. Stewart, D. W. and Shamdasani, P. N., *Focus Groups: Theory and Practice*. Applied Social Research Methods Series, Vol. 20. Newbury Park, CA: Sage, 1990.

25. Based on Interviews with R&D Managers at Kraft Foods Ltd. UK in Banbury, UK, conducted in January 2001.

26. Krueger, R. A., *Analysing and Reporting Focus Group Results*. London: Sage, 1998.

27. Eriksson and Kovalainen, 2008.

28. Emberger and Kromer, 2000.

29. Kepper, 1996.

30. Edmunds, H., *The Focus Group Research Handbook*, New York: McGraw-Hill, 2000.

31. Szwillus, G. and Ziegler, J. (eds.) *Mensch & Computer: Interaktion in Bewegung*. Stuttgart: B. G. Teubner, 2003, pp. 207–218.

32. Wellner, A. S., "I've Asked You Here because…: Online Focus Groups Can Be a Great Way to Get Some Quick-and-Dirty Market Research," *Business Week*, August 14, Issue 3694, 2000, p. 14.

33. Churchill, G. A. Jr., Brown, T. J. and Suter, T. A., *Basic Marketing Research*. 7th edition. Mason, OH: South-Western Cengage Learning, 2010, p. 93.

34. Stokes, D. and Bergin, R., "Methodology or Methodolatry? An Evaluation of Focus Groups and Depth Interviews," *Qualitative Market Research*, Vol. 9, No. 1, 2006, pp. 26–37.

35. Zikmund, W. G., *Exploring Marketing Research*. 6th edition. Fort Worth, TX: The Dryden Press, 1997. In this book, Zikmund summarizes the main advantages of focus groups under the heading the "10Ss", because he summarizes them under ten headings which all start with a "s".

36. Wilkinson, S., "Focus Group Methodology: A Review," *International Journal of Social Research Methodology*, 1999, pp. 181–203.

37. Bryman, A., *Social Research Methods*. 3rd edition. Oxford: Oxford University Press, 2008.

38. Schindler, R. M., "The Real Lesson of New Coke: The Value of Focus Groups for Predicting the Effects of Social Influence," *Marketing Research*, Vol. 4, No. 4, 1992, pp. 22–28.

39. Zaltman, G., *How Customers Think: Essential Insights into the Mind of the Market*. Boston: Harvard Business School Press, 2003, p. 3.

40. The issue evokes associations with Heisenberg's famous Uncertainty Principle. As Heisenberg said, "What we observe is not nature itself, but nature exposed to our method of questioning."

41. Walvis, T., "Avoiding Advertising Research Disaster: Advertising and the Uncertainty Principle," *Journal of Brand Management*, Vol. 10, No. 6, 2003, pp. 403–409.

42. Ibid.

43. Comiteau, J., "Why the Traditional Focus Group is Dying," *Adweek*, October 31, 2005.

44. Rushkoff, D., *Get Back in the Box: Innovation from the Inside Out*. New York: Collins, 2005. Douglas Rushkoff argues that focus groups are often useless, and frequently cause more trouble than they are intended to solve, with focus groups often aiming to please rather than offering their own opinions or evaluations, and with data often cherry picked to support a foregone conclusion.

45. Wellner, A. S., "The New Science of Focus Groups," *American Demographics*, Vol. 25, No. 3, 2003, pp. 29–33.

4   ETHNOGRAPHIC MARKET RESEARCH

1. Arnould, E. J. and Wallendorf, M., "Market-Oriented Ethnography: Interpretation Building and Marketing Strategy Formulation," *Journal of Marketing Research*, Vol. XXXI, November 1994, pp. 484–504.

2. Dane, F. C., *Research Methods*. Pacific Grove, CA: Brookes/Cole, 1990, p. 151.

3. Robson, C., *Real World Research*. Oxford: Oxford University Press, 1993.

4. Leonard-Barton, D., *Wellsprings of Knowledge: Building and Sustaining the Sources of Innovation*. Boston, MA: Harvard Business School Press, 1995.

5. Elliot, R. and Jankel-Elliot, N., "Using Ethnography in Strategic Consumer Research," *Qualitative Market Research*, Vol. 6, No. 4, 2003, pp. 215–223.

6. Frazer, J., *The Golden Bough*. New edition. Basingstoke: Palgrave Macmillan, 2005.

7. Evans-Prichard, E. E., *The Nuer*. Oxford: Oxford University Press, 1940, p. 1.

8. Malinowski, B., *The Argonauts of the Western Pacific*. Long Grove, IL: Waveland Press, 1984.

9. Evans-Prichard, 1940.

10. Kraweski, L. J. and Ritzman, L. P., *Operations Management*. 4th edition. Reading, MA: Addison-Wesley, 1996.

11. Sower, V. E., Motwani, J. and Savoie, M. J., *Classic Readings in Operations Management*. Forth Worth, TX: The Dryden Press, 1995, p. 342.

12. Reese, W., "Behavioral Scientists Enter Design." In Squires, S. and Byrne, B. (eds.) *Creating Breakthrough Ideas: The Collaboration of Anthropologists and Designers in the Product Development Industry*. Westport, CT: Bergin and Garvey, 2002.

13. Ibid.

14. Squires, S., "Doing the Work: Customer Research in the Product Development and Design Industry." In Squires, S. and Byrne, B. (eds.) *Creating Breakthrough Ideas: The Collaboration of Anthropologists and Designers in the Product Development Industry*. Westport, CT: Bergin and Garvey, 2002, p. 104.

15. Badgett, M., Bowen, H., Connor, W. and McKinley, J., "Countdown to Product Launch: Are You Confident Customers Will Buy?" IBM Corporation Report G510–1685-00, 2002.

16. Mariampolski, H., "The Power of Ethnography," *Journal of the Market Research Society*, Vol. 41, No. 1, January 1999, pp. 75–86.

17. Fellman, M. W., "Breaking Tradition," *Marketing Research*, Vol. 11, No. 3, Fall 1999, pp. 20–24.

18. Reese, 2002.

19. Tyagi, P. K., "Webnography: A New Tool to Conduct Marketing Research," *The Journal of the American Academy of Business*, Vol. 15, No. 2, March 2010, pp. 262–267.

20. Kozinets, R. V., "The Field Behind the Screen: Using Netnography for Marketing Research in Online Communities," *Journal of Marketing Research*, Vol. XXXIX, No. 1, February 2002, pp. 61–72.

21. Ronney, E., Olfe, P. and Mazur, G., "Gemba Research in the Japanese Cellular Phone Market" (Nokia Mobile Phones/QFD Institute, May 11, 2000). Available on the Internet.

22. *Ibid*, p. 4.

23. Leonard-Barton, D. and Rayport, J. F., "Spark Innovation through Empathic Design," *Harvard Business Review*, Vol. 75, No. 6, November–December, 1997, pp. 102–113.

24. Atkinson, P., *Research Design*. The Open University, Social Sciences: A Third level Course, Research Methods in Education and the Social Sciences DE304 Block 3B, 1979, p. 52.

25. Elliot and Jankel-Elliot, 2003, p. 216.

26. Arnould and Wallendorf, 1994, p. 498.

27. Shalo, S., "Through Patient's Eyes," *Pharmaceutical Executive*, Vol. 23, No. 11, November 2003, pp. 100–108.

28. Rosenthal, S. R. and Capper, M., "Ethnographies in the Front End: Designing for Enhanced Customer Experiences," *Journal of Product Innovation Management*, Vol. 23, No. 3, 2006, pp. 215–237.

29. Elliot and Jankel-Elliot, 2003.

30. Rosenthal, R. and Rosnow, R. L., *Essentials of Behavioural Research: Methods and Data Analysis*. 2nd edition. New York: McGraw-Hill, 1991.

31. Mariampolski, 1999.

32. Rosenthal and Rosnow, 1991.

33. Hammersley, M., "Data Collection in Ethnographic Research," *Research Design*, The Open University, Social Sciences: A Third level Course, Research Methods in Education and the Social Sciences DE304 Block 3B, 1979, pp. 89–159.

34. Elliot and Jankel-Elliot, 2003.

35. Arnould and Wallendorf, 1994.

36. Dane, 1990.

37. Hammersley, 1979.

38. Rosenthal, Capper, M., 2006, pp. 215–237.

39. Arnould and Wallendorf, 1994.

40. LeCompte, M. and Schensul, J. J., *Designing and Conducting Ethnographic Research*. Lanham, U.S.: AltaMira Press, 1999, p. 18.

41. Arnould and Wallendorf, 1994.

42. Elliot and Jankel-Elliot, 2003.

43. Case based on:—A visit by F. Lemke to Lucci Orlandini Design on December 22, 2006 including an interview with Roberto Lucci—Multiple conversations between Roberto Lucci and F. Lemke in January and February 2010.—The Lucci Orlandini Design website, http://www.lucciorlandini.com/ (accessed in January 2010).

44. Bowen, J. T. and Morris, A., "Menu Design: Can Menus Sell?" *International Journal of Contemporary Hospitality Management*, Vol. 7, No. 4, 1995, pp. 4–9.

45. Mariampolski, H., *Ethnography for Marketers*. Thousand Oaks, CA: Sage, 2006.

46. Dane, 1990.

47. Rosenthal and Capper, 2006.

48. Fellman, 1999, pp. 20–24.

49. Elliot and Jankel-Elliot, 2003.

50. Atkinson, P., "Research Design in Ethnography," *Research Design*, The Open University, Social Sciences: A Third level Course, Research Methods in Education and the Social Sciences DE304 Block 3B, 1979, pp. 41–81.

51. Arnould and Wallendorf, 1994, p. 484.

52. Fulton Suri, J., "Empathic Design: Informed and Inspired by Other People's Experience." In Koskinen, I., Batterbee, K. and Mattelmäki, T. (eds.) *Empathic Design*. Finland: Edita Publishing, IT Press, 2003, p. 53.

53. Johnson, G. and Scholes, K., *Exploring Corporate Strategy*. 5th edition. Edinburgh, UK: Pearson Education Limited, 1999.

54. Mason, E. J. and Bramble, W. J., *Understanding and Conducting Research: Applications in Education and the Behavioral Sciences*. 2nd edition. New York: McGraw-Hill, 1989, p. 300.

55. Arnould and Wallendorf, 1994.
56. El-Amir, A. and Burt, S. "Sainsbury's in Egypt: The Strange Case of Dr Jekyll and Mr Hyde," *International Journal of Retail and Distribution Management*, Vol. 36, No. 4, 2008, pp. 300–322.
57. Rust, 1993.
58. *Ibid.*
59. Arnould and Wallendorf, 1994.
60. Fulton Suri, 2003, pp. 54.
61. Kelly, D. and Gibbons, M., "Ethnography: The Good, the Bad and the Ugly," *Journal of Medical Marketing*, Vol. 8, No. 4, 2008, pp. 279.
62. Kumar, V. and Whitney, P., "Daily Life, Not Markets: Customer-Centred Design," *Journal of Business Strategy*, Vol. 28, No. 4, 2007, pp. 46–58.
63. Sanders, E., "Ethnography in NPD Research—How 'Applied Ethnography' Can Improve Your NPD Research Process," *Visions* (Product Development Management Association), April 2002, http://www.pdma.org/visions/apr02/applied.html.
64. Dane, 1990.

5   EXAMPLE: WAREHOUSE EQUIPMENT RESEARCH

1. Cucka, J., "Scientific Research Not Limited to Anthropology," *Marketing News*, Vol. 33, No. 4, February 15, 1999, p. 4.
2. Case based on interviews with Ceri Batchelder and Neil Stainton of Smith & Nephew, 2007–8 and partly on Batchelder, C., Pinto, C., Bogg, D., Sharples, C. and Hill, A., "Capturing Best Practice in Establishing Customers' Hidden Needs for Smith and Nephew," Manchester Business School, International Business Project 2006, December 2006.
3. Stolzoff, N. C., "Mindless Action Sells Research Short," *Marketing News*, Vol. 38, No. 2, February 1, 2004, p. 36.
4. Orban, A., "The Truth about Ethnography: A Rebuttal," *PDMA Visions Magazine*, Vol. XXXI, No. 1, March 2007, pp. 6–7 (quote on p. 7).

6   REPERTORY GRID TECHNIQUE

1. Fransella, F. and Bannister, D., *A Manual for Repertory Grid Technique*. 2nd edition. Wiley: Chichester, 2004, p. 6.
2. Kelly, G. A., *The Psychology of Personal Constructs*, Vol. 1 and 2, New York: Norton, 1955.
3. Frost, W. A. K. and Braine, R. L., "The Application of the Repertory Grid Technique to Problems in Market Research," *Commentary*, Vol. 9, No. 3, July 1967, pp. 161–175 (quote on p. 175).
4. In 2007 Cranfield School of Management telephoned ten leading European market research agencies and found that none of them use repertory grid technique.
5. Grunert, K. G., Sorensen, E., Johansen, L. B. and Nielsen, N. A., "Analysing Food Choice from a Means-end Perspective," *European Advances in Consumer Research*, Vol. 2, 1995, pp. 366–371.
6. Coshall, J., "Measurement of Tourists' Images: The Repertory Grid Approach," *Journal of Travel Research*, Vol. 39, No. 1, August 2000, pp. 85–89.
7. Riley, S. and Palmer, J., "Of Attitudes and Latitudes: A Repertory Grid Study of Perceptions of Seaside Resorts," *Journal of the Market Research Society*, Vol. 17, No. 2, 1975, pp. 74–89.
8. Embacher, J. and Buttle, F., "A Repertory Grid Analysis of Austria's Image as a Summer Vacation Destination," *Journal of Travel Research*, Vol. 27, No. XX, 1989, pp. 3–7.
9. Pike, S., "The Use of Repertory Grid Analysis to Elicit Salient Short-break Holiday Destination Attributes in New Zealand," *Journal of Travel Research*, Vol. 41, No. 3, February 2003, pp. 315–320.
10. Goffin, K., "Understanding Customers' Views: A Practical Example of the Use of Repertory Grid Technique," *Management Research News*, Vol. 17, No. 7/8, 1994, pp. 17–28.

11. Goffin, K. and Koners, U. "Tacit Knowledge, Lessons Learned and New Product Development" Accepted for publication in the *Journal of Product Innovation Management* in Vol. 28, No. xx, March 2011.

12. Khan, A., "Perceived Service Quality in the Air Freight Industry," *PhD Thesis,* Cranfield School of Management, UK, 1993.

13. Bender, M. P., "Provided versus Elicited Constructs: An Explanation of Warr and Coffman's Anomalous Finding," *British Journal of Social and Clinical Psychology,* Vol. 13, 1974, pp. 329–330.

14. Ryle, A. and Lunghi, M. W., "The Dyad Grid: A Modification of Repertory Grid Technique," *British Journal of Psychiatry,* Vol. 117, 1970, pp. 323–327.

15. Fransella and Bannister, 2004, p. 35.

16. O'Cinneide, B., "The Cheesecraft Case." In O'Cinneide, B. (ed.) *The Case for Irish Enterprise.* Dublin, Ireland: Dublin Enterprise Publications, 1986.

17. Landfield, A. W., "Meaningfulness of Self, Ideal and Other as Related to Own versus Therapist's Personal Construct Dimensions," *Psychological Reports,* Vol. 16, 1965, pp. 605–608.

18. Case based on market research conducted for Fascia Mania by one of the authors in 2005.

19. Pope, M. L. and Keen, T. R., *Personal Construct Psychology and Education.* London: Academic Press, 1981 p. 46.

20. Hudson, R., "Images of the Retailing Environment: An Example of the Use of the Repertory Grid Methodology," *Environmental Behaviour,* Vol. 6, No. 4, December 1974, pp. 470–494.

21. Case based on an interview in 2001 with the UK business development manager for Eucerin.

22. www.beiersdorf.de

23. Goffin, K., Lemke, F. and Szwejczewski, M., "An Exploratory Study of 'Close' Supplier-Manufacturer Relationships," *Journal of Operations Management,* Vol. 24, No. 1, 2006, pp. 189–209.

24. www.idiogrid.com/

25. http://tiger.cpsc.ucalgary.ca/

26. Smith, M., "An Introduction to Repertory Grids—Part Two: Interpretation of Results," *Graduate Management Research,* Vol. 3, No. 2, Autumn 1986, pp. 4–24.

27. Rocchi, B. and Stefani, G., "Consumers' Perception of Wine Packaging: A Case Study," *International Journal of Wine Marketing,* Vol. 18, No. 1, 2006, pp. 33–44.

28. Jankowitz, D., *The Easy Guide to Repertory Grids.* Chichester: Wiley, 2004, p. 145ff.

29. www.qsrinternational.com

30. Goffin, K., "Repertory Grid Technique." In Partington, D. (ed.) *Essential Skills for Management Research,* London: Sage, 2002.

31. Open University, *Block 4 Data Collection Procedures,* DE304 Research Methods in Education and the Social Sciences Series. Milton Keynes: Open University Press, 1979, p. 30.

7   INVOLVING THE USER

1. Melillo, W., "Inside the Consumer Mind," *Adweek,* January 16, 2006, p. 12 (Quote from Professor Gerald Zaltman).

2. NESTA, *The New Inventors, How Users Are Changing the Rules of Innovation.* National Endowment for Science, Technology and the Arts (NESTA) Research Report, 2008.

3. Lüthje, C., Herstatt, C. and von Hippel, E., "The Dominant Role of 'Local' Information in the User Information. The Case of Mountain Biking," MIT Sloan Working Paper No. 4377–02, July 2002.

4. Von Hippel, E., "Lead Users: a Source of Novel Product Concepts," *Management Science,* Vol. 32, No. 7, 1986, pp. 791–805.

5. Based on an interview with Ryan Jones on December 27, 2009; http://www.pg.com/en_US/brands/beauty_grooming/index.shtml (accessed January 2010); http://www.hugocreate.com/en/home (accessed January 2010).

6. Tuomi, I., *Networks of Innovation,* Oxford: Oxford University Press, 2002.

7. Tiemann, M., History of the OSI. Open Source Initiative, 2006. www.Opensource.org/history. Retrieved February 2010.

8. Sonali, K. S., *Open Beyond Software.* Open Sources 2. Edited by Danese Cooper, Chris DiBona and Mark Stone. Sebastopol, CA: O'Reilly Media, 2005.

9. Postigo, H., "From Pong To Planet Quake: Post-industrial Transition from Leisure to Work, Information," *Communication & Society*, Vol. 6, No. 4, 2003, pp. 593–607.

10. Tyagi, P. K., "Webnography: A New Tool to Conduct Marketing Research," *The Journal of the American Academy of Business*, Vol. 15, No. 2, March 2010, pp. 262–267.

11. NESTA, 2008.

12. Piller, F., VDI Nachrichten, *Weltmeister Magazin* 1/2009, RWTH Aachen, 2009, p. 23.

13. Schilling, M. A. and Hill, W. L., "Managing the New Product Development Process: Strategic Imperative," *Academy of Management Executive*, Vol. 12, No. 3, 1998, pp. 67–81.

14. Brown, S. L. and Eisenhard, K., "Product Development: Past Research, Present Findings, and Future Directions," *Academy of Management Review*, Vol. 20, No. 2, 1995, pp. 343–378.

15. Von Hippel, E., "Has a Customer Already Developed Your Next Product?" Working Paper, MIT Sloan Management School of Management, Vol. 18, 1976, pp. 63–74.

16. Case based on a CNN news report on Sunday March 21, 2010: http://edition.cnn.com/video/#/video/international/2010/03/17/quest.united.uniform.cnn.

17. Füller, J., Bartl, M., Ernst, H. and Mühlbacher, H., "Community Based Innovation: How to Integrate Members of Virtual Communities into New Product Development," *Electron Commerce Res*, Vol. 6, No. 1, 2006, pp. 57–73.

18. Lüthje, C., "Methoden zur Sicherstellung von Kundenorientierung in den frühen Phasen des Innovationsprozesses." In Herstatt, C. and Verworn, B. (eds.) *Management der frühen Innovationsphasen: Grundlagen—Methoden—Neue Ansätze*. Wiesbaden: Gabler, 2003.

19. Case based on: Multiple visits by F. Lemke to Sample U between 2009 and 2010. Interview with Craig Bongart (former President and CEO of Sample U) conducted by F. Lemke on January 9, 2010. Conversation between David Deal (current CEO of Sample U) and F. Lemke in March 2010.

20. Magnusson, P. R., "Exploring the Contributions of Involving Ordinary Users in Ideation of Technology-based Services," *Journal of Product Innovation Management*, Vol. 26, No. 5, 2009, pp. 578–593.

21. Prahalad, C. K. and Rangaswamy, V., "Co-opting Customer Competence," *Harvard Business Review*, Vol. 78, No. 1, 2000, pp. 79–87.

22. Boutellier, R. and Völker, R., *Erfolg durch innovative Produkte. Bausteine des Innovationsmanagements*. München: Hanser, 1997.

23. Slater, S. G. and Narver, J. C., "Customer-led and Market-Oriented: Let's Not Confuse the Two," *Strategic Management Journal*, Vol. 19, No. 10, 1998, pp. 1001–1006 (quote on p. 1003).

24. Rogers, E. M., *Diffusion of Innovations*, New York: Free Press, 2003.

25. Herstatt, C. and von Hippel, E., "From Experience: Developing New Product Concepts via the Lead User Method: A Case Study in a 'Low-Tech' Field," *Journal of Product Innovation Management*, Vol. 9, No. 3, 1992, pp. 213–221.

26. Koerner, B. I., "Geeks in Toyland," *Wired* 2, 2006, pp. 108–150.

27. Herstatt, and von Hippel, 1992, pp. 213–221.

28. Goffin, K. and Mitchell, R., *Innovation Management. Strategy and Implementation using the Pentathlon Framework*. London: Palgrave Macmillan, 2nd edition, 2010.

29. Cooper, R. G. and Edgett, S. J., *Generating Breakthrough New Product Ideas: Feeding the Innovation Funnel*. Product Development Institute, Ancaster, Canada, 2007.

30. Herstatt, C. and von Hippel E., (1992).

31. Schmookler, J., *Innovation and Economic Growth*. Cambridge, MA: Harvard University Press, 1966.

32. Rogers, E. M. and Shoemaker, F. F., *Communication of Innovations. A Cross-Cultural Approach*. 2nd edition. New York: The Free Press, 1971.

33. von Hippel, E., Thomke, S. and Sonnack, M., "Creating Breakthroughs at 3M," *Harvard Business Review*, Vol. 77, No. 5, September–October 1999, pp. 47–57 (quote on p. 50).

34. Case based on: Multiple visits by F. Lemke to Nubert electronic GmbH from 2003 and 2008. Interview with Roland Spiegler conducted by F. Lemke on January 7, 2010. Multiple conversations between Roland Spiegler, Daniel Belcher and F. Lemke in February and March 2010.

35. The term "brand community" was established by Albert Muniz Jr. and Thomas C. O'Guinn in 1995. Their article published in 2001 in the *Journal of Consumer Research* is heavily cited: Muniz, A. M., O'Guinn and T. C., "Brand Community," *Journal of Consumer Research*, Vol. 27, 2001, pp. 412–432.

36. Sawhney, M., Verona, G. and Prandelli, E. (2005). "Collaborating to Create: The Internet as a Platform for Customer Engagement in Product Innovation," *Journal of Interactive Marketing*, Vol. 19, No. 4, pp. 4–17.

37. McKinsey & Company—German Office (2008). Acht Technologietrends, die Sie im Auge behalten sollten. www.mckinsey.de (accessed on 16.6.2008).

38. Jeppesen, L. B. and Frederiksen, L., "Why Do Users Contribute to Firm-hosted User Communities? The Case of Computer-Controlled Music Instruments," *Organization Science*, Vol. 17, No. 1, 2006, pp. 45–63. Muniz, A. M., O' Guinn, T. C. , "Brand Community," *Journal of Consumer Research*, Vol. 27, No. 4, 2001, pp. 412–432. Williams, R. L. and Cothrel, J., "Four Smart Ways to Run Online Communities," *Sloan Management Review*, Vol. 41, No. 4, 2000, pp. 81–91.

39. Lave, J. and Wenger, E., *Situated Learning: Legitimate Peripheral Participation*. Cambridge University Press, Cambridge, 1991.

40. Bartl, M., Hück, S. and Landgraf, R., "Netnography erschließt Online-Communities als Innovationsquelle," *Research&Results*, Vol. 1, 2008, pp. 28–29.

41. Werry, C. and Mowbray, M., *Online Communities*. New Jersey: Prentice Hall, 2001.

42. Howe, J., "The Rise of Crowdsourcing," *Wired*, 2006, www.wired.com/wired/archive/14.06/crowds.html

43. Ibid.

44. Kleemann, F., Voß, G. and Rieder, K., "Un(der)paid Innovators: The Commercial Utilization of Consumer Work through Crowdsourcing," *Science, Technology & Innovation Studies*, Vol. 4, No. 1, 2008, pp. 5–26.

45. Bradshaw, T., "Original Ideas Prove Customer Knows Best," *Financial Times*, London, January 4, 2010, p. 4.

46. Whitla, P., "Crowdsourcing and Its Application in Marketing Activities," *Contemporary Management Research*, Vol. 5, No. 1, 2009, pp. 15–28.

47. Kleemann, Voß and Rieder, 2008.

48. Bonabeau, E., "Decisions 2.0: The Power of Collective Intelligence," *MIT Sloan Management Review*, Vol. 50, No. 2, 2009, pp. 44–52.

49. Thomke, Stefan. H., *Experimentation Matters: Unlocking the Potential of New Technologies for Innovation*. Boston: Harvard Business School Publishing, 2003, p. 6.

50. Thomke, S. and von Hippel, E., "Customers as Innovators: A New Way to Create Value," *Harvard Business Review*, Vol. 80, No. 2, March–April 2002, pp. 74–81.

51. Andreasen, A. R. and Smith, W. A., *Marketing Research That Won't Break the Bank: A Practical Guide to Getting the Information You Need*. 2nd edition. San Francisco: Jossey-Bass, 2002.

52. Sequeira, J. T., "Take a Chance on Experimenting," *Business Week*, September 21, 2009.

53. This well-known anecdote about the Walkman product is not mentioned in the official history of the product on the Sony website http://www.sony.net/Fun/SH/1–18/h3.html (accessed March 2010).

54. Dahlsten, F., "Hollywood Wives Revisited: A Study of Customer Involvement in the XC90 Project at Volvo Cars," *European Journal of Innovation Management*, Vol. 7, No. 2, 2004, pp. 141–149.

55. Huxold, S., *Marketinforschung und strategische Planung von Produktinnovationen*. Berlin: Erich Schmidt Verlag, 1990.

56. McKay, L., "Where Does Innovation Come From?" *Customer Relationship Management*, Vol. 14, No. 1, 2010, pp. 24–30.

57. Lilien, G. L., Morrison, P. D., Searls, K., Sonnack, M. and von Hippel, E., "Performance Assessment of the Lead User Idea-Generation Process for New Product Development," *Management Science*, Vol. 48, No. 8, 2002, pp. 1042–1059.

58. Case based on: Interviews with Vernon Mortensen conducted in January 2010 by F. Lemke and several conversations in February and March 2010 between Vernon Mortensen and F. Lemke.

59. Iansiti, M. and MacCormack, A., "A Developing Products on Internet Time," *Harvard Business Review*, Vol. 75, No. 5, 1997, pp. 108–118.

60. Goffin, K. and Mitchell, R., "The Customer Holds the Key to Great Products," *Financial Times*, March 24, 2006, pp. 10–11 (quote on p. 10).

61. Cranfield School of Management is currently (2010) working with a major manufacturer of medical devices that has used lead user technique (with top surgeons in teaching hospitals) but has

been disappointed by the resulting products that have not sold widely. The company, which for obvious reasons wants to remain anonymous, is now applying other techniques to identify the hidden needs of more typical hospitals.

62. McKinsey & Company—German Office. "Acht Technologietrends, die Sie im Auge behalten sollten." www.mckinsey.de 6.16.2008.
63. Cooke, M. and Buckley, N., "Web 2.0, Social Networks and the Future of Market Research," *International Journal of Market Research*, Vol. 50, No. 2, 2008, p. 267.

8 CONJOINT ANALYSIS

1. Kessels, R., Goos, P. and Vandebroek, M., "Optimal Designs for Conjoint Experiments," *Computational Statistics & Data Analysis*, Vol. 52, No. 5, 2008, pp. 2369–2387 (quote on p. 2369).
2. Luce, R. D. and Tukey, J. W., "Simultaneous Conjoint Measurements: A New Type of Fundamental Measurement," *Journal of Mathematical Psychology*, Vol. 1, No. 1, 1964, pp. 1–27.
3. Green, P. E. and Rao, V. R., "Conjoint Measurement for Quantifying Judgemental Data," *Journal of Marketing Research*, Vol. 8, No. 3, 1971, pp. 355–363.
4. Green, P. E. and Srinivasan, V., "Conjoint Analysis in Consumer Research: Issues and Outlook," *Journal of Consumer Research*, Vol. 5, No. 2, 1978, pp. 103–123.
5. Wittink, D., Vriens, M. and Burhenne, W. (1994) Commercial Use of Conjoint Analysis in Europe: Results and Critical Reflections. *International Journal of Research in Marketing*, 11 (1), 41–52.
6. Naudé, P. and Buttle, F., "Assessing Relationship Quality," *Industrial Marketing Management*, Vol. 29, No. 4, 2000, pp. 351–361.
7. For ranking, the *median* is a better measure of central tendency than an average. The disadvantage of rankings is that most statistical operations, including arithmetic averages, are not valid. So in this case median values are better. Note that where there are only two values, the arithmetic mean and the median are the same.
8. Case based on interview with Kiran Parmar conducted by F. Lemke on January 25, 2010 and several conversations in January and February 2010.
9. Louviere, J. J., Hensher D. A. and Swait, J. D., *Stated Choice Methods: Analysis and Application.* Cambridge: Cambridge University Press, 2000.
10. Ibid.
11. Churchill, G. A. J., *Marketing Research: Methodological Foundations.* 6th edition. London: The Dryden Press, 1999.
12. The example comes from a leading manufacturer of washing machines and the specific list of factors/attributes as well specific details are shortened for illustrating the Conjoint Analysis technique in this chapter.
13. Veisten, K., "Willingness to Pay for Eco-labelled Wood Furniture: Choice-based Conjoint Analysis versus Open-ended Contingent Valuation," *Journal of Forest Economics*, Vol. 13, No. 1, 2007, pp. 29–48.
14. Number of matrices = number of attributes (number of attributes−1) / 2. For example, with 10 attributes you get 45 matrices.
15. Miller, G. A., "The Magical Number Seven, Plus or Minus Two: Some Limits on Our Capacity for Processing Information," *The Psychological Review*, Vol. 63, No. 2, 1956, pp. 81–97.
16. Huber, J., *What We Have Learned from 20 Years of Conjoint Research: When to Use Self-Explicated, Graded Pairs, Full Profiles or Choice Experiments.* Sawtooth Software Research Paper Series, 1997.
17. Keppel, G. and Wickens, T. D., *Design and Analysis: A Researcher's Handbook.* 4th edition. Upper Saddle River, NJ: Pearson Prentice Hall, 2004, pp. 76–79.
18. Hahn, G. J. and Shapiro, S. S., *A Catalog and Computer Program for the Design and Analysis of Orthogonal Symmetric and Asymmetric Fractional Factorial Experiments.* General Electric Research and Development Center. Technical Report: 66-C 165, 1966.
19. PASW (Predictive Analytics Software) was formerly called SPSS (Statistical Package for the Social Sciences). It is a statistic- and analysis-program, which was developed in the end of the 1960s and

has undergone various amendments over the years. Today, PASW/SPSS represents a worldwide-accepted standard for statistical software.

20. The box case is based on: Brown, G. and Vandenbosch, M., *Bayernwerk A.G. (A): Responding to Deregulation.* IMD Case Study: IMD-5–0590, 2003; Brown, G. and Vandenbosch, M., *Bayernwerk A.G. (B): Aquapower.* IMD Case Study: IMD-5–0599, 2003; http://www.eon-bayern.com (accessed May 29, 2008); http://www.yellostrom.de (accessed May 29, 2008), and http://www.rwe.com (accessed May 29, 2008).

21. Adaptive Conjoint Analysis (ACA) software by Sawtooth Software, Inc. is a computer-based interactive conjoint package that is well established in the industry.

22. This section on calculating utilities is based on: Orme, B., *ACA User Manual Version 5.* Sequim, WA: Sawtooth Software, Inc, 2002.

23. The box case is based on: Lipke, D. J., "Product by Design," *American Demographics,* Vol. 23, No. 2, 2001, pp. 38–41. http://www.motorola.com (accessed February 19, 2010); and http://www.populus.com (accessed February 19, 2010).

24. Detailed mathematical description about the analysis model can be found in the recommended reading list, which is provided at the end of the chapter.

25. Walley, K., Custance, P., Taylor, S., Lindgreen, A. and Hingley, M., "The Importance of Brand in the Industrial Purchase Decision: A Case Study of the UK Tractor Market," *Journal of Business and Industrial Marketing,* Vol. 22, No. 6, 2007, pp. 383–393.

26. Respondents can be overwhelmed with the CA task when the full profile method with more than six attributes is applied. The respondent would have to evaluated all attributes at the same time. The complexity can be avoided with a bridging design, where all attributes are split into several sets and the reduced numbers are noted on profile cards. In the sets, at least one attribute should be identical. With this method, the variety of attributes is reduced. With the help of attributes, which can be found on all sets (so-called bridging-attributes), the results of the single sets can be put in relation and the results can be summarized across all sets. Apart from that, it is also possible to summarize single attributes in a superior meta-attribute, in order to reduce the number of attributes (a description can be found in: Oppewal, H., Louviere, J. J. and Timmermans, H. J. P., "Modeling Hierarchical Conjoint Processes with Integrated Choice Experiments," *Journal of Marketing Research,* Vol. 31, No. 1, 1994, pp. 92–105). We have not described this technique in this book, because in practice, the Adaptive Conjoint Analysis (ACA) program by Sawtooth Software can deal with this limitation and is established as the standard.

27. Rao, V. R. and Sattler, H., "Measurement of Price Effects with Conjoint Analysis: Separating Information and Allocative Effects of Price," In Gustafsson, A., Herrmann, A. and Huber, F. (eds.) *Conjoint Measurement: Methods and Applications.* Berlin: Springer-Verlag, 2001, pp. 47–66. Orme, B. K., *Three Ways to Treat Overall Price in Conjoint Analysis.* Sawtooth Software Research Paper Series, 2007.

9 COMBINING THE TECHNIQUES: DESIGNING BREAKTHROUGH PRODUCTS AND SERVICES

1. von Hippel, E., Thomke, S. and Sonnack, M., "Creating Breakthroughs at 3M," *Harvard Business Review,* Vol. 77, No. 5, September–October 1999, pp. 47–57 (quote on p. 47).

2. Case adapted from Goffin, K. and Mitchell, R., "The Customer Holds the Key to Great Products," *Financial Times,* FT Mastering Uncertainty, Friday, March 24, 2006, pp. 10–11.

3. Modified and extended from: Deszca, G., Munro, H. and Noori, H., "Developing Breakthrough Products: Challenges and Options for Market Assessment," *Journal of Operations Management,* Vol. 17, No. 6, 1999, pp. 613–630.

4. *Ibid.,* p. 613.

5. Case based on an interview with Kate Blandford by K. Goffin on January 6, 2010 and http://kate-blandfordconsulting.com/ (accessed January 2010).

6. Batchelder, C., Pinto, C., Bogg, D., Sharples, C. and Hill, A., "Capturing Best Practice in Establishing Customers' Hidden Needs for Smith and Nephew," Manchester Business School, International Business Project 2006, December 2006, p. 27.

7. Chisnall, P., *Marketing Research*. 4th edition. London: McGraw-Hill, 1992, p. 34.

8. Zaltman, G. and Coulter, R. H., "Seeing the Voice of the Customer: Metaphor-Based Advertising Research," *Journal of Advertising Research*, Vol. 35 No. 4, July/August 1995, pp. 35–51 (quote on p. 39).

9. Griffin, A. and Hauser, J. R., "The Voice of the Customer," *Marketing Science*, Vol. 12, No. 1, Winter 1993, pp. 1–27 (quote on p. 19).

10. At the time of writing (August 2010) we are conducting live market research for a number of organizations. At each of these companies we are taking 100 customers, dividing them randomly into 5 groups and then applying 5 different market research methods in parallel—including a survey, focus groups, and repertory grid interviews. If you are interested in this research check http://www.som.cranfield.ac.uk/som/p1400/Research/Research-Centres/The-Centre-for-Innovative-Products-and-Services/

11. Cooper, R. G. and Edgett, S. J., "Ideation for Product Innovation: What Are the Best Methods?" *PDMA Visions Magazine*, Vol. XXXII, No. 1, March 2008, pp. 12–17 (quote on p. 12).

12. Ibid, p. 12.

13. Griffin, A. and Hauser, J. R., 1993, pp. 1–27.

14. Hargadon, A. and Sutton, R.I., 'Building an Innovation Factory', *Harvard Business Review*, Vol. 78, No. 3, May-June 2000, pp. 157–167 (quote on p. 157).

15. Couger, J.D., *Creative Problem Solving and Opportunity Finding*, Danvers, MA: Boyd and Fraser, 1995.

16. Thomke, S. and Fujimoto, T. 'The Effect of 'Front-Loading' Problem-Solving on Product Development Performance'. *Journal of Product Innovation Management*, Vol. 17, No. 2, March 200), pp. 128–142.

17. Amabile, T.M., Hadley, C.N. and Kramer, S.J. 'Creativity Under the Gun', *Harvard Business Review*, Vol. 80, No. 8, August 2002, pp. 52–61.

18. Mascitelli, R. 'From Experience: Harnessing Tacit Knowledge to Achieve Breakthrough Innovation'. *Journal of Product Innovation Management*, Vol. 17, No. 3, 2000, pp. 179–193 (quote on p. 186).

19. Case based on interviews with Angelique Green and Julian Gwyn-Owen, conducted by K. Goffin in September 2009. See also: http://www.boxercreative.co.uk/

20. Case based on an interview with Massimo Fumarola, conducted in 2005 by K. Goffin.

21. Couger, 1995.

22. Verganti, R. (2009). *Design-Driven Innovation—Changing the Rules of Competition by Radically Innovating what Things Mean*. Boston, MA: Harvard Business Press.

23. Goldenberg, J. and Mazursky, D., *Creativity in Product Innovation*, Cambridge: Cambridge University Press, 2002.

24. Altshuller, G. *And Suddenly the Inventor Appeared*. Worchester, MA, Technical Innovation Center Inc: 1996.

25. Zhang, J., Chai, K-H. and Tan, K-C. 'Applying TRIZ to Service Conceptual Design: An Exploratory Study', *Creativity and Innovation Management*, Vol. 14, No. 1, (March 2005), pp. 34–42.

26. Case based on an interview with Peter Elvekjær conducted by K. Goffin on 15th January 2010 and the website www.grundfos.com (accessed January 2010).

10 CREATING A CULTURE FOCUSED ON HIDDEN NEEDS

1. Inglehart, R. *Culture Shift in Advanced Industrial Society*. Princeton University Press: Princeton, New Jersey, 1990, p. 428.

2. Case based on:
    —Multiple visits by K. Goffin to Bosch Crailsheim from 2003–2009.
    —An MBA team project led by Hector Martinez and Alejo Ribalta (2003).
    —In-depth interviews with Klaus Ullherr, Klaus Schreiber, Werner Mayer and Markus Kurz conducted by K. Goffin on 28th September 2009.
    —The Bosch website, http://www.boschpackaging.com/boschpackagingworld/eng/index.asp (accessed in October 2009).
3. Batchelder, C., Pinto, C., Bogg, D., Sharples, C. and Hill, A. Capturing Best Practice in Establishing Customers' Hidden Needs for Smith and Nephew. Manchester Business School, International Business Project 2006, December 2006.
4. Ibid p. 58.
5. For a detailed explanation of *open innovation* see Chapter 4 of: Goffin, K. and Mitchell, R. *Innovation Management: Strategy and Implementation Using the Pentathlon Framework*. Basingstoke: Palgrave Macmillan Academic Publishers, 2nd edition, March 2010.
6. Jaruzelski, B. and DeHoff, K. 'The Customer Connection: The Global Innovation 1000', *Strategy + Business*, Issue 49, (Winter 2007), pp. 69–83.
7. Case based on an interview conducted with Johann Gessler by K. Goffin at the Gulkeweise Austria in December 2009 and http://www.audi.com/com/brand/en.html (accessed January 2010).
8. Based on: Mathew, M. and Donepudi, A. 'Innovation at Whirlpool: The DNA of Corporate Culture', *ICFAI Business School Case Development Centre*, 2006, ECCH European Case Clearing House: Cranfield, UK, code 306-504-1, pp. 1–12. And: Information found on http://www.whirlpool.com/

Index